THE WORD AND THE WAY

Alliance of Confessing Evangelicals
600 Eden Rd., Lancaster, PA 17601

Manuscript prepared from messages delivered at the Keswick Convention

Except where stated, Scripture quotations are from THE HOLY BIBLE: AUTHORIZED VERSION, International Bible Society.

ISBN: 978-1-969723-98-8

Eric Alexander was an ordained minister in the Church of Scotland for over 50 years, spending many of those years as senior pastor in the historic St. George's-Tron Church in Glasgow. He studied at the University of Glasgow, graduating with a Master of Arts in 1954 and Bachelor of Divinity in 1958. Throughout his ministry, and in his retirement years, he preached at conferences such as the Keswick Convention and the Philadelphia Conference on Reformed Theology. He is the author of *Our Great God and Savior* and *Prayer: A Biblical Perspective*, both published by Banner of Truth Trust. His sermons can now be heard on the Alliance podcast Hear the Word of God.

THE WORD AND THE WAY

Living the Christian Life

Eric Alexander

600 Eden Road
Lancaster, PA 17601

Contents

Foreword

I can remember vividly the first time I heard Eric J. Alexander preach. I was a young Christian in my second year at University in Glasgow. Mr. Alexander (as I then called him) came to speak at the Inter Varsity group in the University. He spoke on Christian discipleship, and I was gripped from beginning to end. That evening, a friendship began that lasted until Eric went to glory in 2023. All through my student years and into my forty years of gospel ministry, Eric's friendship and preaching indelibly impacted my life. He was always available to take my phone calls; always ready to listen to my questions, and at times my frustrations; always ready to encourage me with a word in season. He truly was a man of God, in life as well as in the pulpit. One of my vivid memories of Eric's funeral service, which I was so privileged to attend, was to hear Eric's son Ronald say, 'What our father was in the pulpit, was exactly what he was at home'. Eric's ministry was an overflow of his life, an extension of who he was. For me, he epitomised everything that a gospel preacher should be.

God blessed Eric Alexander with a magnificent, mellifluous voice, but even more with a godly, Christ-loving life that permeated everything he said and did. I know that Eric would be the first to say that his wife Greta and his children, Jennifer and Ronald, enriched his life and, under God, enabled him to fulfil his calling to 'preach the word'.

Written sermons rarely capture the Spirit-anointed moment when they were first preached, but in *The Word and the Way*, you will quickly sense not only the compelling clarity of Eric's exposition of God's word, but also the inner passion with which that word was first preached. In these pages, you will encounter biblical truth that will instruct your mind, warm your heart, and compel you to bow down and worship.

— Ian Hamilton
Professor of Historical Theology
Westminster Seminary UK

Editor's Preface

Rev. Eric Alexander was one of the most gifted preachers of the latter twentieth century, possessing an engaging and compelling command of language, and combining that with a careful exposition of the Scriptures and a penetrating ability to apply it in all of life to the glory of God. Rev. Alexander was therefore something of a modern-day Puritan. He not only dealt with how to properly apply the Word of God in one's behavior as a Christian; he also urged upon the hearer the need for the Bible to govern their thinking and affections. When Eric preached, it was more than the mind that was exercised; the heart was stirred and moved to wonder, love, and praise for who God is and all that He has done for needy, helpless, and rebellious sinners. Rev. Alexander's handling of the Scriptures sought to exalt the triune God, and encouraged all to worship, serve, and love Him wholeheartedly.

This book addresses the great themes that pertain to the Christian life. A Christian is not one who merely believes certain doctrinal facts, or who is relying upon their baptism or church membership, or on their having signed a card or having come down an aisle for a gospel invitation decades ago. A Christian is one who is trusting in the Person and work of the Lord Jesus Christ alone for their salvation, and whose life is demonstrating that saving faith by obedience, repentance, growth in holiness, and consecration for God's service. A Christian bears witness in their words, deeds, attitudes, and affections to the reality of the indwelling Holy Spirit who produces spiritual fruit in all those who are converted. This is the abundant life that is only available to God's people, giving peace and joy while we reside in this world, as we make our way with expectant hope as pilgrims who are traveling toward the eternal city, "whose designer and builder is God" (Heb. 11:10).

On June 15, 2000, Dr. James Boice, pastor of Tenth Presbyterian Church and the founder of the Alliance of Confessing Evangelicals, went to be with the Lord. Eric Alexander was asked to preach the sermon for the memorial service. The title of the message, taken from Philippians 1:21, was "To Live Is Christ and to Die Is Gain." How appropriate for a Christian's memorial service. But it is also appropriate for us who are still living, because God has work for each of us to do for Him. For believers, Christ is our life. We live to honor Him, to praise Him, to do His will, to be a blessing to others in His name, and to make known to our lost world the glory of His saving grace. Eric's life and ministry truly exemplified Paul's own testimony and motivation.

May this book deepen your love for our Savior. And may it cause you to abound in hope, joy, and thanksgiving for who you are in Christ, and for the glorious destiny that awaits the people of God. And until that day, as Peter exhorted his readers, "As obedient children, do not be conformed to the passions of your former ignorance, but as he who called you is holy, you also be holy in all your conduct, since it is written, 'You shall be holy, for I am holy'" (1 Pet. 1:14-16).

— Michael Roberts

Editor

Alliance of Confessing Evangelcals

BOOK ONE

Righteous Beginnings– Hearing and Response

Chapter 1
TAKE HEED HOW YOU HEAR

He that hath ears to hear, let him hear.
— Mark 4:9 —

Great multitudes had gathered together by the Sea of Galilee. In Luke's account of this story, they came out from every city to gather in this beautiful part of the world. There was among the people a stirring air of expectancy and eagerness, an atmosphere which was derived from the purpose for which the people had gathered together, and that purpose was that they might meet with the Lord and wait for His word. There is a wonderful sense in which across all these years we are united in heart and mind with them, and it seems to me that we need to begin where Jesus began with this great multitude who had gathered by the lakeside.

At the very outset of what appears to have been a sustained period of teaching, our Lord lays across the threshold of everything that He had to say the critical issue on which it seems everything was going to depend. In a very real sense this is the critical issue, I believe, for today—and that issue was the *right hearing of the Word of God.* Luke crystallizes the whole question for us in these words: "Take heed … how ye hear" (8:18).

In this parable that has become, perhaps, too familiar to us, our Lord begins with divine insight to sketch the true character of the hearts into which the good seed of the Word is going to be sown. This is, of course, a description of His own ministry and of precisely what is happening whenever and wherever the good seed of the Word is thrust into the hearts of men by the Holy Spirit.

I want to point out to you that this is a parable which does not simply refer to that initial preaching of the gospel and that initial response of the human heart which we call conversion—for the whole of the Christian life, and the whole of progress in the Christian life, is marked by a continual responsiveness of heart to the Word of the living God, akin to the response that the seed meets in the soil. We, therefore, need to be continually reminded of this pivotal issue of the right hearing of the Word of God.

We are here to meet with God in His Word. It is possible to come rather with the vague idea that we have come for a blessing. But we do not believe in blessings which are not anchored in, and ministered through, the Word of God. We must submit ourselves, heart and mind and spirit, to the Word of the living God through which He blesses His people.

The two things are gathered together by the psalmist in that cry from the depths, in Psalm 130:5: "I wait for the LORD,… and in his word do I hope." I suggest to you that these are the two great longings that need to swell up from our hearts, because it is in the Word of the Lord that the Lord of the Word is to be met.

Perhaps the basic truth of this parable is that the Word of God has a twofold action. According to the words of Jesus, it has, first of all, a *dynamic* action. This is one of the lessons of the whole picture of the seed. Within this small, despised seed, as Jesus amplifies later on, there is life that is ready to burst forth into a great harvest. Where previously there has been nothing but barrenness and wasteland, the coming of the seed, where the conditions are right, brings an abundant fruitfulness.

There is a dynamic in this little seed to produce something far beyond what the untrained eye looking upon it might imagine.

"The word of God is quick, and powerful" (Heb. 4:12) is the New Testament's witness and the experience of so many of us, is it not? If, as you read the following chapters, God is going to grip your life by His Word through His Spirit, there is no limit to what God may do for you, whoever you are, however burdened and longing and even barren and needy your heart may be. If you let God's Word grip your life, there is no limit to what may happen.

The Word of God not only has a dynamic action, but it also has a *discerning* action, because it was the seed itself which discovered the truth, you will notice, about these different soils, three of which most probably looked indistinguishable from each other. It is the Word itself which sifts men out and discovers their true condition. "The word of God," the writer of the Epistle to the Hebrews reminds us, "is a discerner of the thoughts and intents of the heart" (4:12). It is because of this that Jesus describes these different situations that this Word meets. And this comes right into our own situation—the different kind of heart into which His Word is sown.

I want, as God shall help us and His Spirit lead us, to take these pictures that Jesus paints for us of the kinds of heart into which the Word comes and to say before God, "Which of these represents the truth about me?" We used to have a doctor in my family who always greeted his patients with the words, "And how do I find you today?" And I believe that God is meeting with every one of us, and His word to us is "How do I find you?" He is the great heart knower, the great *kardiognostes*, the "knower of the hearts of men," who is here to look into our hearts and to assess for us the possibilities.

So Jesus paints the picture, first of the *hard heart*, then of the *shallow heart*, then of the *divided heart*, and lastly of the *open heart*.

THE HARD HEART

Will you look with me, first of all, at the *hard heart*? Some seed, says Jesus, "fell by the way side" (v. 4). But the trouble was that the wayside was so exposed to the traffic of the world and the constant comings and goings of the feet of men that it became, over the weeks and months and years, as hard as concrete; and no seed ever penetrated it.

Let me remind you that in this parable Jesus is not speaking about those who have never heard His Word, or who stay away from His Word, or who are even inattentive to His Word. The parable does not deal with them. He is speaking here about those who actually hear, but in His description of the hard heart Jesus is speaking of the man or woman who sits and listens to the Word of God with a heart that is utterly impenetrable and is like that wayside path—so exposed to all the traffic of the world that it is like concrete to the Word of God.

That heart, says Jesus, is ideal ground not for Him but for Satan. "These are they by the way side, where the word is sown.... Satan cometh immediately, and taketh away the word" (v. 15). Some scholars think that Jesus is specifically thinking here of one group of people on whom it seems, from the testimony of the Gospels, the words of our Lord made absolutely no impression. They think He is speaking about the Pharisees who, because of that smug self-righteousness that characterized their lives—that deep-seated sense of satisfaction with themselves and thanksgiving that they were not like other people—had provided for themselves an armor plating against the word of the Lord. That may be so; it may be that some of us need to hear that word from God.

What is quite clear is that there is some real significance in this parable in the very position of the wayside. Notice it is actually withdrawn from the Sower's path; it is in the position, rather, of the spectator of all that the Sower is doing than of a participator of what He is doing. The falling of the seed is almost a casual, incidental thing. It brushes off upon the wayside; it is not where the Sower is making His pathway; it is not in the line of His purpose. I wonder if you grasp the point. I wonder if there are not some of us who are just like that—here as spectators, and they have withdrawn themselves, perhaps over a whole lifetime, from the pathway of God's purpose and from the word that He speaks.

It may be that you are an interested spectator but determined to keep yourself out of the line of anything that God may be going to do. May I simply say to you in the Lord's name, let His love break that barrier down, and let Him bring you from the sidelines into the path of His Word and of His purpose for your life.

THE SHALLOW HEART

But there is another picture here which Jesus draws—the picture of the *shallow heart*: "Some fell on stony ground" (v. 5), or ground where there was a thin covering of earth beneath which was the rock. There are two words in verse 5 and two in verse 6 which sum up the problem of this kind of ground and this kind of heart when the word of Jesus is seeking to penetrate it. The two words in verse 5 are "no depth," and the two words in verse 6 are "no root." The problem lies, you see, below the surface. If it was, in the first case, a stubborn resistance which was the barrier to the Word, in the second picture it is a superficial reception which is the barrier to the Word. If, in the first place, the seed could not get in, then, in the second place, it could not get down.

Outwardly, you see, there is a great show of response to the seed—a great show of response to the Word. Jesus means us to understand and have enthusiasm about it. "These are they … which are sown on stony ground; who, when they have heard the word, immediately receive it with gladness" (v. 16). I should think this is the kind of life which is deeply involved in Christian work, deeply instructed in evangelical truth, perhaps even respected in evangelical circles, but it is all a covering. And beneath the surface there is a heart of stone.

I believe that if there is a need to face in this critical hour in the church's history, it is this, right at the heart of the evangelical world. On the surface, you see, there was undoubtedly so much convincing speech among this kind of person of whom Jesus is speaking; and He is warning them about the utter impossibility of the living God penetrating into the vitals of their lives if they remain like this. So much convincing speech, but it is just empty talk!

Is it not true that much of our evangelical talk is just Christian chit-chat, betraying the shallowness of our lives? We go away from meetings and from services, and we say, "Lovely word! A fine message!" And our hearts beneath the surface are saying, "We shall not be moved!" Is that not true? I tell you diffidently, with the urgency of this fact in my soul that the place where this same spirit so often afflicts us is in the pulpit, when ministers believe that we have discharged our duty to the Word of God simply by preaching on it. "Oh, that's a great truth. I'll need to preach on that!" And we actually deflect the Word of God from the depths of our own souls.

I believe that we need to humble ourselves before God about this whole question of the shallow heart. May I say that this may be a shallowness that belongs to the world of a barren intellectualism as well as of a superficial emotionalism. It does not matter what the covering is if it hides that stony heart. The seriousness of this is that a man can live a lifetime at this level, deceiving and being deceived, and all the time he has never really faced and counted the cost of discipleship. He is ready for all the spiritual picnics, but when God begins to drive His Word deeper into his heart, so that "deep calleth unto deep" (Ps. 42:7), and to exercise him in the ways of adult godliness, the shutters are up, and he says, "Thus far and no further!"

THE DIVIDED HEART

Will you look with me briefly at the third picture of the *divided heart*? Here the seed really does get a deep hold, says Jesus, but the trouble is that it is not an undisputed hold. That means that the Word of God is not able to accomplish the purpose that the Holy Spirit means it to accomplish. The seed got in, and it got down, but it could not get room. The trouble was that there was a rival crop there which was left undisturbed. Gradually it grew and became dominant, and the good seed of the Word which once had seemed to be going down into the depths of the soil—and everything was set for a fruitful life—was strangled. And that field was ultimately left a wilderness.

It thereby becomes a picture of multitudes of once-promising lives. Like many an overgrown garden, that wilderness was not the result of deliberate cultivation, but it was the result of neglect. You just try neglecting your garden the way my predecessor did before I came into the house I am living in now, and I can tell you what the results are— the good seed had been strangled.

God is going to meet with you in these days, to make you, as this sick and lost world so desperately needs, a fruitful child of His and a fruitful servant of His. And it may be that He will make you face such issues as these.

> Is there a thing beneath the sun
> That strives with Thee my heart to share?
> Ah! tear it hence, and reign alone,
> The Lord of every motion there.[1]

Are you a barren child of God with a soul that is a wilderness? Have you, through neglect maybe, seen the Word stifled? We shall be

---

1 From Gerhard Tersteegen's hymn (translated by John Wesley), "Thou Hidden Love of God Whose Height."

finding that weeds, like "the cares of this world ... and the lusts of other things entering in" (v. 19), need radical treatment.

THE OPEN HEART

You will be relieved to turn with me to the last picture of the *open heart*. Some seed "fell on good ground ... and brought forth" (v. 8). It did so because this good ground is everything that the others are not. Here the seed can get in, and it can get down, and it can get room. After much patience and endurance—it is the endurance that Luke reminds us of—it bursts forth with all the glory of a new fruitfulness. The interesting and significant thing is that the same sun which scorched and burned up the plants in the shallow soil is the sun—be it tribulation, or the cost, or whatever it be—which ripens the grain in the deep soil.

I do not know why you have picked up this book and still less what is hidden away in your heart. You may be weary and worn, having gone through testing and tribulation, with a heart that is well-nigh torn with the sheer pressure of things. Or perhaps you know the virtue that has been slipping out of you over the years, and you have been in conflict with the powers of darkness. Then again, perhaps you are scarcely conscious of these things in the first place.

It does not matter that we do not know about one another. We do know this: that if we are going to let the Word of God get down into the depths of our being—if we are going to see it having free course in our hearts to probe and pierce and penetrate—we shall know its quickening power in our lives, and we shall prove the reality of the wilderness and the solitary place rejoicing and the desert blossoming like a rose (Isa. 35:1) and barren hearts which will know a new fruitfulness. There may be hard hearts ready to let the ploughshare of God's Spirit break up the fallow ground today. And I tell you, the outcome of this cannot be measured by man's mind.

I have a friend who is a minister. When he was a bachelor he had a notice which he used to put up on his study door for the benefit of his housekeeper at certain times of the day to ensure that he had privacy and quiet. It said quite simply, "Not Available." Anybody who came in or passed his door at that time knew that he was not accessible to anybody under any circumstances, except the most urgent. I have a feeling that, as God turns the searchlight of His eye upon our hearts, here and there are notices like that over our lives—ready for something, for some word that we may think we may need, but in some areas of our lives "Not Available" to God. May we let the Word of Christ dwell in us richly, for the glory of His name.

Chapter 2

SUMMONED BEFORE GOD

Also I heard the voice of the Lord, saying,
Whom shall I send, and who will go for us?
Then I said, Here am I; send me.
— Isaiah 6:8 —

I well remember one of the earliest Inter-Varsity Fellowship conferences that I ever attended as a student, when on the opening night a note was struck which stayed with us through the coming days. It was struck by the lady who was the gracious hostess in our midst, Mrs. J. O. Fraser, the widow of J. O. Fraser of Lisuland. As she spoke to us briefly on the first evening, these were the words that she used to focus the purpose of our coming together: "To what end is it if we dwell in Jerusalem and see not the face of the king?"

The point is that the real driving intention of a conference is not merely that we should come together to enjoy the blessing of fellowship with one another, or to go away thrilled with messages that are helpful, but that we should meet with God. And it is so very easy for us to evade or miss this basic concern. "To what end is it if we dwell in Jerusalem and see not the face of the king?"[2]

---

2   Editor's note: Eric Alexander applied his thoughts here to conferences, but it equally applies to Sunday worship services.

One of the classic accounts in the Bible of such an encounter with God comes to us in Isaiah 6:1-8. There is some doubt as to exactly when this experience of Isaiah's took place. John Calvin thinks that it came at the outset not of his ministry but of a particular part of his ministry. It came as a turning point in the man's experience, giving both his life and his ministry a new direction and a new impetus. But whenever it took place, there is no question that this was an experience that left the profoundest mark upon this man's life. He could never be the same man again. It left a mark, too, upon the place that he occupied in the purposes of God.

I want to look at four of the characteristic marks—four of the conspicuous features of this critical hour in the life of the prophet as he met with God. The first of these features of this experience of Isaiah comes in the introductory phrase of chapter 6, and it concerns the *death of Uzziah*.

DEATH OF UZZIAH

I have little doubt that this is the basic thing which solemnized the mind of this young man as he was brought into the presence of God in this hour of his life and ministry. You see, behind these sparse words, "In the year that king Uzziah died," there lies a tragic story—the story of a man who had known the anointing of God upon his life, the prospering hand of God leading him and the whole nation through him into days of blessing and prosperity unparalleled since the time of Solomon; a man who had risen to great heights with the hand of God upon his life and upon his reign. It is the story of a man who at the height of his career was beguiled from his earlier consecration and from his humble dependence upon God, and he became spiritually a back number.

George Adam Smith speaks of King Uzziah as the man with "a glorious reign with the ghastly end."[3] He has gone down in the history

---

3   George Adam Smith, *The Book of Isaiah: Vol. 1* (New York: A.C. Armstrong, 1899), 59.

of the people of God—gone down through the ages—as one of the great might-have-beens. The shadow of his life hung over this young man Isaiah in these days as he met with God—the shadow of a man who faded out of history when he was spiritually past his best, a man of whom it could only be said, "Oh, what he might have been if only, if only…!"

Have you noticed how often one comes across this kind of tragedy in the Bible—the tragedy of a man who either fades out of God's picture and God's purposes or who is set aside by God, over whose life there is written that frightening word "Ichabod … the glory is departed" (1 Sam. 4:21)? You remember Samson, Israel's mighty man of power in battle, who played with fire and ended his days as the clown of the Philistines. And he rose up to say, "I will go out as at other times before.… And he wist [knew] not that the LORD was departed from him" (Judg.16:20).

It was thus that Uzziah had faded from the scene, and there is no doubt that a man of Isaiah's spiritual perception must have known his heart solemnized and trembling before God by all this. His soul must have ached with the cry, "How are the mighty fallen!" If it could happen to a man like this, whom the young Isaiah probably raised on to a pedestal as the savior of Israel, who among men in Israel could stand?

What was it that caused the eclipse of Uzziah? What was this shadow which lay over Isaiah's life at this hour? There is a significant description of what happened to him in 2 Chronicles 26:15. God helped him and made him to prosper, "and his name spread far abroad; for he was marvellously helped, till he was strong." It was in that hour that the corruption set in in the life of this man Uzziah. In King Uzziah's case the corrupting thing was prosperity and the power that prosperity brings. He represents in the Bible the tragedy of men in every generation whose hearts are slowly—almost imperceptibly at first, but decisively nonetheless—being seduced away from God by materialism, by place and position and reputation and everything that is going to minister to the love of ourselves.

How often one has watched this tragedy enacted within Christian fellowships. Issues which were once crystal clear are now rather grey. "Oh, I used to think that way. I used to see things like that. But I've grown out of that now." The keen edge of a life of great spiritual promise blunted! I wonder if you know this kind of thing; I wonder if you know men whose spiritual victory could be described in one sentence: "He was marvellously helped, till he was strong."

My dear Christian friend, I wonder if you are spiritually past your best. You look back to former days and say, "Oh, that it were as it has been!" You have a testimony of something that happened years ago—of the impact of your life within the Christian fellowship—but the life that you now live is a life that has been, or is being, put aside by God. And I wonder if the cause of it in your experience could be the seduction that the world so often exerts upon God's children.

Do you find your heart over the years—not dramatically, so that people would notice too much yet, but gradually—being sucked away from your first love? Oh, the danger, the deadly danger, that things represent to the child of God! Do you remember that man who makes his appearance in the New Testament from time to time in the most select company? "We send you our greetings," the Apostle Paul says again and again. "Luke, the beloved physician, Mark, and Demas, my fellow worker; we send you our greetings." And "Demas, who labors with me in the Lord, sends his greetings." But by the time Paul is writing to Timothy there is an awful word that comes at the end of 2 Timothy: "Demas hath forsaken me, having loved this present world" (4:10). Do you know men like that, and could that man be you?

VISION OF GOD

Well, this was the shadow that overhung Isaiah. But the second characteristic mark of his experience was not the memory of Uzziah but the *vision of God*: "In the year that king Uzziah died I saw also the Lord sitting upon a throne, high and lifted up, and his train filled the temple" (v. 1). And that vision was, of course, the vision of God in His sovereign majesty. "I saw also the Lord sitting upon a throne," and no doubt the point that God was impressing upon the trembling heart of His servant was that although the throne of Uzziah was empty, God had not abdicated His throne. He was bringing to His servant the encouragement that God brings in every age to His children—in days of darkness and difficulty and doubt, when things have collapsed around them—by assuring them that He is King of kings and Lord of lords and is in control of all that He has made. "Mine eyes," says Isaiah, "have seen the King" (v. 5). And that vision can be a great comfort and blessing to God's people in days of despair.

But Isaiah did not find it so. Do you notice his reaction to this vision? It is the reaction of a man who finds himself utterly confused and "undone," as he says. And the reason is that Isaiah—in the midst of the crumbling collapse of the nation under the shadow of the judgment of God upon the life of a man who had risen to such heights and been cast out as a leper—found that one of the things that the sovereignty of God meant was the reign over all things of a God who is infinitely holy. One of the seraphs "cried unto another, and said, Holy, holy, holy, is the LORD of hosts" (v. 3). This is the thing that God is seeking to burn into the heart of His servant in this critical hour when He sees the possibilities of a life that could fade out into spiritual oblivion.

You may know that in Hebrew usage it is a common thing to repeat a quality to intensify the meaning of it. But this use of the word "holy" is the only place in the Old Testament where a characteristic is repeated, and repeated again, to give us some impression of something that is far beyond our understanding, deeper than our mind can grasp. The idea behind it is that the holiness of God is lifted right out of the realm of anything else that is known to men. That is what Isaiah saw flashing forth from the throne of God: the burning glory of a God who not only exhibits holiness but also demands it of His creatures. You see, to a man who has been trifling with God, the sovereignty of a holy God who does not refrain from intervening in the affairs of His children permanently is a very solemn and terrible fact.

SIGHT OF HIMSELF

That leads us to the third mark of this experience: not only the memory of Uzziah and the vision of God but also the *sight of himself*—for the effect of becoming aware of God's holiness is seen in two ways at the beginning of chapter 6. The effect of the holiness of God is seen in these sinless, heavenly creatures called the seraphim, who react in awe and wonder to this vision. It is something that is too great and too glorious for them, and with two of their wings they hide their faces, covering themselves from God's glory and holiness.

But the burning majesty of God has an entirely different effect upon the sinful creature. Isaiah describes his reaction to it like this: "Woe is me! for I am undone." As if to underline the truth of it, the very earth beneath him heaves as though it is convulsed with the holiness of God: "The posts of the door moved at the voice of him that cried, ... Woe is me! for I am undone" (vv. 4-5).

Then you will notice something that follows which almost seems to be an anticlimax: "Woe is me! for I am undone; because I am a man of unclean lips!" Would you have thought that he would have reacted so violently?—because this is something that has been exposed by the holy fire of God burning out from the throne of God to this man. A man of unclean lips? That is something that is rather an amiable weakness to us. But the point is, you see, that this is the place of reality for the child of God. This is why God summons us in the Scriptures to consider the holiness, the flaming glory of His character. It is because there, and there alone, do we see ourselves as we really are: where all our hypocrisy and pretense is burned up, and we are exposed before God. This is the God with whom we have to do.

We sing, sometimes glibly, "Give me a sight, O Savior!"[4] God knows if we came into His presence and saw Him in His glory, we should be thrust into the dust, and our foolish little proud spirits would be burned down before Him.

Was it not Robert Murray M'Cheyne who said, "What a man is alone on his knees before God, that he is, and no more"[5]? What kind of a man does that make you, with all reputation gone, with every kind of outward façade down?

Well, there is the sight of himself which Isaiah was given, but it was a sight that God gave him not merely to depress him, not because He was some cruel tyrant gloating over the misery of His creature, but so that it might be burned out with the live coal from off the altar, and that Isaiah might face the last of the characteristics of this experience.

THE CHALLENGE

And that is the challenge of the hour—the challenge of *how far he was going to be available for God*. And I think that this, too, comes under the shadow and within the context of all that he was remembering of Uzziah the king, who had faded out in such spiritual ignominy. There comes the challenge to God's servant: "Whom shall I send, and who will go for us?" And Isaiah cries, "Here am I; send me" (v. 8).

---

4   From Katherine Kelly's hymn, "Give Me a Sight, O Savior."

5   Quoted in D.A. Carson, *A Call to Spiritual Reformation: Priorities from Paul and His Prayers* (Grand Rapids, MI: Baker Academic, 2006), 16.

A missionary whom I respect very much—who has been in some of the new churches in Africa in the last ten years—came home some time ago and, having spent some of his time going round the churches in Great Britain, came to a meeting which I was attending. I said to him, "Would you be able to describe the difference you notice between the spiritual life of the Christians in Africa, among whom you have been working, where you have seen the Spirit of God moving, and Christian life in this country?"

"Oh," he said, "it is very simple. The difference is that in Africa the Christians are whole-hearted; in this country they are half-hearted."

I think he had put his finger upon the basic disease of the church of God in Britain in our time.[6] And the challenge of this hour, men and women, I believe is this: In your own life, in your own sphere of service, whatever age you may be, how far are you available for God?

In these days when the very moral fabric of our nation is crumbling—in these days of spiritual decline and darkness—how far are you available for God? How far are you accessible for Him? If God should break in upon your life in all His sovereign majesty and divert the whole course of your future from what you had planned, are you available for God? For this was the challenge of the hour for Isaiah, and he responded, "Lord, here am I; send me."

May it be that the same Lord of glory may so summon us before His holy throne that He may burn out of our hearts all coldness and every kind of unwillingness, draw us back from the seductive influence of every lesser thing, and lead us into the joy of being in the very center of His good and acceptable and perfect will.

---

6   Editor's note: Sadly, this disease has spread throughout Europe and also infects the church in America.

Chapter 3
A Heart-Cry concerning Sin

Create in me a clean heart, O God;
And renew a right spirit within me.
— Psalm 51:10 —

I suppose few of us have not in these days known something of the probings and the prunings of the Spirit of God as He has turned His Word upon our hearts and begun to search us and try us. We have come to see more clearly what we really are like. I do not doubt that some of us have one cry in our hearts, and it is the cry of the psalmist: "I am a worm, and no man" (Ps. 22:6). Having seen something of the blackness of my heart and of my sin, how can I find the way to restoration—to fellowship with the God whom my life and character have offended? When there has been so much that has grieved Him and cut me off from Him, how can I find the way back to the place of blessing?

I wonder if that is the language of your heart. It is because I believe some of us are saying these very things in the secret place of our soul that I want to turn to Psalm 51. The reason we turn to it is this: if these things are the language of your soul, then here in the psalm is a man who is speaking the same language—a man who has the same heart cry. It is the cry of a man who has discovered that there is only one thing that he can ask of God; there is only one plea that can find its way on to his lips, and it is a plea for mercy:

> Have mercy upon me, O God, according to thy loving kindness: according unto the multitude of thy tender mercies blot out my transgressions. Wash me thoroughly from mine iniquity, and cleanse me from my sin.… Create in me a clean heart, O God; and renew a right spirit within me (vv. 1, 2, 10).

"Oh," says David, "the sight of my own blackened heart is more than I can bear! O God, I want to know the way to cleansing. Make me clean!"

You will recollect the context of the psalm. David is a man who is bowed down beneath an awful load of shame. The psalm, we are told, was written "when Nathan the prophet came unto him after he had gone in to Bathsheba"; there is the dark beginning and background against which these words are breathed. David had thought that the whole thing was over and done with after Uriah was gotten out of the way. He had got rid of Uriah very conveniently and rather cleverly. It was all past and hushed up, and he would never hear anything more about it—so he thought.

But notice that terribly solemn postscript in 2 Samuel 11:27, where it seems as if God takes the divine pen in His hand and writes the postscript to the story: "The thing that David had done displeased the LORD." And David was to discover that that was the thing that really mattered about his sin.

Do you remember how he discovered that "there is nothing covered, that shall not be revealed; neither hid that shall not be known" (Luke 12:2)? It was when Nathan, the faithful prophet, came to him with the word of God; however costly it might be to declare it, he came to David with it. God knows how many of us have cause to be eternally grateful to faithful prophets who have crossed our paths. Nathan came to David and began to describe to him his own sin—only, as if in the life of another man. He told him the parable of the man whose sheep, his only one, was taken by the strong and wealthy. As David listened to the story, his heart was filled with hatred for this man of whom Nathan was speaking, and he cried out, "The man that has done this thing shall surely die!"

How often it happens among evangelical Christians that we rise up in damning judgment against the sin in the lives of other men and women which is the very thing that is eating the heart out of our own spiritual lives. Do you know that kind of hatred?

Then came the withering blast of reality, in Nathan's words: "Thou art the man!" (2 Sam 12:7). I wonder if that is what God has been saying to you, maybe in the quiet of your own soul, as some word that you have often applied to other people has been coming to your heart, and the breathings of the Spirit of God in your life have been saying but one thing: "Thou art the man!" Well, it was at such a moment of awful darkness that David poured out the words of this psalm. There are two notes in the psalm which I want us to consider together: *the cry from the heart of David* and *the concern in the heart of God.*

THE CRY FROM DAVID'S HEART

The great value of the Psalms, as I never tire of reminding myself, is that they are not primarily theological treatises but the authentic heart yearnings of men with whom God is dealing. They are not the polished phrases of the study, but they are the heartaches of men who are being dealt with by a holy God. There is no time there for artificiality. That is why you and I turn to the Psalms in the dark hours of our own lives. That is why, when a man is really seeking for God and seeking the way out of the state of his own heart, he so often turns to the Psalms because the psalmist does this one thing: he cries, "Come and hear, all ye that fear God, and I will declare what he hath done for my soul" (66:16). That is what David is doing here: he is declaring what God has done for his soul. And those who walk the same pathway may discover the same gracious God doing it again for them.

Notice first that this cry of David's reveals the *enormity of his sin*. That was the one thing which he could not ignore and which he could not free from the very center of his gaze. "Against thee," says David, "thee only, have I sinned, and done this evil in thy sight" (v. 4). That was the terrible thing about it, to David. On the surface, of course, that is not really true. We would say it was against Bathsheba, against Uriah, and against the child. But David says no, that is not the thing that makes it as black as hell. It is "against thee" that he has done it; he has "done this evil in thy sight."

That, says David, is the enormity of his sin. He had discovered, you see, that the root of the thing that has blighted and blasted his life was a rebellious and willful self that had risen up against the Lord of glory and cast its rebellion in His very face. He discovered what you and I have to discover if we are to find the place of blessing: that sin not only breaks God's law, but it also breaks God's heart. And David comes to the place where he has nothing else to say than "against thee, thee only have I sinned, and done that which is evil in thy sight, so that [and this is the proper translation] thou art justified in thy sentence and blameless in thy judgment" (RSV). He says whatever the sentence that is brought upon his blackened life, whatever the judgment, he has no quarrel with it: "Thou art justified in thy sentence and blameless in thy judgment."

This psalm is often called a Psalm of Confession, and that is what confession is. David has got to the place where he is agreeing with what God has to say about his sin. Did you know that the meaning of the Greek word in the New Testament for "confession," the word *homologeo,* is quite simply "to say the same things as"? David has discovered that as he has encountered God, he is saying the same things about his sin that God is saying; he has discovered the enormity of his sin.

It seems to me that perhaps the one thing which, more than many others, the church of Christ today is needing to recover is a sense of the enormity of sin. During the time of the prophets it was said that one of the ways by which the people of God were being led away from Him was that there was a healing of the heart which was too light. They cry, "Peace, peace; when there is no peace" (Jer. 6:14). David's cleansing came on the pathway of discovering the enormity of his sin.

Secondly, from the cry from the heart of David we discover the *reality of his seeking*. That is perhaps the key to David's restoration. Within his heart there is now a seriousness of purpose in finding the way back to God. Whatever God would do with him, whatever the cost of the cleansing, he says, "O God, I am ready for it." Have you noticed the words of verse 2? There are two words in the Hebrew for "washing." One means "rinsing lightly, dipping," and the other, rightly translated, means "to pummel." It is the word used for ingrained dirt—for drastic treatment. That is the cry on David's lips: "Wash me thoroughly, O God. Be it by water or by fire, make me clean."

That is the cry of a man who is serious about getting right with God—about getting back to the place of cleansing—whatever it costs. And I tell you, there is no heart that has become thus serious with God which is turned away. "Ye shall seek me, and find me, when ye shall search for me will all your heart" (Jer. 29:13). There was the reality of his seeking, the cry from the heart of David. But there is another side to the psalm.

THE CONCERN IN GOD'S HEART

Notice, first, the *sphere in which He works*. That is the thing which David has come to see as he moves on through this prayer. There is a question, you see, at the very outset, and it is this: What is the fundamental concern in the heart of God? Where is it that God does His work? What is the sphere in which He works? David says, "O God, sham that I have been all down the line, and all through this time, I have discovered now that thou desirest truth in the inward parts. The longing of my heart, O God, is that Thou wilt create in me not a clean reputation, not a clean semblance which will convince other people. Create in me a clean heart, O God; and renew a right spirit within me." That is the sphere in which He works. "Thou desirest truth in the inward parts" (v. 6), and oh, how desperately we need to learn that! We are living in an age of appearances, and that disease is eating its way into the heart of the Christian church, so that the great concern which masters and dominates our life is far too often the impression we make rather than the characters we have. And the word of the Lord is that it is character that counts with God. That is the sphere in which He works.

Do you remember how Jesus, with breaking heart, warned the people who gathered closest to Him against this very thing? He said, "If there is one type of man I long that you will not be like, it is the hypocrite." But what did that word mean to the ears of His disciples? It was a very common word in Jesus's time and meant an "actor." In the theatre they could cry, "What a grand *hupokritēs*!"—yes, what an effective hypocrite. One of the greatest tragedies of evangelical Christendom is surely this: that we have become past masters in the art of acting before other men, acting before ourselves, and we even have a try at acting before God.

But the sphere in which God works is the inward parts: "In the hidden part thou wilt make me to know wisdom" (v. 6). One of the greatest tragedies that could happen here would be for you to go away without giving God the chance really to work in the sphere in which He does His work. "Man looketh on the outward appearance, but the LORD looketh on the heart" (1 Sam. 16:7).

Secondly, there is the *sacrifice for which God waits*. David has discovered, as he draws near to the end of these heart breathings, that there is one condition of heart in his circumstances which is acceptable to God, and that is brokenness. This is the beginning of the way back. The sight of his own sin and the shame of his heart rebellion and the brokenness of the heart of God as He has looked down upon His servant in this morass of shame—all that awful burden has crushed and broken David. And the prayer that we have been reading and meditating upon is the prayer of a broken man.

I do not doubt that there were many people around him—and among them the people of God—who were very ready to despise David and whose barbed tongues would be eager to attack him who made capital out of his shame. But at that very moment there came the most blessed word that David could ever have heard. He says, "The sacrifices of God are a broken spirit: a broken and a contrite heart, O God, [such a broken man as I] thou wilt not despise" (Ps. 51:17).

Do you see the eternal pattern of the dealings of God with men being worked out here? The way to resurrection is ever through the brokenness of the cross. And the place of healing is the place that David found which foreshadowed the eternal place of healing for all men—the place of brokenness of heart at the foot of the cross. The cross is the answer to the psalm, to the need of David's heart, and to the need of my heart and of your heart. It is through death and brokenness that a resurrection into healing and health and newness of life comes. And God has come to lead us to that place. Our hearts have been made sore because of the probing of God's sword of His Spirit. Then He has brought us to the place where "the Sun of righteousness [shall] arise with healing in his wings" (Mal. 4:2) because it is the place of the cross for broken men and women. We have the eternal assurance of God that the broken and contrite heart He will not despise—thank God! May God in His mercy bring us there today.

Chapter 4
The Work of Christ

For the love of Christ controls us.
— 2 Corinthians 5:14 (RSV)[7] —

I suppose that almost all of us have some particular chapter or passage in the Bible which has a special place in our hearts for some reason or other. The second half of 2 Corinthians 5 is one such passage for me. I suppose it may well be because it was there that I first began to understand what it really meant to have a saving experience of the Lord Jesus Christ—what it really meant to be a true Christian. There was a period in my life when it seemed as if every preacher that I went to hear had conspired with every other preacher to preach on 2 Corinthians 5. They said, "The place that I want you to turn in your Bibles is," and I could have almost said to them, "Second Corinthians, chapter five!"

When I was thinking, therefore, of our need to begin by facing ourselves with some of the great fundamental issues of the Christian gospel, you may not be surprised that it is to this passage in 2 Corinthians that I found my mind turning, until it became God's insistent word in my heart.

---

7   Unless otherwise stated, Scripture quotations in this chapter are from THE HOLY BIBLE: REVISED STANDARD VERSION, International Bible Society.

It is very much with the things that lie at the foundations of the faith that the Apostle Paul is concerned in verses 14 to 21. Some pretty fundamental questions had been asked in Corinth about Paul and his ministry. Some of them had been asked by people with a pretty vitriolic line of criticism, and Paul was under fire in Corinth. He wrote this letter in answer to some of the questions and criticisms that had been raised about his life and his ministry.

"What is the man really living for?" they were asking. "What's the real motive behind his ministry? What is this message that he is preaching really deriving from?" It is in answer to these questions that Paul opens up his heart in a very personal way. Sometimes we feel that he is opening his heart diffidently, and almost reluctantly, but he wants to tell them what the key secret of his mind is—and the core and kernel of his ministry.

He does so in these six words of verse 14: "The love of Christ constraineth us," or in the RSV, "The love of Christ controls us."

It is important to notice what this love is that Paul is speaking about as he introduces this personal testimony to what the gospel of Christ—the whole Christian faith—really is. It is not Paul's love for Christ, for that is an evidence of salvation. The ground of a man's salvation is not his love for Christ but Christ's love for him. This is what Paul is speaking about in 2 Corinthians 5:14. It is Christ's love for him in a special way, not a vague sentimental feeling about Christ's love but a definite and a specific understanding of the love of Christ in what He has done by His death on the cross. "The love of Christ constraineth us," he says, "because we thus judge" (AV). We see it this way; we are convinced of this truth: that He died for all.

It is there that the love of Christ is displayed for the apostle. Indeed, in the whole of this passage he is absolutely absorbed with all that Christ has done *for* us: "He died for all" (v. 15); what He has done *in* us:

"If any one is in Christ, he is a new creation; the old has passed away, behold, the new has come" (v. 17); and what He is to do *through* us: "We are ambassadors for Christ, [God making His appeal through us]" (v. 20). That is the threefold work of Christ for the believer, and it is this threefold theme that I want to take up from this passage.

THE WORK OF CHRIST FOR US

These things lead us right to the very foundations of what the Christian gospel really is. I would first draw your attention, therefore, to what Paul has to say about what Christ has done *for* us. What is it that Christ has done for us, then? Well, Paul says, "He died for all." It is crystal clear in the New Testament that the work that Christ has done for us centers upon His death. What had gripped Paul's soul was the love of Christ seen in the death of Christ. But it is not simply that the death of Christ displays the love of Christ in a vague kind of general way. He loves so much that He was ready to go to the extent of dying on the cross. It is what God was doing there in the death of Jesus that really matters to the apostle. That death was actually accomplishing something for us.

In order to explain this, the Apostle Paul uses a variety of vivid word pictures in the epistles. Sometimes, for example, he uses the metaphor of the *law courts*. He pictures the whole of humanity summoned before the last assize[8] of God, and the heart of man is turned inside out in the presence of God. You know how people's lives are turned inside out in the law court. The whole of what we really are—not what we pretend to be, not what we keep up appearances to suggest that we are, but the real nature of man's heart—is poured out before God, and all his guilt and all his transgression is laid before

---

8   Editor's note: In law, an assize is a trial in a court of justice.

the judgment seat of the Holy One who searches into the hearts of men. And God declares the whole world guilty before Him. Man's great need as he stands before God's assize—as every single one of us shall do one day—is for pardon and acquittal, for what the Bible calls justification. The glorious, good news of the gospel is that by His death the Lord Jesus Christ has procured that. We are justified by faith, freely by His grace.

But sometimes Paul draws not from the world of the law courts but from the *slave market,* and he sees that sin not only brings men under judgment and into condemnation, but it also brings them into slavery and bondage. His great need, therefore, as he is in shackles, "fast bound in sin and nature's night,"[9] is for freedom—release from this bondage—for what Paul calls redemption. And Christ brings this: "In him we have redemption through his blood" (Eph. 1:7).

He breaks the power of cancelled sin,
He sets the prisoner free.[10]

But here in 2 Corinthians 5 Paul uses a third metaphor to tell us what Christ has done for us in His death, and it is the *domestic* metaphor which you find five times over in these verses. In verse 18, for example: "God, who through Christ reconciled us to himself and gave us the ministry of reconciliation." That is the picture which deals not with the problem of guilt or of bondage but with the problem of alienation and estrangement. The great need to which it points is the need for reconciliation.

What Paul is speaking about is not just man's estrangement from his fellows, or his alienation from society (although these are very

---

9   From Charles Wesley's hymn, "And Can It Be That I Should Gain?"
10   From Charles Wesley's hymn, "O for a Thousand Tongues to Sing."

real factors in the world in which we live). They are a symptom of something, and it bids us well to look to them and to understand what these symptoms are.

Jimmy Reid, the highly articulate Communist leader of the Upper Clyde Shipbuilders, was once chosen by the students of Glasgow University to be their rector. At his installation he delivered a remarkably penetrating rectorial address in which he was trying to assess and tease out the problems of modern society. And he summed them up in one word, which is the title of his address: "Alienation." He speaks of the alienation that there is in the world, the sense of estrangement—of black from white, of employer from employee, of children from their parents, of young people from society, this sense of an alienation that goes the whole way through life—and of that deeper alienation which seems to estrange people from themselves, so that you discover young people wondering who they are. Some of today's pop songs express this uncertainty. There is this great sickness throughout society of an alienation of spirit and heart and life.

Jimmy Reid was absolutely right. Alienation remains one of the great factors of our time, and the evidences of it are all around us: in literature, in art, in music. But where he is wrong (and tragically wrong, because so many people listen to him) is in not recognizing that these things are only the symptoms of an infinitely deeper disease: the ultimate estrangement and alienation in the universe—the alienation of man from God. That is the root of all the agony in the hearts of men, of the nations, and of the world in our generation.

It is this estrangement of man from God which meets you in the earliest chapters of the Bible. That is where you have got to go to understand the sicknesses of the modern world: to the Bible, to discover that man was made for fellowship with God—to bear His image, to share His presence, to enter into the knowledge of the Lord, and to live for Him. But by his rebellion against the Lord, and by his pride and his revolt, he is removed from the presence of God. Do you remember it? The Lord God drove Adam and Eve out from the garden and from His presence. The mark of Cain—the curse upon humanity—is that man became a fugitive and a wanderer on the earth. That is man's real sickness, beloved. And all the evidences of it are the evidences of the human spirit exiled from God, crying out for home, and unable to find it.

Aleksandr Solzhenitsyn, the Russian Nobel Prize winner for literature, in one of his books pictures man in the midst of a society where he says there are no signposts because there is no place to go—the homelessness of the human spirit.

Now, when God sets about dealing with that, He does not just medicate the symptoms, but He goes right to the root of the problem—He gets down to the heart of the disease. When we ask what God has done for us in Jesus Christ, the answer is in 2 Corinthians 5:18: He has reconciled us to Himself. What Christ was doing, therefore, by His death, was accomplishing a reconciliation between God and man. He was, therefore, dealing with that root from which all the symptoms spring. You will see now why I say that the most relevant thing for the modern world in all its sickness is the Christian gospel. It is all very well for men and women to diagnose the symptoms of our disease, but it is a very poor doctor who spends his time medicating symptoms. He wants to get at the root of the thing and put it right, and that is what the Lord Jesus Christ does.

How does His death do this? Well, Paul's emphasis in these verses is not on the physical suffering of Jesus's death and what He bore; it is rather on what He became for us. In verse 21: "For our sake he made him to be sin who knew no sin, so that in him we might become the righteousness of God." Do you see that exchange, which Paul says is the essence of what is happening on the cross? "He made him to [become] sin who knew no sin, so that in him we might become the righteousness of God."

To grasp the meaning of this, you really need to go back into the Old Testament where this truth is symbolized and prefigured. In Leviticus 16 you get the great picture of the Day of Atonement, when God arranged this great prefiguring of the death and sacrifice of our Lord Jesus Christ. On that Day of Atonement there was not one animal but two animals taken—two goats. One of them was killed and offered as a sacrifice on the altar. The other was kept alive and was called by a name which has entered into our everyday vocabulary. It was the "scapegoat," and the whole point of the scapegoat was that the sins of the people of Israel were taken, and by symbol in the hands of the priest they were laid on the scapegoat.

Listen to what happened to this scapegoat:

Aaron shall lay both his hands upon the head of the live goat, and confess over him all the iniquities of the people of Israel, and all their transgressions, all their sins; and he shall put them upon the head of the goat and send him away into the wilderness by the hand of a man who is in readiness. The goat shall bear all their iniquities upon him to a solitary land [or as the Authorized Version puts it, rather more pointedly, "a land not inhabited"] and he shall let the goat go in the wilderness (Lev. 16:21-22).

You see the point of this figure. Our Lord Jesus Christ, of course, is the great fulfillment of both of these pictures. He is the Lamb slain, but He is also the fulfillment of this other picture—of this goat upon which all the sin of the people was laid. And then it was taken by the hands of a fit man out into the wilderness, without the camp. It was taken to the place of isolation; it was taken to the place of being cut off from man and from God, in a land not inhabited.

That is the shadow of which Jesus is the fulfillment in His death. What is happening on the cross is that He is identified with our guilt and our sin and our shame and all that it has brought into the universe and has done between man and God. He was led without the camp, into the no man's land of being isolated and separated from God and from men.

Do you remember how that is prefigured in Gethsemane, and Jesus is withdrawn from them? Some of them could come a certain distance, and then He says to them, "Sit here, while I go yonder and pray" (Matt. 26:36). He is cut off from man by His holiness. And ultimately on the cross, as He cries out from that agony of desolation, "My God, my God, why hast thou forsaken me?" (Matt. 27:46), He is cut off from God by our sin. That, says Paul, is where the reconciliation has been accomplished. That is where he has found the love of Christ, and it set his heart on fire, beloved. He entered into all that it meant to be isolated from God, even for these moments which were an eternity, in order that we might know what it was to be brought nigh, and brought back, and know that fellowship with the Father for which we were born. That is the work of Christ for us.

THE WORK OF CHRIST IN US

Let me say something to you about the work of Christ *in* us, for the glory of this gospel to Paul is not that God has just done something at a certain point in history, but it is that He has brought the riches of His grace into your life if you are a Christian. The nature of Christ's work in us is so radical, so glorious, and so cataclysmic that the only adequate parallel for it is the creation of the world at the beginning. Do you see this? In 2 Corinthians 5:17: "Therefore, if any one is in Christ, he is a new creation; the old has passed away, behold, the new has come." Again in 2 Corinthians 4:6, Paul says that "it is the [same] God who said, 'Let light shine out of darkness,' who has shone in our hearts to give the light of the knowledge of the glory of God in the face of Christ." He says that the same God who spoke out into the void at the creation and said, " 'Let there be light,' and there was light," is doing it again, this time in the heart of the believer. He is saying, "Let there be light," and "the light of the knowledge of the glory of God in the face of Christ" shines into my heart, hitherto estranged from Him, and brings me to know Him.

Oh, I want you to see this! If you are a child of God, beloved, what has happened in your heart is not that one day you made up your mind to follow the Lord Jesus. That did happen, and blessed be God for that day, but what has really happened in your heart is a miracle of God's grace akin to the creation of the world. It is not just that you have got a bit of religion mixed up with your life, and that perhaps someday that bit of mixture may get out, and you'll be back where you started again. The apostle says, "He is a new creation; the old has passed away, behold, the new has come."

Let me try to illustrate this from my school days which, as my children are constantly reminding me, were "not yesterday, Daddy!" I went to a school that had a special emphasis on science; and these poor people, for whom I now have the greatest sympathy, tried to teach me chemistry and physics. There was one thing that stuck in my mind, however, and it was the experiment whereby they taught us the distinction between a compound and a mixture. Do you know what the distinction is?

Well, they taught us it by taking two things, iron filings and sulfur. What happened was this: the iron filings and the sulfur were mixed together—that's a mixture. But a mixture is something that is reversible, and the way it can be reversed is demonstrated by taking a large magnet and putting it over the mixture of iron filings and sulfur; and the iron filings leap up to the magnet, of course, and you can get all the iron filings out. In other words, you can put it back to what it was like before.

But if you put the iron filings into the sulfur, and then put a burner underneath them, something quite different happens. The iron and the sulfur come together not as a mixture but as a compound; and you get a new substance called ferrous sulfide. It is something new, and the important thing about it is that it is irreversible.

You see, that is the distinction between having a little bit of a mixture of religion in your life, which can be taken away with a change of circumstances, or advancing years, or a change of thought, or something of the kind, and having a work of grace done in your heart, where God makes you a new creature. If you are a child of God, settle your heart on this: this work of grace is irreversible. It is a relationship that has been forged for all eternity. That is the ground on which you can be sure that you are a Christian. It is something that God has done, that you have come to Him in Jesus Christ and received His grace in the gospel; it is something that forges a relationship which is eternal.

This new creature finds that he has been created for a special purpose, and this is part of the work of Christ in us. The description of the new creature is in verse 15: "He died for all, that those who live might live no longer for themselves but for him who for their sake died and was raised." What is the transformation that takes place in a man when the grace of God touches him, brings him from being a stranger to God and Christ, and reconciles him to God? The transformation is this: the mark of the new creature is that he is no longer living unto himself, but unto Him who died for him and rose again. That's what a Christian is.

A Christian is not somebody who has necessarily got what we call "a testimony" about the date and hour when he was converted, although thank God if you have got that; I am not despising it. But what I want to say is something even more important than that. A Christian is somebody who has seen the change take place in his life whereby he now no longer wants to live for himself, but for Christ. That's what it means to be a new creature: that we live no longer to ourselves, but unto Him.

THE WORK OF CHRIST THROUGH US

Finally, a word about the third of these areas in which the work of Christ applies to us. It is the work of Christ *through* us. Paul says that God has not finished when He has brought us to Himself and reconciled us to Him through the cross. He not only gives us the reconciliation, but He also gives us a ministry. This is the ministry: "We are ambassadors for Christ, God making his appeal through us. We beseech you on behalf of Christ, be reconciled to God" (v. 20). That is the work of Christ through us. Here is a glorious thing, beloved: that the same God who has devised the reconciliation and procured it for us in Jesus Christ has chosen to proclaim it to the world through people like you and me.

That is what your life is for: that God may make His appeal through you to the world. I tell you, it never ceases to amaze and astonish me, knowing my own heart as I do, at least a little, that God is able even this moment to make His appeal through these words to you—that the Lord Jesus Christ is able to come and stretch out His hand through me and reach to you. Maybe it is here that He wants to speak to you, because right down at the very foundations you have never been brought to God through Christ. God making His appeal through us!

It may be that you are here at this very moment for that very reason. Then that passage could become very real for you, too, and you might go out from this time forward blessing God that He brought you to this point—to bring you to Jesus and to bring you everlasting life. May God grant it to be so, for His name's sake.

Chapter 5
The Foundation of Faith

But he was wounded for our transgressions, he was bruised for
our iniquities; the chastisement of our peace was upon him;
and with his stripes we are healed.
— Isaiah 53:5 —

All Christians are united by two basic truths. The first is that we have been born into the family of God by faith in our Lord Jesus Christ; and we are able, because of this, together to call Him our Father. The second truth that binds us together is that, having been born into the family of God, we have in some measure a desire and a hunger to grow up as His children. And this is our concern. Our aim will be that we might seek not some emotional experience, nor some shortcut to spiritual maturity, but to try to learn from the truth of God the means by which we may grow up in our spiritual lives, be established in the faith, and become mature men and women of God.

This means that there is one thing which is necessary. Remember my minister friend in Glasgow who, before he was married, had the little notice "Not Available" which he used to pin up outside his study door? Of course, now that he has a wife and children, he knows better than to put notices like that outside his door!

But, you know, ever since I first saw it, I have thought that there are many of us who find it quite possible to have unseen notices written over our hearts: "Not Available to God"—available for some of the things that He may want to say to us, but quite unavailable for others. I think it would be a wonderful thing if we were to immediately take down every such barrier to God, so that whatever He may want to say to us now, we may be accessible to Him.

Now, I said that the concentration of our attention will be upon spiritual growth, but it will be immediately obvious to you that both in the physical world and in the spiritual world, the very possibility of growth depends upon birth. A baby cannot begin to grow until it has been born. And until men and women have been born of God spiritually and begun a new life in Jesus Christ, spiritual growth is equally impossible for them.

There are always some people who discover themselves looking at the whole thing from the outside—who find themselves somehow or other, in all this talk about spiritual growth and going on to know Christ better day by day, not participators in the Christian life but spectators of it. They discover that they are viewing from without. My concern is to focus our thinking, for this reason, on the things that lie at the very foundation of our faith. That is why we are looking at Isaiah 53, that we might come to what lies at the root of the matter and address ourselves to discover the very basis of our life as Christians. This will not only be something of great importance to those who find themselves detached from all that seems to mean so much to others, but it will also be of tremendous importance to committed Christians, that we may come again to be sure of our foundations.

The reading of Isaiah 53 seems to impose a strange solemnity on people's hearts, partly, I suppose, because it is describing in such detail the death of Jesus eight hundred years before it took place, but partly also because there is something in our hearts that responds instinctively to the central figure in the Christian message—to Jesus Christ, and specifically to this whole matter of His death on the cross. There is nothing so central in the Christian message; there is nothing that lies more truly at the foundation of our faith than this.

This is what the whole Bible is insistently pointing us to. You find that in the Gospels the imbalance of their presentation of Jesus's life is quite remarkable—a far greater proportion of the account of Jesus's life is taken up with the story of His death than with the details of His life on earth. You find that Jesus Himself insisted upon this. He spoke about something He called "mine hour," which He repeatedly described as having "not yet come," and only when He is in the very shadow of the cross do we hear Him say, "The hour has come." In other words, the supreme hour for which He had come into the world was the hour associated not with His triumphant deeds in His life but with the giving of Himself in His death.

We find the apostles continuing this; this was the preaching of the Christian message. "We preach Christ crucified.... I am determined," says the Apostle Paul, "not to know any thing among you, save Jesus Christ, and him crucified" (1 Cor. 1:23; 2:2). This was their message, and this is the message that I want us to look at.

Isaiah 53 is basically a statement of belief about the death of Jesus, but you will notice that it begins not with a statement about belief but with a statement about unbelief. It begins with a question which is posed in such a way that it expects a particular answer: "Who hath believed our report?" And the answer is that not very many have believed it. So the two themes of the passage are not simply Christ as the One in whom men gladly believe but also Christ in whom so many men and women find it impossible to believe. It is first a statement about unbelief and then a statement about belief. And it is centered in both cases upon Christ; first, on *Christ the stumbling block*, and second, on *Christ the substitute and the Savior*.

CHRIST THE STUMBLING BLOCK

Let us look, first, at *Christ who is the stumbling block* to so many. The first thing we discover as we turn to this fifty-third chapter of Isaiah, in all its beauty and wonder and power, is that the message of Jesus Christ crucified for the sins of men is not a message which men and women find it natural to accept and believe. "Who hath believed our report?" This Jesus, says the prophet, is One who has no form nor comeliness; when we shall see Him, there is no beauty that we shall desire Him. Instead of being gladly accepted and received by men, He is despised and rejected by them—the One from whom we have hidden, as it were, our faces.

This was written eight hundred years before the advent of Jesus into the world, and it ought to have prepared us, as nothing else could do, not to be surprised at unbelief. When the apostles began to preach the death of Christ as the central fact of history—as the basic thing with which men and women needed to reckon—they discovered that to the Jews this message, this Jesus, was not a Savior but a stumbling block. To the Greeks, this message of the need of a Savior who had died on the cross was folly. And it is a very good thing for us to recognize this, as we seek to bring this message of Jesus to other people. There is by nature in every man and woman something which blinds them to the true reality of who Jesus Christ is. He is One from whom we hide our faces—whom men reject and despise.

The Apostle Paul gives us the answer to this situation in 2 Corinthians 4:3:

If our gospel be hid, it is hid to them that are lost; In whom the god of this world hath blinded the minds of them which believe not, lest the light of the glorious gospel of Christ, who is the image of God, should shine unto them.

Why, then, is it that your friends find it impossible to believe? University students come to me, as I move here and there in the universities, and say, "I am persuaded that the reason why some people find it possible to believe in Jesus Christ is that there is a certain section of the human race who are more gullible than others." And in the quiet of their minds, I believe, there are many people who are quite persuaded about this.

But the Apostle Paul opens up the reason to us. There is not only a power at work in the hearts of men, seeking to open their eyes to who Jesus is as the answer to the basic human dilemma. There is another power at work in our hearts to blind us to Him: "The god of this world hath blinded the minds of them which believe not." And when people say to me, in rather a superior manner sometimes, "I just don't see it that way; that's the way you see it, but I don't see it that way," they are speaking much, much more literal truth than they imagine, for the great problem is that until a man has found his way to Jesus Christ, he just cannot see.

So Isaiah turns us to the answer to this problem in verse 1: "Who hath believed our report? and to whom is the arm of the LORD revealed?" In other words, this truth about who Jesus Christ is, in all the wonder of His ability to come into the hearts of men and reclaim them from the ruin of their own sin, is something that is not arrived at merely by the exercise of intellectual ability, although it is certainly far from irrational, but it is arrived at by the revelation of God to the heart and mind. That is why you find people suddenly saying—sometimes the most thoughtful of people who have sought to think their way through all this—"Ah, I see it now!"

You remember in Matthew 16 when Jesus asked the disciples, "Who do men say that I am?" and then, "Who do you say that I am?" they began to give confused answers; they hardly knew. Then Peter came out with it: "Thou art the Christ, the Son of the living God." Immediately Jesus said, "Simon, flesh and blood has not revealed this to you, but my Father."

That is one of the most humbling things for us ever to realize, is it not? Can man by searching find out God? And the answer really is, no, although that does not mean that we have not to seek. It means that because there is a darkness over our hearts and minds, it takes nothing short of the same kind of command from the lips of God that came at the creation of the world, "Let there be light," to dispel that darkness and let us see this Jesus. That is why Paul goes on to say in 2 Corinthians 4, "For God, who commanded the light to shine out of darkness, hath shined in our hearts, to give the light of the knowledge of the glory of God in the face of Jesus Christ" (v. 6).

CHRIST OUR SUBSTITUTE AND SAVIOR

Isaiah 53:5 summarizes the teaching of *Christ our substitute*. Whatever else one may say of the Bible's teaching on the meaning of Jesus's death as it is summarized in this verse, it is patently obvious that this death of Jesus has something to do with Him, and it has something to do with us.

You catch the sense of this even in the language of verse 5: "He was wounded for our transgressions, he was bruised for our iniquities: the chastisement of our peace was upon him; and with his stripes we are healed." You see how it moves backwards and forwards: He was wounded—our transgressions. He was bruised—our iniquities. His chastisement—our dispeace. His stripes—our sickness.

This is the whole point of the Bible's teaching about the meaning of the death of Jesus. It is not just in an impersonal sense the sin of the world that Jesus is doing something about from a distance, but it is my sin and my transgression. It is the sickness of your life and the ills of your heart that Jesus Christ is not just looking at but taking to Himself and dealing with there on the cross.

You notice that in verse 5 we find four descriptions of human need and four descriptions of Christ's answer to that need. Of ourselves it is said that we have *transgressions, iniquities, dispeace,* and, finally, a *sickness* from which we need to be healed. Of Jesus it is said that He was *wounded,* He was *bruised,* He was *chastised,* and He *suffered stripes.* In each case these truths about ourselves and about Jesus move from the circumference of the truth into the center, for transgression is sin in its outward expression and moves into a sickness that belongs to our inner being. And Jesus's suffering is described first as wounding—an outward assault on His body—and goes on to the stripes which cut to the very quick of His spirit, to deal with the depths of our sickness.

Let us briefly look at them together. You notice that our human need is described, first, as *transgression,* which is sin of conduct—the public and outward act of sin. This God has dragged out into the open afresh at the cross; this is sin specifically as it relates to the breaking of God's commandments—God's law.

The word "transgression" is just the anglicizing of a Latin word meaning "to go across, to travel across." This is what it means in reference to the law of God. It means the cutting across God's law, despising it, casting it aside. It is important to recognize this, in these days when men and women are gaily casting aside law and restraint. But the Word of God states unequivocally that there is a permanent character about the law of God, and that men and women are going to be faced with its demands on Judgment Day.

You remember the words of Jesus: "Whosoever … shall break one of these least commandments … shall be called the least in the kingdom"

(Matt. 4:19). In other words, Jesus's judgment of men is concerned with how they fare over against the law of God. This is tremendously important. It is the first description of human need that we discover here. And, of course, we find it so easy to send these outward acts of transgression down into the murky past of our own ability to forget.

But do you know the word in the Scripture which disillusions us about our own ability to cast so much behind us that has offended against God's holy law? "God requireth that which is past" (Eccles. 3:15). At the cross of Jesus this is the primary fact that is declared about human sin: that it matters to God that men and women break His law.

But the second description takes us further in. If the first, transgression, was a description of sin in our conduct, the second word, *iniquity*, is a description of sin in our character. It goes beyond our outward habit of breaking the law of God to seek below the surface for the reason for this disposition of our lives. And that is what iniquity is. This is the condition which produces the act. It is traced in the Bible to the fundamental problem of man, namely that his will is inverted and perverted against God—the inward rebellion which has sought to dethrone God from His rightful place in my life and replace Him with myself. This is the essence of sin: it is playing God. That is what sin is. Primarily, you see, sin is not the outward act, but it is the result of an inward condition which is much more important. And it is a condition which can be found in the most respectable of people.

It was the condition found, you will remember, in the Pharisee in the temple, who was a religious man. The opening sentences of his prayer revealed the kind of man he was. He stood before God with great self-assurance and "prayed with himself." Do you notice this clever juxtaposition of words in the account in Luke? "He prayed thus with himself, God, I thank thee, that I am not as other men [I do this, I do that…]" (Luke 18:11). In other words, the man's god was himself. That is what Paul means as he writes to the Romans in chapter 1: "[They] worshipped and served the creature more than the Creator" (v. 25). That is what sin is, and that is the root of every kind of sin.

Don't believe the man who tells you, "Of course, I'm not a religious character, you know. There are some of us who are religious people; I'm not!" Do you know that men and women are by constitution incurably religious? But some of them have perverted the true point of worship for which they were created. I know some men who worship their motor car. I know others who worship their bank balance. But the basic thing that we worship in place of God is the little god of "me and mine and I." That is the basic thing for which men without Christ will go to a lost eternity. They worship and serve the creature rather than the Creator, "wherefore God … gave them up" (v. 24).

Two other words describe the result of sin in our lives. We have seen its nature; now we see its result. And this is described, first, as *dispeace*, then as *sickness*, or disease.

This *dispeace*, of course, is something which we can see in the lives of men and in the world in our time. The seething unrest among young people today bears witness to this. Why is it that you find this agonizing inability to find something that will satisfy? It is basically because the dispeace in the human heart derives from a lack of peace with God. It derives from our alienation from Him, and everything is out of sorts because of this. Nothing is what it ought to be. The whole world in which we live is unfit to satisfy our hearts. Sin always produces dispeace, and it derives from that fundamental dispeace between God and ourselves. There is an enmity there which has to be dealt with before any other dispeace will be cured.

But it is also a disease, and the word means a *sickness* that leaves no part of our life untouched. That is what our forefathers meant when they spoke of "the total depravity of the human heart." They did not mean that our hearts were as bad as they possibly could be; they meant that there was no part of them which was untouched by the stains of sin. That is a very solemn picture, but it is also very true. But the other side of it is far more wonderful than the other is awful. It is that stage by stage Jesus Christ has met every such need in the hearts of men by what He has done on the cross.

Look at these words with me: "He was wounded"—the word that speaks of an outward assault on His body as He suffered, bled, died, and was humiliated and punished on the cross. "He was bruised"—the word that speaks of His bearing our sin in a far deeper sense than in His physical agony. It speaks of something that is beyond the outward flesh. And this is what the New Testament means when it tells us that the significance of the cross of Christ is not in what He suffered in His body but in what He became. He became sin for us—He who knew no sin, that the righteousness of God might be fulfilled in us (2 Cor. 5:21).

It speaks also of a word which is exclusive in its application: the word "chastisement." You know, of course, that not everybody can chastise. I have two little children, both of whom from time to time need chastising, although I am the softest daddy in the world and find it very difficult, and they can twiddle me round any of their little fingers. You know, a stranger coming into our home could punish them, but he could not chastise them. Chastisement is a father's act.

This brings us to one of the most dreadful things about this message of Christ's death on the cross: that there as He hung, not only was He cut off from men, but He also found Himself cut off from God: "My God, my God, why hast thou forsaken me?" The God of all glory and holiness turned His back, at that instant, on Jesus the Sin Bearer. All this that the great gaping wound of the need of the human heart might be met and healed, and if there had been need in no other heart but yours, it would still have been done.

Well, there is one side of the picture, and there is the other. But how are the two brought together? That is the last thing. Notice the third word in verse 1. Here is the fundamental thing that brings the two together: "Who hath believed our report?" The essence of it, in other words, is in the believing of the message. What does that mean?

There are two kinds of belief spoken of in the Scripture. There is believing *in* something or someone, and there is believing *on* someone or something. The one means that you accept intellectually a certain truth that someone has stated, and you agree that it is true, accurate, and reliable. Or you accept someone as being trustworthy. That is believing *in*. But when the man asked Paul in the Philippian jail, "Sirs, what must I do to be saved?" Paul did not say to him, "Believe in the Lord Jesus Christ," but he said, "Believe *on* the Lord Jesus Christ" (Acts 16:30-31, italics added). There is a difference, because the one involves simply an intellectual acceptance; the other involves a moral obedience of heart and mind and a commitment of life.

I sometimes illustrate it to people by the difference that there would be when someone goes out onto the runway of an airport and sees a plane that is going from one destination to another. When they hear about this plane and where it was built and how good and airworthy it is, they, of course, believe in it as a vehicle that is worthy of the trust of people who are traveling. But that does not take them from point A to point B. They can go on believing in the plane until they see it soar into the sky and it is gone, and they are still where they are. But when they go out onto the tarmac and step on to the plane, committing themselves to it, they are no longer spectators; they are participators.

Which are you?

Chapter 6

Reconciled to God

All this is from God, who through Christ reconciled us to himself
and gave us the ministry of reconciliation.
— 2 Corinthians 5:18 —

We should now look at some of the great issues that face us in seeking to live the Christian life. But at the very beginning it would be unwise of us not to recognize a most obvious fact: that it is impossible for a man to live the Christian life without having the Christian life to live. It is impossible for a man to grow in the Christian life until he has been born into the Christian family. And so I want to face, first of all, some of the great priorities in this matter of living the Christian life.

I want us to look at the fundamentals of our faith—at the answer to the question, How can I become a Christian? And I want you to imagine, if you will, that you have never heard all this before, for many of us have grown so accustomed to the Christian message that somehow or other we begin to think, whenever we hear it, "I've heard all that long, long ago." I want us to seek to hear God's message as though it were the first time that it had come to us.

One of the most striking things that an intelligent man who is reading the New Testament for the first time discovers is the sheer disproportion that he finds in the Gospels. They are declared to be the life story of Jesus Christ—His biography—yet when you begin to read the Gospels for the first time, you discover that there is an extraordinary disproportion about the space they allot to different areas of the life of Jesus. For instance, the man who is intelligently reading the Gospel of Matthew would discover that one-fifth of the whole of the story was taken up with matters concerning Jesus's death; in the Gospel of Mark the proportion is one-third; in the Gospel of Luke, two-fifths; and when we come to the Gospel of John, we discover that practically one-half of the Gospel is concerned not with the life of Jesus but with His death.

This is a very strange thing because every historian who sets about writing the life of someone who is important concerns himself with the matters of the man's life—with the things he said and did, with the peculiarities of his personality, and with the whole story of his time here on earth. But the extraordinary thing about the story of Jesus in the New Testament is that its great emphasis is not upon His life but upon His death. Not only so, but we also discover, when these men in the New Testament go out to preach the Christian message, that the apostolic message is concerned primarily not with the life of Jesus but with His death. We find the Apostle Paul, for instance, telling the Corinthians that He preaches "Christ crucified."

We discover that Jesus Himself, during all the days of His earthly ministry, is supremely conscious that He has come into the world for one hour above every other hour, the hour that He calls "mine hour." Again and again throughout Jesus's life we discover Him using words like these: "Mine hour is not yet come"; "The hour is not yet come." Only when Jesus is within sight of the cross do we find Him saying, "The hour is come, that the Son of man should be glorified" (John 12:23). In other words, Jesus sees His life as being deliberately measured out, under the sovereign purpose of God, to an hour when He will come to the cross of

Calvary. Of course, men and women who were gazing on—His enemies among the Jews and the Roman soldiers—think this is just some kind of accident that has befallen a young man in the prime of his life, but Jesus said, "This is the hour for which I have come into the world."

There must be something uniquely significant about this, when we discover that the life history of Jesus is centered not upon His life but upon His death, and we find that the whole of the New Testament is in concord with this disproportion. Out of all proportion to its seeming significance to men, the New Testament emphasizes beyond everything else the fact that Jesus came into the world supremely to die.

So the crucial question about the whole of the life of Jesus is, Why is this so? What is the meaning of the life and death of Jesus Christ, when He is supremely conscious that He has come into the world not to live but to die? When the true significance of His life is to be found in His death, what is the meaning of the death of Jesus?

Notice that the New Testament uses a number of picturesque words to describe the death of Jesus Christ and the significance of it not just for Christians but for the whole world. The New Testament uses pictorial words to show us what the message that Jesus was declaring to us from Calvary really is. Most of them are words that come from different spheres of life.

For instance, we discover the Apostle Paul using a word that comes from the *legal world,* the word "justification," which we might translate in our modern language "acquittal." Justification, and the picture that Paul paints as he uses this word again and again, is the picture of a law court where the people in the dock are the whole of mankind. The apostle seems to be bringing the whole of humanity before the judgment seat of God and begins to hear the witness for the prosecution—in other words, the case against man. He even pictures himself, you, and me— every one of us—in the dock before God.

Paul's concern is to set down the case that God has against man. He begins in Romans 1 to 3 the great, vast indictment that God brings before man and says, "How can you answer this? Here are the things that God has against you. Here are the things that an all-seeing God has discovered in your life that offend Him, and that are worthy of His condemnation. How can you answer it?" Paul waits for the witnesses for the defense to come and then discovers that there is no voice raised in defense of the charges that are brought against man. The result is "that every mouth may be stopped, and all the world may become guilty before God" (Rom. 3:19).

Then Paul paints the wonderful picture of how, from the throne of God, there comes a message to the man in the dock that the charge, the verdict, and the penalty are not going to be worked out and paid in the life of sinful, hopeless, and helpless man but are going to be paid in the Person and work of the Son of the Judge Himself, even Jesus Christ. So that by Him, says Paul—and this is the message that Paul takes out to the world— we have freedom from the condemnation of God, so that "there is therefore no condemnation to them which are in Christ" (Rom. 8:1).

He uses another word, from the *slave market* this time—the word "redemption." Here, Paul's picture is of the whole world not judged before a holy God but bound in bondage, chain, and fetters from which man cannot break free. Paul, as you may have noticed, has this deep insight into the nature and the reality of the life of men. He discovers that the truth about man—despite all his vaunted boasts, despite all his achievement and all his discovery—is that he is in shackles to a bondage from which he cannot break free. Paul sees beyond the outward façade to the realities of men who are sitting in bondage—the most erudite and the most ignorant, the richest and the poorest—discovering that there is a bondage from which they cannot free themselves. Paul tells them of One who comes into this slave market with the ransom price to give to those in bondage freedom and liberty. This is the message that comes from the cross of Jesus.

But the word that he uses in 2 Corinthians 5:19 is neither of these. It is a much more homely word and a word that we still use in our vocabulary today: "reconciliation." It is a word we often use about two people who are estranged from each other; something has brought a gulf between them, and we say there is the need for reconciliation.

Now, says the apostle, this is precisely the situation that exists between man and God. Man discovers when he is honest with himself—and above all when he has listened to the Word of God—that he is a stranger to God. Paul pictures the need for reconciliation not just between men and men and nation and nation but supremely and most deeply between man and God.

This estrangement that Paul speaks about is the result of man's disobedience. It is not because of anything that is in God that we are broken away from Him, drifted, and at a distance from Him. Paul describes elsewhere in the New Testament how we ourselves have rebelled against the government of God over our lives. We have cast Him from His rightful place in our lives; we have worshipped and served the creature rather than the Creator. We have broken His law; we have transgressed His commandment; we have offended against Him. We have sought to live our lives for ourselves and have refused to acknowledge that we were created not for ourselves and for our own pleasure and satisfaction but for God. Because of this, says the apostle, we find ourselves aliens and enemies and strangers to God.

You remember how this was illustrated in the beginning of the Old Testament, when Adam and Eve rebelled against God's word that He had given them. He had told them how they were to live in the world, and they rebelled against Him. And when they did, they discovered that something happened in their experience. Life did not go on as it had before; it never does after sin! Adam and Eve discovered that they were driven out of the garden, and God put cherubim with a flaming sword at the end of the garden so that they would not come to the tree of life.

Every Jew who went up to the Temple in Jerusalem in days to come discovered that there was a great veil that shut out God from him, and he might not go through it. You remember that the day when that veil was torn down was the day when Jesus died upon the cross.

This separation between God and man is not something simply that the Bible teaches, but this is something that experience confirms to every honest man, woman, boy, and girl. They discover that God is desperately unreal. Young people today in my church in Ayrshire come and say to me, "You know, all this talk about God is utterly irrelevant in my situation, in my life. You are not with it! You don't understand! This God you talk about is a theory; He is ancient; He doesn't mean anything to us."

Not only so, but many people who are of a very different turn of mind also say, "You know, when I got into a jam, and things seemed to be tumbling in upon me, I tried to pray. When I tried, it seemed as if I was talking to somebody I didn't know—somebody who was far away. And it all seemed so desperately unreal." My friends, that is simply experience confirming what the Bible has been teaching all along: that God and man have been cut off from each other and need to be reconciled.

The result of that central fact about human experience ramifies out into a thousand different sicknesses of the human heart and of the whole of society. It stems from this one thing: that man and God have been separated from each other. This is what the apostle is concerned to answer in 2 Corinthians 5:11-21. How is it that man and God may be brought together again, after this mutiny on the part of men against

God? How may they be reconciled? When God Himself has driven man from Him, how may we be brought back to Him?

Well, that is the same question as, How may I become a Christian? The apostle answers it in four different ways. First, he says that *the author of this reconciliation is God Himself*: "All this is of God" (v. 18, RSV). The only hope that men have of being brought back to God from the place of banishment, says Paul, lies in whatever God may do, or has done, in order to bring it about. There is no hope for any man of himself finding his way back to God when he has been banished from Him.

The apostle says it all depends upon God, and the reconciliation that He offers to men is something of which God alone is the author. The one who has taken the initiative —and this is Paul's good news, or gospel—is God. What He has done through Jesus Christ is done by Him and is finished before ever we hear the good news about it. So the apostle is coming, you see, not with a message that says to people, "You must do this, and you must do that before God will be prepared to receive you back to Himself." He tells them about something that has happened—something that God has already done in Jesus Christ.

Now I suppose this is one of the hardest lessons that any of us can ever learn. There is something like an indestructible weed that grows in the heart of man, a conviction that he must earn his acceptance with God—that there is something he must do, something he must work at, some kind of standard he must try to achieve before God will receive him back again.

This misunderstanding—this lie of the devil—makes religion such a desperate burden for the majority of people in our land and in our time. They have been told, you see, that all they need to do to be acceptable to God is to try to keep the Ten Commandments, or as many of them as they can manage (like the boy who wrote at the top of them, "Only six of these are to be attempted!"), or try to keep the Sermon on the Mount and live by the standard that Jesus sets for people. And what happens? Back from their failure, men and women come consistently and say, "You know, what I need is not a lecture but a Savior!" They come back with the words of Studdert Kennedy on their lips:

> It is not finished, Lord.
> There is not one thing done,
> There is no battle of my life,
> That I have really won.
> And now I come to tell Thee
> How I fought to fail,
> My human, all too human, tale
> Of weakness and futility.[11]

This is the story of the lives of so many of us, is it not? We discover that we cannot live by a lecture—we need a Savior. So the deepest need of man's life is precisely what God has sent in Jesus Christ. But it is God who has sent it. The whole summary of what He has done in sending Jesus is in the one word "grace" (2 Cor. 6:1); and grace in the New Testament speaks of unmerited, unearned love and mercy and favor. This, says Paul, is what God brings in Jesus Christ. This is why you have to come to God, with all the pride that marks out so much of our life, and allow God to crush and smash it—because a proud man is the one who will never receive the gift that is given to empty hands.

> Not the labor of my hands
> Can fulfill Thy law's demands;
> Could my zeal no respite know,

---

11 From Geoffrey Studdert Kennedy's poem, "It Is Not Finished."

Could my tears forever flow,
All for sin could not atone;
Thou must save, and Thou alone.

Nothing in my hand I bring,
Simply to Thy cross I cling.[12]

The author of this reconciliation is God Himself.

Notice that Paul goes on to say that *the agent of it is Jesus Christ*. The reconciliation is of God, and through Jesus Christ: "All things are of God, who hath reconciled us to himself by Jesus Christ" (v. 18). How did He bring this reconciliation to men? The apostle says, "He died for all, that they which live should not henceforth live unto themselves, but unto him who died for them, and rose again" (v. 15). He died for all, and in that one phrase the apostle encompasses the whole meaning of the death of Jesus.

There are two words that describe it for us. The first word is "substitution"—He died for all. In other words, He died as a substitute in place of all men; and the whole emphasis of this chapter is on the fact that Christ has taken our place on the cross—in the dock, before the judgment of God—and paid the penalty of our sin, so that the cause of our estrangement from Him might be taken away.

You see, it is not enough to say that Christ died to show me, and to show all men, how much God loved us. That would be very impressive. We could have a lecture about that, but it would not save us. You can see this in an illustration. A young couple are walking along a pier, and the young man wants to demonstrate to the girl how much he loves her. He says, "To show how much I love you, I am going to jump off the end of that pier and get drowned in the sea." What do you think

---

12   From Toplady's hymn, "Rock of Ages, Cleft for Me."

she would say to that kind of demonstration of love? This would be altogether pointless.

But here is another occasion. The same fellow and girl have gone to the same place, and somehow the girl has fallen into this sea and is in mortal danger of drowning. The fellow looks down at her, in her predicament, and jumps down in order to save her from death that seems certain—for she's unable to swim—and in saving her he loses his own life. Certainly this is a demonstration of love; and ever after the girl is able to say, "I am alive because he has died; he has given his life in place of me, and I live because he died."

This is something altogether different, and this is what Paul says Jesus has done. He has not died simply to demonstrate that God loves men so much as to sacrifice His Son, but He has died in order that Jesus Christ might rescue us from the peril in which we stand apart from that one act. This is the Christian message:

He died that we might be forgiven,
He died to make us good,
That we might go at last to heaven,
Saved by His precious blood.[13]

Now I do not know about you, but I am not interested in a Christian gospel that cannot break the power of sin in my life, save me from the effects of it, and deliver me from the bondage in which I live. That is the message I wanted. And I am happy to be able to tell you that that is the message of the Christian gospel.

The other word that explains what Jesus did is "identification." Paul says that He who knew no sin was made sin for us, to bring us to God (v.

---

13   From Cecil Frances Alexander's hymn, "There Is a Green Hill Far Away."

21). What does that mean? It means that Jesus on the cross was bearing the wrath of God against our sin. He not only looked at it, but He also became sin for us. He took it upon Himself. He took it from us, clasped it to Himself, and became sin. He identified Himself with all in us that had caused God to drive us from His presence. And because of this, says Paul, He was made sin that we might be made righteous. He was cast out from God as He cried on the cross, "Why hast thou forsaken me?" He was driven from God and knew the agony and the horror of being banished from His Father, with whom He had held fellowship in all eternity, in order that we might be brought into fellowship with this same God. The author of it is God; the agent of it is Jesus.

Very briefly, there are two more things: *the availability of this reconciliation is universal.* What does the apostle say in verse 15? "He died for all." In other words, there is not a man, woman, boy, or girl whose plight is too deep or too dark, or whose bondage is so great, that the grace of God in Jesus Christ cannot reach him and set him free. There is no man whose life is beyond the grace of God; and there is not one fellow who may not know beyond any shadow of doubt that he has received the reconciliation, is united with God, and is brought back into fellowship with Him not only for this life but also for the life to come. The availability of it is universal.

Finally, *the acceptance of it is vital.* Paul says that the reconciling work of Jesus on the cross is not something that is automatically applied to every man. Some of us hear this kind of message of the Christian gospel, and we say, "This is very wonderful; this is all very nice, that Jesus has done this for me, and that we are all reconciled to God again." The apostle says that is not true. He says he has to come among men and plead with them, beseech them in Christ's stead, that they be reconciled to God. Paul says, "We are ambassadors for Christ, as though God did beseech you through us. We pray you [we plead with you] in Christ's stead, [receive the reconciliation] be ye reconciled to God" (v. 20). He says, "God has done it. He has worked it out on the cross, and He has commissioned ministers and messengers in order that they might go among men and say to them, 'Hear this word that God has sent, and receive the reconciliation.' "

Paul does not hand this out to men with a metallic fist. He does not say, "This is a fine piece of theological insight that I have received, and here it is; take it or leave it." He says, "We plead with you." There is a sense of urgency about the apostle's message, because he has discovered that the plight of man is so serious—the position of man is so desperately solemn—that his reception of the Christian message is desperately urgent. So Paul says, "Receive the reconciliation. Here it is; receive it."

BOOK TWO

Growth and Development

Chapter 7

The Christian's Walk

I therefore, the prisoner of the Lord, beseech you
that ye walk worthy of the vocation wherewith ye are called.
— Ephesians 4:1 —

We have so far concerned ourselves with the right beginning to the Christian life, which requires hearing from our God and responding to His Word. We should now explore the subsequent growth and maturity in the Christian's life.

We will begin with the Christian's walk—the life that the Christian ought to be living. In Paul's letter to the Ephesians, the subject of the fourth chapter is, very clearly, the Christian's walk. Notice one very important word, the second word in that chapter, which occurs several times in Paul's epistles: the little word "therefore," that Paul uses again and again to tell us that he has come to a special point in his letter.

Many of the letters of Paul are divided into two sections. He deals, in the first section, time and again, with the subject of doctrine—of belief, of the things that Christians ought to learn and believe if they are going to stand and go on in their Christian lives. Then he goes on, in the second half of his letters, again and again, to the way Christians ought to behave—how they ought to live if these are the things they believe. And the word that joins the two sections together, again and again, is this word "therefore."

You get this in Romans 12. Paul has been talking about the creed of Christians—the doctrines that their faith is founded upon. Then he goes on to talk about the conduct of Christians—the kind of disciples that the doctrine which he has been teaching ought to produce. And in Romans 12:1 Paul proceeds, "I beseech you therefore, brethren, by the mercies of God, that ye present your bodies a living sacrifice."

This is something that we find Paul is doing, not simply in order to construct his letters in a special way but because he believes something very basic about the lives of Christians—about the gospel that God has given us to preach—and that is that it has these two sides to it. It has the side of truth, which the apostle proclaims—doctrine which he believes Christians ought to know. On the other hand, it has a quality of life which ought to proceed out of this doctrine. This is what Paul calls the walk of the Christian. "I beseech you [because of all that I have been saying] that ye walk worthy of the vocation wherewith ye are called" (Eph. 4:1).

BASIS OF THE CHRISTIAN'S WALK

Notice that it is the Christian's walk, for it is obvious that a dead man can't walk. To command a dead person to get up and walk is just as irrelevant as to say to someone who has never been truly converted to Jesus Christ, "This is how you ought to live as a Christian." In Romans 12 the apostle says that it is on account of all the mercies of God that he had been opening up to them in chapters 1 to 11 that they have got to present their bodies to Jesus Christ. In other words, the root and foundation and *basis* of your walk as a Christian is the great and glorious fact of the doctrines of the Christian faith. That is the thing that will make you live as a true and stable disciple of Jesus Christ.

We shall be noticing presently how many times Paul talks about "the truth," and learning and knowing and understanding the truth, so that Paul says, "Before you are ever able to become a real disciple of Jesus Christ whose walk is right with God, there are certain great foundation stones on which your life will have to be built, and these are the truth of God." This is brought out in verses 20 and 21. He talks about them having learned Christ. They are making mistakes in their Christian lives, and Paul says, "Ye have not so learned Christ; If so be that ye have heard him, and have been taught by him, as the truth is in Jesus."

It would be a very good thing to go through the New Testament and see in how many places there is this emphasis upon getting to know the truth. The ignorant Christian is one of the devil's easiest prey. The basis of the Christian's walk is all the wonder of the Christian truth upon which Paul has been basing his appeal. You see, the trouble is that if he had left out chapters 1 to 3 in Ephesians and chapters 1 to 11 in Romans, he would have nothing to appeal to them about. They would have had no reason to present their bodies to Jesus Christ. The motive for it all is the wonder of the truth of God that Paul has been expounding.

SPHERE OF THE CHRISTIAN'S WALK

Secondly, we see the *sphere* of the Christian's walk. "I therefore, the prisoner of the Lord," and the Greek really has, "I therefore, the prisoner *for* the Lord" (italics added). This was physically true when Paul was writing. He was bound with chains, and this reminds him of something that is more deeply true about his life than his physical bonds. He says, "I am a prisoner for the Lord." He is there in servile bondage, as it seems, in Rome, but it is far more than just having the shackles of a Roman bondage around him. He is a prisoner for the Lord, and it is because of his relationship to Jesus Christ that Paul is in Rome at all.

What is that relationship? There is one word that Paul delights to use to describe himself. He begins the Epistle to the Romans in this way: *Paulos, doulos*—"Paul, a slave." What he meant was that his relationship to Jesus Christ was such that he had yielded himself. He was a purchased man; his life was purchased by Jesus Christ; he was not his own. And he writes to them as a slave of Jesus Christ. He was a man reserved.

You know how frustrating it is to go into a place and discover on seats a notice, "Reserved," and the implication is that they are reserved for another. Well, Paul had that notice not over his life outwardly but written indelibly into his heart. He was a man reserved for another, and that other was Jesus Christ. That is the sphere of the Christian's walk. It is not a servile bondage, like the outward chains that Paul wore, but it is the glorious liberty, the only liberty that any man, woman, boy, or girl can ever discover—the liberty of being a glad bondservant of Jesus Christ. That is what Dr. George Matheson meant when he wrote, "Make me a captive, Lord, and then I shall be free."[14] You are never free until you have become a captive of Jesus.

AIM OF THE CHRISTIAN'S WALK

Thirdly, there is the *aim* of the Christian's walk. "I therefore, the prisoner of the Lord, beseech you that ye walk worthy of the vocation wherewith ye are called." To discover the aim of the Christian's walk, Paul looks back to the eternal purpose of God in calling him and calling all who are His disciples. He discovers that there is something that has been working in the counsels of God before Paul was born that brought Paul into the knowledge of Jesus Christ on that day on the Damascus road.

The calling of God in the Bible is twofold; there are two senses in which people are called by God. There is one that is general and one

---

14   From George Matheson's hymn, "Make Me a Captive, Lord."

that is particular. The one that is general is the one in which Paul talks about all of us being "called to be saints." This is God's purpose, says Paul, for every child of His. He is called by God in order to bear the very image of Jesus in his own life, so that the great purpose of God from all eternity in bringing us into the knowledge of His Son was not simply to change our eternal destiny but that our lives might be changed into the image of Jesus. We are called to be saints, or holy.

The particular sense in which the Bible talks about calling, however, is the one which Paul speaks of when he says, "I am called to be an apostle"—called to be an apostle, or called and sent. God calls us all, in order that we might grow up into the likeness of Jesus. Then He calls us particularly to special tasks. Part of the trouble, when some of us are seeking guidance from God about specific things in our life, is that we give attention to the particular calling of God but not to the general calling of God. No man has any right to seek the particular calling of God for his life in one sphere until he has become obedient and begun to understand the general calling of God to make him like Jesus. So that is the basis, the sphere, and the aim of the Christian's walk.

FEATURES OF THE CHRISTIAN'S WALK

Here now are the *features* of the Christian's walk. "I … beseech you that ye walk worthy of the vocation wherewith ye are called, with…" With what? Let me give them to you in single words. First, with *humility*: "with all lowliness and meekness, with longsuffering, forbearing one another" (v. 2).

We have noticed that one of the first marks of sin in the life of Adam was pride, and the essence of sin is pride. It is that which puffs us up, which gives a man great ideas about himself, and which puts himself in the forefront. Paul says that the first thing that the grace of God in Jesus Christ ought to do in your life is to reverse that process. That is why in 2 Corinthians 5:15, Paul says that Jesus Christ has "died for all, that they which live should not henceforth live unto themselves, but unto him"—in other words, that pride might be attacked in their life. So the first mark or feature of the Christian's walk is humility; the bubble of his own opinions of himself has been severely burst.

The words "lowliness and meekness" (v. 2) originally meant, in pagan Greek, a groveling attitude—a groveling disposition, rather like that of Uriah Heep whom Charles Dickens depicts as "so 'umble." But this is not what the New Testament means. New Testament humility is not this outwardly paraded humility like that of the man who wrote the book, *Humility and How I Achieved It*. The New Testament's form of humility is not something that men can acquire of themselves and try to gather about their lives, but it is specifically a Christian grace, and it derives from seeing ourselves as God sees us.

That is why Martin Luther once came to the vicar general of the order in which he was a monk, before he was converted, and, having been in his cell reading the Word of God, said, "Sir, having gazed into the depths of my own heart, and begun to see what God sees, I can scarcely lift my head again." The meaning of Luther's discovery was just this: he had begun to see himself as God saw him. The man who has done so is a man who has begun to discover what it means to know Christian humility. The fact is, of course, that this is one of these unconscious qualities which makes the rather strange situation that probably the humblest man in the world is the man who thinks he's the proudest.

The second feature is *unity*:

With all lowliness and meekness, with longsuffering, forbearing one another in love; Endeavoring to keep the unity of the Spirit in the bond of peace. There is one body, and one Spirit, even as ye are called in one hope of your calling; One Lord, one faith, one baptism, One God and Father of all (vv. 2-6).

You will notice how many times the word "one," the expression of unity, comes out in these verses. Paul says that a mark of the life of the Christian ought to be unity. The outworking of the inward spirit of humility will produce unity.

But notice three things about this unity. First, they are to *keep* it, in the church, not create it: "Endeavoring to keep the unity of the Spirit in the bond of peace." So the true unity that exists among Christians is not something that we create but that God has already created in bringing us into the knowledge of His Son; we are told to keep, not to make it.

Secondly, this unity is *doctrinally based*. Paul says we have "one Lord, one faith," and the word used there is the word that is used again and again in the New Testament to speak about the body of faith or doctrine that has been committed to us by God—as Jude says, "the faith that was once delivered unto the saints" (1:3). True New Testament unity is doctrinally based—that is, it exists among people whose lives are grounded on the same truth. It is wise for us to remember that this New Testament unity is something that is not achieved at the expense of throwing the truth overboard, but it is achieved on the basis of the truth and is already there among those who are all one in Christ Jesus.

Notice, thirdly, that it is unity in *diversity*. "Unto every one of us is given grace according to the measure of the gift of Christ" (v. 7)—that is, we are enabled in all the diversity of our own backgrounds. Coming together, for example, from many different kinds of homes, situations, jobs, and churches, we are able to discover that we have this glorious unity that God gives to those who are "one in Christ Jesus," although we ourselves are so different. That is why it is very wrong for us to try to ape somebody else in the Christian life. God has a purpose and a specific plan for your life that is different from everybody else's. Never try to ape someone else, except in his seeking to be like our Lord Jesus Christ.

The third feature of the Christian's walk is *maturity*. Paul says, "He gave some, apostles; and some, prophets; and some, evangelists; and some, pastors and teachers" (v. 11). This means that the calling of so many of the people of God is quite diverse from one to the other. It does not mean that we all become ministers, although it does mean that many of us might have to think very seriously as to whether God doesn't want us in some form of calling like that. It means that we discover our calling to be diverse. All the diversities of God's calling of people in the church are given for one purpose:

> For the perfecting [the maturing] of the saints, for the work of the ministry, for the edifying of the body of Christ: Till we all come in the unity of the faith, and of the knowledge of the Son of God, unto a [mature] man, unto the measure of the stature of the fulness of Christ: That we henceforth be no more children, tossed to and fro, and carried about with every wind of doctrine, by the sleight of men, and cunning craftiness.... But speaking the truth in love, may grow up into him in all things, which is the head, even Christ (vv. 12-15).

That is Paul's concern for the Christians in Ephesus: that they may grow up. It is a very wonderful thing to see someone born into the family of God and coming to know all the wonderful things that new birth into God's family brings before our eyes. Of course, we all love the attributes of a baby. Paul talks about those who are "babes in Christ," as we all have been at one time. But if the attributes of babyhood remain after the years have gone by, you have nothing but tragedy. That is not something that anybody admires or is glad to see. So Paul says that whatever happens in your Christian experience, see that you do not stand still.

It is the Christian's walk, you will notice, not the Christian's remaining where he was when he became converted. The language of the Christian life in the New Testament is this language of growth, and Paul's great concern is for their maturity in Jesus Christ. One of the tragedies that Paul sees in the lives of those to whom he is writing is that they have not been going on spiritually; they have not been growing in the faith.

I always remember, very early in my ministry, an occasion when I had to go to a hospital to see a child of a man who was a member of the congregation in which I was serving. He told me—a man of about seventy years of age—that his little girl was in hospital, and I was surprised at him talking about a "little girl," being a man of such seniority as he was. But I went to the hospital to see her, and I shall never forget the reaction in my heart and mind when I looked into the room where that girl was—who was approaching 40—to discover her sitting on the floor playing with her dolls.

The tragedy is that it is possible, if he cannot stop us being converted, that the devil will seek with all his devices to stop us growing up in the Christian life. You ought to be expecting, every week, every month, every year of your life, that there are new things opening out to you in the things of God, and that you are no more being children, tossed to and fro, carried about with every wind.

Notice some of the characteristics of immaturity that the apostle lays down in these verses. One of them is that they are like children who are "tossed to and fro, and carried about with every wind of doctrine." One of the things that I notice about my little girl, who is not yet a year old and exhibiting some of the signs of original sin—and some of it is very original—is that she can never be kept at the one thing for any length of time. Her eyes are always roving to and fro around the room, or from one thing to another; she cannot stick at anything for long. And, you know, there are many Christians like that. After years in the Christian life, they cannot stick at anything. And Paul says, don't be like that. So give yourselves to God, to the study of His truth, and to a concern to growing up into Him, that you will become stable, and you will be the kind of person who will endure in your Christian experience.

May I ask you in this connection about your church attendance? What about your attendance at the church prayer meeting and at the Sunday services, morning and evening? Are you the kind of Christian that your vicar or minister can rely on to be there every Sunday to be built up in the solid teaching of the Word of God? Or are you the kind of person who, like the moth, flits to and fro to the bright lights—you cannot stick at anything? Oh, be sure that the devil does not lure you away from the solid, steady increasing in the knowledge of God and of His truth!

The last thing is the relation of truth to maturity—the means by which we grow up into Him. This, says Paul, is why the ministry is given to us: that we "may grow up into him" (v. 15). If you are neglecting to sit under the teaching of such men as Paul talks about, week by week with regularity, you are avoiding growing up in the faith.

Look how many times Paul uses words to do with truth: "Till we all come in the unity of the faith, and of the knowledge of the Son of God" (v. 13); "with every wind of doctrine" (v. 14); "speaking the truth" (v. 15). He says the reason that so many have gone astray is because they have empty minds: "the vanity of their mind" (v. 17). In verse 18, he says that they have had their "understanding darkened." In verse 20, he talks about having "learned Christ." In verse 21, he speaks about having "been taught by him, as the truth is in Jesus."

We need never be away from the Word of God, from building our lives upon it, and from feeding upon it—studying it with the labor of students. Do you give as much diligent attention to the study of the Word of God as you do to subjects that will only last a lifetime? Do you so concern yourselves with building your life on the truth of God and growing up into Him that when we go to appear before Him, having been changed by His grace from glory into glory—having grown nearer to His likeness—we shall discover that when He appears we shall be like Him? May God help us so to give ourselves to Him and to His Word that we may grow in the faith.

Chapter 8
Christian Growth, Maturity, and Service

Unto the measure of the stature of the fulness of Christ.
— Ephesians 4:13 —

Ephesians 4:7-16 has as its background the glorious picture of the ascending Christ who, having spoiled principalities and powers and made an open exhibition of them, goes in triumph into the presence of God, bearing the spoils of His victory with Him. And now at the right hand of God, as the first fruits of His ascension, Paul tells us that the heart of the ascended Lord turns toward His flock on earth. We discover in these words the same concern burning in the heart of the now risen and victorious Savior, which we find in John 17 when in that great High Priestly Prayer Jesus cries, "Father,... I pray not for the world, but for them which thou hast given me.... Keep them.... Sanctify them through thy truth: thy word is truth."

The result of this concern of the ascended Christ is that He bestows gifts upon men. "Wherefore he saith, When he ascended up on high, he led captivity captive, and gave gifts unto men" (v. 8). The ascended Lord, bent upon the blessing and upbuilding of His people and equipping them for service, gives gifts to His church. What are these gifts? Well, they are described in verse 11, and they are, in summary, the gifts of the ministry of the Word. This is the great activity of the ascended Christ as He has risen in triumph, taking the spoils of His majestic victory with Him. He comes now from these spoils to send gifts to His church, and they are gifts of the ministry of the Word. That is how the ascended Lord knows that His people, in all their frailty and weakness, are going to be built up and secured in Him.

The object of this gracious gift of Christ to His people is described in these verses both negatively and positively. God's design is quite clearly that we should cease to be one thing and that we should become something else.

We will turn, first of all, to the negative side of this teaching. Notice in verse 14 what it is that we are henceforth no longer to be: "no more children, tossed to and fro, and carried about with every wind of doctrine, by the sleight of men, and cunning craftiness, whereby they lie in wait to deceive." In other words, the first ministry which these gifts that the risen and ascended Christ has given to His church ought to produce concerns *an immaturity that we are to avoid.*

Let me say that that does not suggest that we will never be children. It does not suggest that we will never be babes in Christ, for the very figure of speech which the New Testament uses to describe the beginning of spiritual experience necessitates this. We have in Christ by the Holy Spirit a new birth, and when we have a new birth, naturally we become babies. The task of the people of God and of the church of God, when babes in Christ are to be found among them, is to care for them, nurture them, yearn over them, guard them, and watch them with all the constant attention of a mother over her newborn child.

This is a challenge to the church of God in these days and to us as individual Christians. It is one thing, you see, to be gladly willing to go out to attend meetings, or to take some prominent public part within the church of God; but there is a costliness about taking someone under your wing who is newly born, with all the awkwardness, weakness, and sheer stupidity, at times, of the newborn creature. I am persuaded that there is a ministry here which is costly and secret but very precious in the eyes of the Lord—the ministry of the man or woman within the church of God who is ready to take the newborn and nourish and nurture them into growth and maturity.

But of course the apostle is speaking about the next stage from this. We are all agreed that the attributes of babyhood are very attractive in babies (although there have been times at 3 o'clock in the morning when I have begun to wonder). But when these same attributes are continued into adult life, you have nothing but abysmal tragedy. And what the Apostle Paul is speaking about here is the parallel in spiritual experience to this prolonged adolescence and babyhood in physical life.

MARKS OF SPIRITUAL ADOLESCENCE

What are the marks of this spiritual adolescence which was clearly a problem in the churches to which Paul wrote? Well, there are several of them that he points out for us here.

The first is a *lack of stability*. Verse 14: "That we henceforth be no more children, tossed to and fro, and carried about with every wind." In other words, these people are like a ship without a rudder; they lack a real sense of direction. You see this kind of thing, of course, in children in so many ways. It is a mark of childishness to be like the moth, attracted to every new bright light that appears. They find it difficult to stick at anything for very long. That is one of the marks of spiritual adolescence, says the apostle. God has given these gifts to His church in order that we may grow out of these.

My dear people, there is a desperate need today for evangelical Christians who have the marks of stability about their lives. How easy it is for us to be keen and effervescent on special occasions! Multitudes of evangelical Christians are wonderful people on the occasion of a conference, a crusade, or something of that kind; but when it comes to the thing that is infinitely more vital—the regular work and witness of the local church—they are utterly useless and unreliable. You look for them at the prayer meeting; one night they are there, and the next week they are not. You look into the church, and you do not say, "Of course they'll be there." You say, "Where will they be today?" I am persuaded that one of the great needs of our time is that we should grow up out of this childishness which is marked by the absence of stability.

Another form of the same thing is the Christian who lives from thrill to thrill in his spiritual experience—the kind of person who has no general progress in his spiritual life but depends, like the drug addict, on an injection from time to time. There are people who travel round conferences with this very motive, in order that they might get an injection at one to do them until they get to the next. That is not the stuff out of which our forefathers were made! That is not the stuff out of which the men of God who have toiled for God in the mission field are made! The call of God is for the kind of man who spiritually has his roots down into a stable hold on Christ, and we are in desperate need of Christians who are delivered from an invertebrate condition.

One of the reasons for physical instability is malnutrition. The man who has not been fed and nourished properly becomes weak and unable to withstand the winds and the storms of which Paul is speaking. I am persuaded that, so often, this is precisely the problem among us spiritually. May I say, in great humility and love, that I am disturbed and alarmed in these days at the trend of Christian appetites among us—at the kind of appetite that is confined to spiritual titbits and that has no real hunger for solid food. The only thing that that produces is prolonged adolescence. You do not expect a baby to have a solid meal; you would not try to give it to the baby. But you do not expect someone who has been on the road for years still to be sipping milk.

The second mark of this immaturity, says the apostle, is *lack of discernment*. This whole question of instability, you will notice, is closely linked with doctrine: "That we henceforth be no more children, tossed to and fro, and carried about with every wind of doctrine, by the sleight of men, and cunning craftiness, whereby they lie in wait to deceive." Again it is a mark of the child that it is easily deceived. That is why "let's pretend" stories are so much fun—they find it difficult to distinguish between reality and unreality. But such is not for the mature Christian when handling God's truth, as John Newton made clear:

> They who study the Scriptures,… by treasuring up the doctrines, precepts, promises, examples, and exhortations of Scripture, in their minds,… grow into an habitual frame of spiritual wisdom, and acquire a gracious taste, which enables them to judge of right and wrong with a degree of readiness and certainty, as a musical ear judges of sounds.[15]

That is the mark of maturity. It involves discernment, and the reason why so many of us within the evangelical church these days are so easily seduced away by some false teaching is just this: that we have been undernourished in the truth of God. Do you remember the Berean Christians who must have delighted the apostle's heart, who searched "the scriptures daily to see if these things were so" (Acts 17:11, RSV)? Oh, my dear people, are you an easy prey to deception? Well, these are some of the marks of immaturity, says the apostle: a lack of stability and a lack of discernment.

MARKS OF MATURITY

But now to the positive side of these gifts that God has given and

---

15 John Newton and Richard Cecil, *The Works of the Reverend John Newton … With a Life of the Author by the Rev. Richard Cecil* (London: George Virtue, 1839), 88.

their purpose. If this is the immaturity we are to avoid, what is the maturity that we are to seek? Well, notice how the apostle speaks of it: God has given us these gifts, he says, in Ephesians 4:12-13,

> For the perfecting [or as the other versions translate it, "the maturing"] of the saints, for the work of the ministry, for the edifying of the body of Christ: Till we all come in the unity of the faith, and of the knowledge of the Son of God, unto a perfect [mature] man, unto the measure of the stature of the fulness of Christ.

And in verse 15, "Speaking the truth [or perhaps better, 'holding the truth'] in love, may grow up into him in all things, which is the head, even Christ." So the first thing about this maturity we are to seek is *growth*.

John Stott once emphasized this when he spoke about the fruit of the Spirit and the way it appears:

> not as a sudden flash of lightning, but as something that has demanded first that the seed was sown, that there was growth and the evidence of life, and then the bud, and then the flower. It is the flower with all its show that comes suddenly, but it doesn't last long, and it doesn't do you much good; it is the fruit that takes a long time to appear, and while it hasn't the show of the flower, it is what nourishes you.

Generally, therefore, spiritual maturity comes about gradually. Of course, in the figure of physical growth there are stages in our physical life when we grow much more than we do at other times; but the overall pattern is a gradual growth. May I warn you against any attempt to seek some kind of quick shortcuts to spiritual growth and maturity.

There are people who have had dramatic crisis experiences in their lives—who have been faced with some sin, and that has been in the nature of a spiritual surgical operation. But to say that, therefore, every Christian needs that kind of experience is like saying that everybody needs their appendix out. The operation is in order for health to be possible. It removes the hindrances; it does not produce the health. There have been men who have dramatically met with God in a crisis of their lives as He has exposed something that has been hindering their growth. But then they have got to go out and begin to grow; that is the point. And that is the first thing: it is growth.

The second thing about this maturity we are to seek is that it is the *"measure of the stature of the fulness of Christ"* (italics added). What a glorious phrase this is; would that we had time to linger over it! Verse 13: "Till we all come in the unity of the faith, and of the knowledge of the Son of God, unto a perfect [or mature] man, unto the measure of the stature of the fulness of Christ."

That is the pattern of our growth: we are to grow in the sense that day by day it is in the purpose of God to recreate us into the image of Jesus. This, and this only, is biblical salvation. Biblical salvation is that process by which God restores in us the divine image that we lost at the fall. And a holy God will never be satisfied with doing anything less than this. He has chosen us in Him, says the apostle, that we might bear what J. B. Phillips calls in his translation of Romans 8:29 "the family likeness" of Jesus. There is God's precious purpose: that day by day He might draw us on, build us up, nourish us, mature us, and bring us to obedience and grace so that there might be seen in us the very reflection of the Savior.

Notice, thirdly, that this growth and maturing into the likeness of Christ is closely and intimately bound up with the *truth*. This gracious purpose of God is the explanation of some of the tribulations and trials which many of us may have been passing through. You know, of course, how it is that the silversmith gets the silver purified to the right kind of consistency. He puts it to the fire, and it is when the fire roars around it that he is able to see all the impurity coming to the surface; and he takes it away. Then he puts the silver into the fire again, and again takes the impurities away, and again to the fire, until the time comes when he is satisfied because he can see in it an undistorted likeness of himself. Is that a word from God some of us need to hear?

It may be a word for the days that are to come, but all this is so closely bound up with the truth, says the apostle. Notice the number of occasions in these few verses that words for the Word of God and the truth of God recur. In verse 13 it is "till we all come in the unity of the faith, and of the knowledge of the Son of God." In verse 14, the trouble is that we are "carried about with every wind of doctrine," and we are deceived in this realm; and the answer in verse 15 is, "[holding] the truth in love." In verse 20, the apostle chides them: "Ye have not so learned Christ"; and in verse 21: "If so be that ye have heard him, and have been taught by him, as the truth is in Jesus."

That is just because the prayer of Jesus was "Sanctify them through thy truth: thy word is truth." That means, you see, that we are not sanctified under the wisdom of God through some emotional experience—that is not sanctification—but we are sanctified through the truth.

Lastly, this maturity we are to seek is *the restoration of a true humanity in us by the grace of God*. The word in verse 12 for the maturing or "perfecting of the saints" is a word which speaks of restoring something to its true condition. It is the word used, for instance, in Matthew 4:21, for the mending of nets which have been torn, broken, and destroyed from their true condition. The word in the Greek means that the gifts which God has given to His church have been given in order that the people of God might be restored to the true condition that sin has marred. That means that they will find the sanctifying work of God in their lives day by day being marked by the restoration of a true humanity.

You see, the gracious work of the gospel of Christ is not to make us spiritual oddities. It is all too often literally true that the Lord's people are His peculiar people! But you know, Christ's life which is to be reproduced in us is a perfect humanity as well as a glorious deity. He again and again warns His disciples against the very kind of stilted inhumanity and unreality which so often marks our lives.

How strangely inhuman some keen Christians can be! Do you remember how Jesus expressed it so beautifully in Matthew 6 when talking to the disciples about the Pharisees? "Ye shall not be like them," He says, as He talks about almsgiving, or the service we render to others; about prayer, our life toward God; and about fasting, the disciplines of our own attitude to ourselves. Says Jesus, "Be not as the hypocrites. Avoid at all cost their unreality, for when they fast they like to distort their appearance that they might appear unto men to fast." Says Jesus, "They are being unnatural. When you pray, when you give alms, when you serve, when you fast, be real; be yourself."

God save us from the kind of repulsive unnaturalness that so often drives people away from the Savior rather than drawing them to Him. There is a winsomeness, a warmth, and a reality about the true life that is being brought into the likeness of Jesus that the world can never copy. God never intends to destroy your personality when He is making you like Jesus.

There was a godly man in America whose life toiled for God most graciously, and a lot of young men came under his tutelage and leadership, and they thanked God for him. But that man was troubled by a physical disability which made him stoop; and do you know, all these young men developed what came to be known in America at the time as the "evangelical stoop"! You can see what was happening: they were being unnatural. The purpose of God is to restore a real humanity in your heart and life and not destroy it. It is through real manhood and real womanhood that the beauties of Jesus will be seen.

MEANS OF MATURITY

Now, what about the *means of this maturity*? It is inescapably bound up with the Word of God. But the particular sense in which it is bound up with the Word of God relates to the ministry of the Word of God— the gift of Christ the ascended Lord looking down with great love and longing upon His people in all their needs. The gift of God is the ministry of apostles, prophets, evangelists, pastors, and teachers. We haven't time to go into the meaning of these words except to say that most probably apostles and prophets were temporary ministries that were given; evangelists, pastors, and teachers represent to us the ministry of the Word within the church of God. And if you would grow spiritually, the most fundamental thing is that you should be under a biblical ministry—not just for a week, but that this should be the very character of your life and the sphere of your growth. This is God's provided means for our growth in Him. He has given gifts unto men, and the gifts are evangelists, pastors, teachers—the ministry of the Word.

A friend of mine recently had someone come to him in his church, greatly troubled, confused, and mixed up with a very difficult history. She said, "Could you help me? Could you lead me into something that would help me from this?" He spoke to her for quite some time, and light began to dawn; but the words that he spoke to her as she left were these: "Now listen. The main thing I have to say to you is to just keep coming under the ministry of the Word, and its healing power will heal your soul and your mind." And that girl lived to discover that to be gloriously and wonderfully true.

But somebody says, "I haven't such a ministry." I know that many of you have not. God knows too, which is much more important. I know also that there are other means of grace that God has given to His people. He has given us His Word and promised us His Spirit. He has provided for us means by which, if we have the hunger and taste for it, we can get down to the truth of God and let it minister to our souls. He has given us the written page that it might minister to us. One of the greatest blessings would be His people beginning to get down to solid reading some evenings, instead of the TV. God will provide the means and the ministry where there is the taste and the hunger.

Our theme is Christian continuance and service, and maybe you are wondering, "What about the service?" Well, of course, what a man is determines what he does. My character determines my service, and real service for God, out into which He will thrust you in the days to come, is much more a matter of overflow than overwork. The great and wonderful thing is that, like the Apostle Paul who found himself being taken away into the silence of Arabia (like Elijah who had the word from God, "Go hide thyself" before he ever heard the word, "Go show thyself"), we will find that when God has begun to do His gracious work in us—the very fact of our being in the world as the people of God, as He sends us out into all the appalling need of the hour in which we live—the very overflow of the life of Jesus in whatever area of the church of God He trusts us with His work will draw men to Him. That is the meaning of that wonderful verse 16. It is much clearer in the RSV than in the AV: "From whom [that is, from Christ] the whole body, joined and knit together by every joint with which it is supplied, when each part is working properly, makes bodily growth and upbuilds itself in love."

Oh, may God take us out into the world and make us the kind of men and women whose lives tell for Him! But primarily, may He make us to hunger and thirst that we might "grow up into him ... which is the head, even Christ" (v. 15)—that we may grow into His likeness, and that we may find our experience as the man of God long ago who said, "I shall be satisfied, when I awake, with thy likeness" (Ps. 17:15).

Chapter 9
THE LIFE OF FAITH

I have been crucified with Christ; it is no longer I who live, but Christ who lives in me; and the life I now live in the flesh I live by faith in the Son of God, who loved me and gave himself for me.
— Galatians 2:20 (RSV)[16] —

There are few verses in the Bible into which so much doctrine and teaching are packed as Galatians 2:20. The letter in which the verse is found was written to Christians who appear to have been going astray spiritually. Everything seems to have been going well for a period, but now Paul has to write to them, "I am astonished that you are so quickly deserting him who called you in the grace of Christ and turning to a different gospel" (1:6). Again in chapter 3 he points out the fact that, though they are converted, though they began the Christian life, they seem to have been seduced by some folly. "O foolish Galatians! Who has bewitched you, before whose eyes Jesus Christ was publicly portrayed as crucified?" (v. 1). The point of Paul's letter is to help these Christians to recover the ground they had lost— to set them again on the true foundation for living the Christian life.

---

16   Unless otherwise stated, Scripture quotations in this chapter are from THE HOLY BIBLE: REVISED STANDARD VERSION, International Bible Society.

Notice that he is speaking to those who are already Christians, who have somehow or other lost the way. This is a word whose purpose is spiritual restoration—not spiritual beginnings here but spiritual restoration. In this particular verse, Paul seeks to restore the Galatians who have erred from the faith by reminding them of certain things which they do not seem to have understood fully and for the lack of which they are going astray. This may be summarized by saying that Paul is setting down before them what exactly happened when they became Christians, or the nature of their Christian life.

This is a frequent thing that Paul does throughout his letters. When he is seeking to call people back again to the faith, to restore them and bring stability into their Christian lives as they have begun to wobble, he does so by drawing them back to a new teaching about the very nature of what happened to them when they became Christians. That is why you find here, in chapter 3, these frequent questions. "Let me ask you only this," says Paul in verse 2, and then he goes on to ask them many questions. "Let me ask you only this: Did you receive the Spirit by the works of the law…? Having begun with the Spirit, are you now ending with the flesh? Did you experience so many things in vain?" (vv. 2-4).

We find Paul in Romans 6, again and again, repeating, "Do you not know…?" One of their basic problems is one of *our* basic problems, and it is a lack of knowledge, a lack of instruction, a lack of understanding of exactly what happened when they became children of God.

Of all the very important truths in Galatians 2:20, I want to concentrate on three facts contained in the words:

I have been crucified with Christ; it is no longer I who live, but Christ who lives in me; and the life I now live in the flesh I live by faith in the Son of God, who loved me and gave himself for me.

The first is a fact of *history*; the second is a fact of *experience*; and the third is a fact of *faith*.

A FACT OF HISTORY

You will notice the tense of this first phrase in the RSV, which is different from the AV. In the AV: "I am crucified with Christ." In the RSV: "I have been crucified with Christ." Paul is using his own experience as an example of what has happened to all Christians. He is reminding them not of something further that they must try to do but of something which has already taken place. It concerns the reality that there are ultimately two orders of men. There are in a sense only two men who matter: Adam and Christ, the second Adam. One of our hymns explains this, in the line about Jesus coming to redeem us from the power of sin: "A second Adam to the fight, and to the rescue came."[17]

The point is this: that by nature every man is in Adam. He belongs to the race of men who are under the judgment of God. The result of being in Adam is that we inherit death: "as in Adam all die" (1 Cor. 15:22). But when I am converted, I am redeemed from being a member of the old order, or the old humanity, and made a member of the new order, or the new humanity, of which Christ is the Head. I am incorporated into Christ so that my description now is the basic description Paul gives us of the Christian: a man in Christ. "If any one is in Christ, he is a new creation; the old has passed away, behold, the new has come" (2 Cor. 5:17).

This is something that happened to us when we were converted. This needs to be emphasized and repeated. The basic significance of this is that I thereby enter into all the vast benefits of what Jesus Christ has done in His death. Just as I shared all the ailments of being in Adam, I share all the riches and benefits of being in Christ. This

---

17   From John Henry Newman's hymn, "Praise to the Holiest in the Height."

transfer took place when I was converted. He translated us out of one kingdom into another. This means that I now am the inheritor of all the riches of Christ who is the Head of the kingdom into which I have been translated by His grace.

That means two things. It means that by Christ's death *sin's penalty has been paid*, and we have received pardon from God; we are justified by His grace. Because I have been crucified with Christ, sin's penalty can be required of me no more. Let it be said again that we are to tell this to Satan when he comes as the accuser of the brethren and begins to tell us that our sin has not been cleansed and dealt with, that this time we have gone too far: the penalty has been paid because we are crucified with Christ. We are justified by grace.

But there is a deeper significance in what Christ has done. He has not only paid sin's penalty, but Jesus has also *destroyed sin's power*. Notice that word used in Romans 6:6, translated "destroyed" in the Authorized Version but in the Greek is a military metaphor which means to be stripped of authority or reduced to the ranks. It is the word that is used in Hebrews 2:14 of what happened to the devil. When Jesus Christ died on the cross, there was not only a penalty paid, but there was also a victory won.

> He himself [that is, Jesus] likewise partook of the same nature, that through death he might destroy him who had the power of death, that is, the devil, and deliver all those who through fear of death were subject to lifelong bondage.

That means, you see, that what happened when Jesus died on the cross not only affects the penalty of sin, but it also affects the power of sin. Its power has been broken at the cross, and Satan has been stripped of his authority.

Let me try to explain what that means. It is a picture of a tyrannical general who has a company of men, perhaps away out in the desert, and exercises a terrible control over them. He becomes a tyrant in every sense, making their lives an utter and complete misery as they are under bondage to him. But then one day something happens at the headquarters in the home country. This man who has exercised such tyranny over his men is stripped of his command and all his authority; he is, as we would say, reduced to the ranks.

There is a situation which is true for these men, out there in the desert: that this general no longer has authority to rule over them. His presence is not removed from them—let that be clearly said—but his authority has been taken away. They are no longer under bondage to him. In other words, they have been released from being his prisoners. And when someone comes to bring the good news from the homeland to them, this is the best thing these men have heard: they have been released from his bondage.

This is what has happened to sin as a principle and a power. The message to these men is this, and it is precisely the message of the New Testament to us: I have not to seek to make this so; I have not to try to release myself from this bondage, but I have to recognize that it has been done. That is what these men need to do; they are now free men. And you and I are, in precisely that sense, the Lord's free men who may turn to this tyrant and say, "I have been released from your bondage and tyranny; how shall I live under it any longer? That is now past, not because of something I have done but because of something that has been done by God and Jesus Christ." In other words, what has happened to us is the fundamental thing we need to recognize; we need to realize who we are in Christ.

The metaphor of marriage is used a great deal because it is so much in the Bible. Those of us as clergymen have the task of conducting weddings. After the wedding is over, the clergyman goes to the vestry to get the bride and bridegroom to sign the register, and he says to the bride, "Mrs. Brown, will you come and sign here." She stands and talks away to her husband and looks around for the bridegroom's mother, wondering why on earth she should be signing the register! It sometimes takes quite a bit of convincing to tell her it is she about whom he is speaking, for at that moment she doesn't realize who she is!

This is precisely what Paul is concerned that we should recognize (who we are in Christ), and that we should recognize for ourselves that the old life in Adam is past and gone—that having been liberated from this bondage, how shall we go back to live in it? The whole thing is so utterly unreasonable. And that is why Paul keeps saying, "Do you not know? Do you now understand?"

A FACT OF EXPERIENCE

I want you to look at the phrase, "the life I now live." We have, in other words, not only shared Christ's death, but we have also shared His resurrection, and we have thereby entered into a new life. And that is "the life I now live." What about this life? Well, Paul says two things about it: the first is a fact of experience; and the other is a fact of faith. The first is this, in the three little words "The life I now live *in the flesh*" (italics added).

The point is very important. It is that, although I am no longer the man I was, but a new creature in Christ, I am nonetheless living out this new life in the flesh; that, although the power of Satan—his authority— has been removed, his presence has not been removed. This is the explanation of the basic tension that we experience in our Christian life. We are at the same time, in other words, in Christ but living out this new resurrection life in a world which is under the dominion of him who blinds the eyes of men to the truth.

I wonder if you ever find yourselves discouraged by the kind of Christian who gives you the impression that this is not so—that their Christian experience is just one long spiritual picnic from one thrill to the next. I am amazed at how many people in the evangelical world come to me, when some truth has been explained, and say, "How do you reconcile that with the chorus which says…?" Well, there are some very unbiblical choruses which give you just the impression that living the Christian life is one long experience of bubbling effervescence—we are never cast down or never troubled; it is joy, joy, joy all the time. And there are some people who go to conferences, hoping that they might get some kind of mystical blessing which will produce this in their experience.

The Bible's teaching is that, so long as we are in the flesh, living out the resurrection life of Christ here in this vale of tears, we will always have this tension and conflict. People who are looking for the kind of blessing we have been speaking about are really looking not for a transformation of character here on earth but for a translation to glory. The Bible describes the Christian as a saint, not as an angel.

When you begin to look at the sheer realism and honesty of the Bible, and how important it is for us as Christians to be utterly honest about our own experience, there are a great number of testimonies given that are not true to experience. We are saying what we think ought to be true, or that we would like to be true, or that would be very spiritual if it were true, but we are not telling the truth about ourselves. But the Bible is so gloriously honest. It presents the picture of a man like Elijah, for instance, "subject to like passions as we are" (James 5:17, AV).

That is the glorious thing about God's work in the life of man. When you come to the life of Jesus, you discover that His life was not all effervescence and bubbles. Jesus knew what it was to weep over Jerusalem. Jesus knew what it was to have disappointment in His ministry. "He could there do no mighty work … because of their unbelief" (Mark 6:5-6). He knew some of the real agonies of spiritual loneliness. And even at one point he knew what it was to cry from a heart that was torn, "My God, my God, why?"

Listen to the language of the Apostle Paul as he seeks to describe the normal Christian life—not the defeated Christian life but the normal Christian life. What has God chosen us to be? Paul's answer: He has chosen him to be a soldier. Therefore, the character of our life is that we are to fight the good fight of faith. We wrestle, he says. And look at the catalogue, the description of our wrestling that Paul gives to us: We wrestle not against ordinary enemies like flesh and blood, but we wrestle against principalities and powers—the world rulers of this present darkness, against the spiritual hosts of wickedness in heavenly places (Eph 6:12). We ought to give attention to our weapons in our spiritual life—the sword we are to take, the helmet, the shield. That does not sound like preparation for a picnic, does it?

You see, the point is this: here are men imprisoned, and then suddenly someone comes along from the other side to set them free. What happens then? They are still in the midst of the enemy, held prisoner, but they are set free. That is the very time they are able to fight. They are not able to fight while they are still in bondage. That is why the essence of the Christian's life is that he is engaged in the fight of faith. The man without faith—without Christ—cannot fight against the devil. He is a hopeless dupe of the devil. And so, if you are finding in your experience that there is the conflict with sin, Satan, and the powers of darkness, that is one of the evidences that you are a Christian—not the evidence that you are not.

A FACT OF FAITH

"The life I now live," says Paul, "I live by faith in the Son of God, who loved me and gave himself for me." The life I now live in the flesh is a life by faith. I am in Christ—I live in Christ, I live in the flesh, and I live by faith. These are the three things that are spoken about in this verse. But this third matter brings out that the battle in which we are engaged is not an equal struggle against equal foes, for the ultimate issue is already decided. We engage in this spiritual warfare fighting from victory—not toward victory, but *from* victory. The basic issue has been decided, and this is what Paul means by living in the flesh but by faith in the Son of God.

We have time only to look very briefly at two ideas in this word "faith." The first is a concentration on something or someone outside of myself: it is upon the *object* of my faith. That is why Hudson Taylor, whose motto was "Have faith in God," used to say, "Not my faith [that counts in the long run] but God's faithfulness."[18] And that is where my eyes have to be.

When I am focusing my eyes to look, for instance, at this light, I do not look at the light and say, "How far away is this light? Is it something like thirty feet away? Then I'd better focus my eyes so that I can see thirty feet, and then I'll be able to see that light." Not at all! What I do is concentrate on the object, and the right focus and vision is born because of my concentrating on the object. This is what faith does: it concentrates on the object who is God Himself.

Robert Murray M'Cheyne, a great and godly minister in the Church of Scotland a century ago, used to say to young people, "For one look at yourself, take ten looks at Christ!"[19] That is what faith makes you do.

The other thing that faith means is *obedience*. That is why the two are joined together in the Scripture. It is quite natural in the Bible to

---

18   Dr. and Mrs. Howard Taylor, *Hudson Taylor and the China Inland Mission: The Growth of a Work of God* (London: Morgan & Scott, 1918), 278.

19   Robert Murray M'Cheyne and Andrew Alexander Bonar, *Memoir and Remains of the Rev. Robert Murray M'Cheyne* (New York: W. Middleton, 1846), 240.

speak about the obedience of faith. Faith is not some kind of ecstatic experience. So many of us are looking for this—for some emotional upsurge in our lives. But the essence of faith, in the Bible, is that it is obedience—a committed obedience, a trustful obedience to what God has said.

You find these two things in the life of Abraham. In that great catalogue of the men of faith, in Hebrews 11, the specific characteristics of Abraham are these two: "By faith Abraham obeyed when he was called.... By faith ... he looked forward to the city which has foundations, whose builder and maker is God" (vv. 8-10). By faith he obeyed; by faith he looked. He kept his eyes upon God, not upon himself.

It is what God is—what God has done, what He has promised—that matters. And my response to it is a committed obedience. That is to be the life I now live—not the life I used to live, a year or two ago, but the life I now live in day-by-day committed obedience to His Word.

May God help us, by restoring our minds to the great central truths of the faith, to see our lives transformed by His Word and Spirit into the image of Jesus.

Chapter 10
ABIDE IN ME

I am the true vine, and my Father is the husbandman.... Abide in me, and I in you. As the branch cannot bear fruit of itself, except it abide in the vine; no more can ye, except ye abide in me.
— John 15:1, 4 —

John 15 is one of the most significant places in the New Testament where our Lord speaks about Christian continuance. The context of these words of our Lord is that He is leaving His disciples in a hostile world. Jesus is aware of the pressures that these men are to face as they go out into the world as His ambassadors— pressures both from without, because of the world's hostility (which Jesus never hid from them), and pressures from within, because of their own weakness (which He never denied).

I suppose that we shall never really be able to grasp the depth and tenderness of the Lord Jesus for these men as He sends them forth into the world. Chapters 15, 16, and 17 of John's Gospel are all to be understood in this context of the amazing care and deathless love of Christ for these men whom He has chosen and called, who have spent so much time in the intimacies of His presence, and for whom He has poured Himself out.

This is how Jesus explains the content of chapters 15 and 16. Look at 16:1 in the RSV, which gets much more to the real meaning: "I have said all this to you [that is, all that He has been saying in chapter 15] to keep you from falling away." Then at 16:33: "I have said this to you [that is, the whole of John 16], that in me you may have peace. In the world you have tribulation; but be of good cheer, I have overcome the world." You see the care of Jesus.

Then, at the beginning of chapter 17 our Lord turns His attention away from them. From this ministry of encouraging and strengthening, He now turns to His Father, and before the Father He pours out His soul for them. "I pray for them; I pray not for the world, but for them which thou hast given me.... I pray not that thou shouldest take them out of the world, but that thou shouldest keep them from the evil" (vv. 9, 15).

There is something very wonderful about all this care and concern of the Master for His disciples because, you see, when we too are going back into a hostile world—the hostility of which Jesus never underplays—to seek to live out some of the things that we have been learning so far, it seems to me a tremendous encouragement that the reason why our Lord Jesus Christ is able to save to the uttermost them that come unto God by Him is that He ever lives to carry on this ministry to make intercession for us before the throne of the Father.

We may know something of this even now—that Jesus is engaged even now in this ministry at the Father's right hand, as He looks into the depths of all our weaknesses, all our frailties, and all the failures of the past that come so readily to face us again and again in the future. As He sees the pressures of the world, the flesh, and the devil, He is lifting up His soul afresh to the Father: "Father, keep him now, in that situation, in the hour of darkness, in that moment of special assault— Father, keep him!" That is what Jesus is doing for us. Beloved, we do not think enough about the present ministry of the Lord Jesus. This is what He is doing now—something of what He was telling Peter when He said, "Simon, Satan hath desired to have you, that he may sift you as wheat: But I have prayed for thee" (Luke 22:31-32).

As Jesus turns to the disciples with this burden on His heart for them, He gathers up His concern for them in three frequently repeated words: "Abide in me." I think we can detect at least a recollection here of the three words by which these men were first drawn to Jesus. The words of the Master as they were at their nets, at their fishing, or in the receipt of custom were "Come to me" or "Come after me." These were the words of commitment. But now, here are the words of continuance: "Abide in me." By the words "Come to me," we are drawn through the straight gate. And by the words "Abide in me," we are kept in the narrow way. That is the whole of Christian experience, until that day we see Him face to face.

Have you been drawn through the straight gate yet? Have you entered in to the way of life? God save us from refusing to hear the words of Jesus, "Come to me, that ye might have life" (5:40). But the other words that He speaks to us as we think about going out and continuing with Him are these words, "Abide in me."

One could spend a whole week learning the lesson of this chapter, but I want to focus our attention upon three things which seem to me to be involved with these verses, in a life of continuance and service.

THE ORDER OF THE MASTER'S PRIORITIES

The first thing is *accepting the order of the Master's priorities.* "Ye have not chosen me, but I have chosen you, and ordained you, that ye should go and bring forth fruit, and that your fruit should remain" (15:16). This, said Jesus, is the whole focus and purpose of discipleship: that you should go and bring forth fruit. Whether He is speaking about the eternal election before the foundation of the world, when God chose and called to Himself, or whether He is speaking about their own particular call at the lips of Jesus in their earthly life, the fundamental principle is that the great aim of God in calling men to Himself is that they might bear fruit.

It is interesting to notice that all three persons in the Godhead are involved in this concern. Notice that the Father prunes the branches in order that they may produce fruit; the Son chooses the disciples in order that they may produce fruit; and the Apostle Paul tells us that the Holy Spirit indwells us in order that we may produce the fruit of the Spirit. This, Paul tells us, is the whole point of God's purpose in wedding us to Christ. Do you know that great phrase in Romans 7:4: "Ye should be married ... [in order] that we should bring forth fruit unto God"?

The word "fruit" is used in the New Testament, first of all, of fruit in terms of *Christian character*. This is the thing the gospel is aiming for; this is what salvation is about. This is what every moment of the Spirit of God ought to end with and should be tested by: the fruit of character in the lives of God's children. "Ye have your fruit unto holiness" (Rom. 6:22). He tells the Philippians that he prays they might be "filled with the fruits of righteousness" (Phil. 1:11). And in Galatians, when Paul is describing the character of the child of God, he does so in terms of the fruit of the Spirit.

This is the great burden in the heart of the Master for His children as He sends them out into the world: that in their characters they might bear the fruit of the Spirit and that there might be the signs that God has been at work among them.

Then it speaks also of *service*. Romans 1:13, for instance, says: "I purposed to come unto you ... that I might have some fruit among you also." He is speaking about fruit in terms of the outcome of his service for Christ. The order is, of course, of vital importance.

Basically, you see, it is character which determines service or fruit bearing. The man I am, more than anything else in the world, determines the work that I do.

Beloved, as we think about Christian service in these days of a sick, needy, and dying world, I tell you there is no substitute in the service of God for holiness of character. It is possible in other spheres of service, you see, to divorce the two. I know some men who professionally are very able and competent, and whose life is worthwhile in their own particular spheres, but their character leaves a great deal to be desired. I know some doctors whose personal character is not everything that one would wish. In the service of God you cannot so divorce these two. The man I am, more than anything else, determines the service I render.

This whole question of bearing fruit that will remain, you will notice, is Jesus's great priority as it is His great test. "By their fruits ye shall know them" (Matt. 7:20). We need to make the Lord's priority ours. How shall we do this? Says Jesus, "Abide in me." What does this mean? Notice that it is not a passive word, as we so often imagine when we sing about "constantly abiding."[20] It has nothing to do with the idea of lolling, or a kind of spiritual inertia. The word is an active word.

It rests, of course, on the glorious fact of our union with Christ—the fact that we are in Him. Everything is founded upon that relationship which exists between Christ and those who are truly His. The glorious fact is that we are not, indeed, spectators of all that God has done in Christ; we are participators in it—dead with Christ, risen with Christ, to be glorified with Christ. We are in Him. The New Testament finds it impossible to think of Christ without the believer, or the believer without Christ, so closely are we united with Him. "Your life is hid," says Paul, "with Christ in God" (Col. 3:3).

---

20   From Anne S. Murphy's hymn, "Constantly Abiding."

But the words "abide in Christ" urge us to an ever-increasing intimacy with the Christ with whom we are bound together by grace; and the activity of this word describes an ever-increasing closeness of this bond. You get a hint of this in verse 15 where Jesus says, "Henceforth I call you not servants; for the servant knoweth not what his lord doeth: but I have called you friends; for all things that I have heard of my Father I have made known unto you." Notice how He longs, as He leaves them, to see this increasingly close bond between them and Him; He longs to see them leaving the company of those who are on the periphery of His purposes and being drawn into the center of them. Can you catch something of the desire in the Lord Jesus's heart as He speaks to these men—the longing that He has to draw them into the circle of His intimates?

Now, how is this done? I want to try to be practical, because this is not really something vague, nebulous, and mystical, but it is, rather, something utterly realistic and biblical. Look at verses 7 and 10: "If ye abide in me, and my words abide in you, … if ye keep my commandments, ye shall abide in my love." There is almost a natural interchange in abiding in Him and He in us, in abiding in Him and His words abiding in us, and in our abiding in Him and keeping His commandments. What Jesus is referring to is an ever-deepening knowledge of, and obedience to, His Word.

Oh, my dear friends, I think we need to give ourselves to some new thinking about this. So often our attitude to the Bible is as a kind of prop for our spiritual lives, is it not? We say, "I'm not really interested in reading the Bible except devotionally. You know, what I want the Bible for is for a word at the beginning of the day to help me through the day." Well, do not let me despise this; this is very important and necessary. But do you not think that if this is the only relation a man has to the Word of God, his religion is dreadfully self-centered?

If somebody was only interested in you for what he could get out of you, would you not be inclined to accuse him of cupboard love? We need to remind ourselves afresh that the great purpose of the Word of God is that we might learn of God and come to know Him—that we might discover His commandments, associate ourselves with His purposes, be aligned with His good pleasure, and thus be drawn into ever-deepening fellowship with Him. That is why I pray that we may go to wherever God calls us with a new longing in our hearts to continue to come to know Him through the Word, that we might give ourselves to fulfilling His good pleasure and learn to abide in Christ.

Accepting the order of the Master's priorities, therefore, will lead us to concern for the bearing of fruit in character and service, and for abiding in Christ and letting His words abide in us.

THE SOURCE OF THE SERVANT'S POWER

The second thing that is involved in these words of Jesus seems to me to be *discerning the source of the servant's power*. Notice in verses 4 and 5 how Jesus lays before the disciples this plain biological fact: "As the branch cannot bear fruit of itself, except it abide in the vine; no more can ye, except ye abide in me. I am the vine, ye are the branches.... Without me ye can do nothing."

The service of God is likened to fruit bearing because the production of fruit is a natural outcome of being joined to the vine. This is Jesus's picture of the service that the disciples are ultimately to render. So the source of all true authority and power in Christian service is God. This is the principle: "Without me ye can do nothing"—not just do the job less well than you otherwise would.

Now, behind this there is both a warning and an encouragement. The warning is that which was picked up and enlarged by the Apostle Paul in 1 Corinthians 3. It was precisely this principle that the believers in Corinth had forgotten or neglected. They had begun to be absorbed in personalities; some of them were taken up with Paul, some with Apollos. You know the kind of thing. I can imagine they were having a special series of meetings. They would have said, "You know, Paul did a great job the last time he was here. Let's have Paul back!"

Others said, "No, I prefer Cephas myself."

Somebody else said, "Have you ever heard the oratory of Apollos? We'll have Apollos!"

And Paul says, "Brethren, in the name of God, let this cease. Paul may plant, and Apollos may water, but it is God that giveth the increase." Then, as now, beloved, it is the increase that we so desperately need, evidence not that men are busily engaged in the Lord's service but that the living God has come down upon us in grace and power.

That is the warning that Elijah was given too, in another sense, for his comfort when at Horeb he was taken away to learn some lessons about the service of God. He saw this before him, in 1 Kings 19:

> The LORD passed by, and a great and strong wind rent the mountains, and brake in pieces the rocks before the LORD, but the LORD was not in the wind: and after the wind an earthquake; but the LORD was not in the earthquake: and after the earthquake a fire; but the LORD was not in the fire (vv. 11-12).

A great display, frightfully impressive, but the only trouble was that the Lord was not in them. Then, "after the fire a still small voice." I tell you, the thing that really matters among us today is what Elijah was being taught. The vital factor in every area of Christian life and service is whether the Lord is among us or not; that is the warning.

The encouragement is that if, on the one hand, we need to listen to Jesus saying to us, "Without me ye can do nothing" (v. 5), on the other hand we need to listen to Paul saying the corollary of that: "I can do all things through Christ which strengtheneth me" (Phil. 4:13). That is a great encouragement to the weak believer, conscious of all his frailties, aware of other people who seem not to suffer from them in the same way as he does. And he says, "How can my life be taken and be used by God?" Well, God is not beholden to natural gifts or abilities, or anything else of that kind. Paul says, "I can do all things through Christ who strengthens me." And the logical outcome of this—the warning and the encouragement—is the insistence in the three words "ye shall ask" in verse 7: "If ye abide in me, and my words abide in you, ye shall ask … and it shall be done." And repeated in verse 16: "Whatsoever ye shall ask of the Father in my name, he may give it you."

Have you, perhaps, through a great part of your lifetime felt that you were never able to be involved in active Christian service and in that sense so much less use to God? May I remind you of that vivid story in Exodus 17.

It was Israel's first battle, and the Amalekites had come against them in Rephidim. Moses, contrary to what one would have expected, left the battle field altogether and left Joshua behind to command the troops. And Moses went up into the hillside with Aaron and Hur. The battle commenced, and the fortunes of the battle were extraordinary. Now Israel prevailed, and now Amalek prevailed. Suddenly everything would be going Israel's way, and suddenly the Amalekites turned against them and were beginning to win.

There was no human explanation, nor any military strategy that could have explained the extraordinary battle, until they found that the issue of the day lay not with the fighters on the field but with the intercessors on the mountain top. When Moses lifted up his hands, Israel prevailed, and when Moses let down his hands, Amalek prevailed. It is unnecessary to point out the moral of the story: "God hath spoken once; twice have I heard this; that power belongeth unto God" (Ps. 62:11).

THE COST OF THE FATHER'S PRUNING

The third thing I would suggest to you that is involved in these words of Jesus about the fruitful and fruit-bearing life could be described as *submitting to the cost of the Father's pruning.*

"My Father is the husbandman [or the vinedresser, RSV]." The point is that once the vinedresser sees in the vine signs of growth and potential for fruitfulness, he immediately puts in the pruning knife; and the fruitfulness of the vine depends on the faithfulness of the pruning. Otherwise the possibility is that the life of the vine may be diverted into something less than fruitfulness. Does this not put the tribulation and testing so many of us go back to into an entirely different light? The sign that someone's life is beginning to show possibilities of fruitfulness is that God the Father puts in the pruning knife and begins to cut away and cut back.

Do you know these words of Amy Carmichael's, that woman who went out to India and was such a mighty influence for God—and still is through her writings? Under the heading of "Pruning":

"Rid me, good Lord, of every diverting thing." What prodigal waste it appears to be, to see scattered on the floor the bright green leaves, and the bare stem, bleeding in a hundred places from the sharp steel. But with a tried and trusted husbandman, there is not a random stroke in it all; nothing cut away which it would not have been loss to keep, and gain to lose.[21]

---

21   Quoted in Sinclair Ferguson, *Maturity: Growing Up and Going On in the Christian Life* (Edinburgh: Banner of Truth Trust, 2019), 47.

Does this not put the tribulation of the children of God in a new light? If we really grasped this, it would help many of us. We have fondly believed, and many of us have been mistakenly instructed, that the Christian life is one of freedom from problems, testings, trial, and tribulations—nothing but lovely joy all through the rest of your experience, now until glory. And we have been inclined to feel that these assaults of the devil and the pressures of the whole world of evil that some of us have known in our souls are the sign of something wrong in us.

But this is precisely the reverse of the Bible's teaching. You know these words in Hebrews 12, written to a church in the midst of tribulation:

My son, despise not thou the chastening of the Lord, nor faint when thou art rebuked of him: For whom the Lord loveth He chasteneth, and scourgeth every son whom he receiveth. If ye endure chastening, God dealeth with you as with sons; for what son is he whom the father chasteneth not? ... Now no chastening for the present seemeth to be joyous, but grievous: nevertheless afterward it yieldeth the peaceable fruit of righteousness unto them which are exercised thereby. Wherefore lift up the hands which hang down, and the feeble knees (vv. 5-7, 11-12).

As Jesus says to His disciples in the Upper Room,

If the world hate you, ye know that it hated me before it hated you. If ye were of the world, the world would love his own: but because ye are not of the world, but I have chosen you out of the world, therefore the world hateth you. Remember the word that I said unto you, The servant is not greater than his lord (John 15:18-20).

These very trials, far from being some strange anomaly in Christian experience, are the material of the Father's working in the hearts of His children to bring forth fruit.

I love these words of John Newton. I hope you read John Newton. Get hold of the letters of John Newton and read them, and you will find blessing to your soul:

I asked the Lord that I might grow
In faith and love and every grace
Might more of his salvation know,
And seek more earnestly his face....

I hoped that in some favored hour,
At once he'd answer my request;
And by his love's constraining power,
Subdue my sins, and give me rest.

Instead of this, he made me feel
The hidden evils of my heart;
And let the angry powers of hell
Assault my soul in every part.

Yea more, with his own hand he seemed
Intent to aggravate my woe;
Crossed all the fair designs I schemed,
Blasted my gourds, and laid me low.

Lord, why is this, I trembling cried,
Wilt thou pursue thy worm to death?
"Tis in this way," the Lord replied,

"I answer prayer for grace and faith.

These inward trials I employ,
From self and pride to set thee free;
And break thy schemes of earthly joy,
That thou mayst find thy all in me."[22]

"In the world," says Jesus, "ye shall have tribulation: but be of good cheer; I have overcome the world" (John 16:33). May we, therefore, go forth to abide in Christ, rest in the Lord, and wait patiently for His purposes, aware of all the tribulation that may lie before us, but still more aware that "greater is he that is in you, than he that is in the world" (1 John 4:4). May He make us His fruitful children, grounded and rooted and established in Him, for the glory of His name.

---

22   John Newton and Richard Cecil, *The Works*, 539.

BOOK THREE

Dealing with Difficulties

Chapter 11
Conflict in the Christian Life

Put on the whole armor of God, that ye may be able
to stand against the wiles of the devil.
— Ephesians 6:11 —

Some years ago I remember going to the doctor because I was suffering from that condition which always sounds to me to be a mechanical rather than a medical one of being run down. The sign of my being run down was a plague—a very biblical plague. (I have always suffered from very biblical troubles.)It was a plague of boils. So I went to the doctor to ask him what was wrong. He went into a lengthy and detailed explanation of what was happening inside my bloodstream. He told me about the battle that goes on in the body of every one of us. He said that when germs attack you at specific places in your body, white corpuscles run to the place where the germ is attacking, and they beat it back. This battle goes on in the life of the normal healthy person. There is always a battle which ends in victory for the white corpuscles.

"But," the doctor said, "your trouble is that you are below par. There is something wrong in your life, and the battle at every place where the germs are attacking you is ending in defeat. I'll tell you what's wrong. These white corpuscles, when the message goes to them that the germs are attacking, and the call comes: 'Come on, white corpuscles, come to this place in my body!' the white corpuscles just lie back and raise themselves on one elbow, and say, 'Who, us?' and they never go near. They are paralyzed, and they do not wage the battle; and the result is that the battle is lost. Now, that's what is going on in your body, and we'll need to diagnose why it is that the battle is so constantly being lost, and give you the cure."

You know, there is a battle—not just in our physical makeup— which is always going on like that. There is a battle like that, the Bible teaches us, which is going on in the life of every man, woman, boy, and girl who is really alive spiritually. There is a battle—a conflict— constantly going on.

One of the things that some of us have come to realize (because I think most of us know something about this kind of conflict) is that the result of the battle in our experience has too consistently been defeat. But deep down somewhere in the inner parts of your life, knowing that you were a defeated Christian, you hoped that somewhere, somehow, you might find the answer to that defeat and come to know a victorious Christian life. Just as the doctor had to stop to diagnose where the defeat was coming from, searching and seeking in my physical makeup where the defeat had its roots, so we want to discover together, as God by His Holy Spirit begins to diagnose our defeats, where the reason lies for the fact that many of us have become defeated Christians.

I want to turn, for that reason, to Ephesians 6, where the Apostle Paul begins an instruction and an examination of this matter of the Christian's conflict. I wonder if you have noticed that the Epistle to the Ephesians is an example in one letter of the broad teaching of the whole of the Bible about the Christian life. There are two things, basically, that the Bible has to say about the Christian—two things that it teaches us about his experience—and they are both in this Epistle to the Ephesians.

AT PEACE WITH GOD

The first is that the Christian is a man or woman who is *at peace with God.* That is the first thing that has happened in the life of the Christian. Until you have come face to face with Jesus Christ and received Him in faith, you are a man or a woman at enmity with God. But the Christian is a person who is, first of all, at peace with God. This is the wonderful thing that the Apostle Paul says has happened. In 2:13-16 he tells us:

> But now in Christ Jesus ye who sometimes were far off [from God because we were His enemies] are made nigh by the blood of Christ. For He is our peace, … and hath broken down the middle wall of partition…, so making peace; And that he might reconcile both unto God in one body by the cross.

The kind of people who need to be reconciled are those who are not at peace with each other. And the first thing, says the apostle, that has happened to us who have become Christians is that we have become men and women who are at peace with God. That is the first thing about the Christian, then: his life is a life at peace with God.

AT WAR WITH SATAN

The second thing that the Bible teaches us about the life of the Christian is that it is a life *at war with Satan* (v. 6). So there are two sides to the Christian life. The first great truth about it is that it is a life at peace with God, so that I have nothing to fear from God. I can stand before my fierce accuser and tell him that Christ has died, and I am at peace with God. But there is another side to the Christian life, and that is the life of war with Satan. And Paul tells these Ephesian Christians that. The second basic truth about the Christian experience is that if you are going to live the Christian life, you will discover that you are involved in a mortal conflict with a deadly enemy.

There is a sense, of course, in which this is one of the great tests of the reality of our spiritual experience. The Apostle Paul teaches us, you see, that we ought to be discovering these two things happening in our life as Christians. If your experience of Jesus Christ as Savior is really genuine, you ought to find that, generally speaking, your life is being lived in "accord" with God, and that word means that we are at peace with God—that we are at peace with His purposes, that our will is His will, and that we are living in accord with Him. We ought to be discovering also that the deepest places of our life and experience are at odds with the devil—that we are in communion with God and at odds with Satan. That is the Christian life; that is the healthy Christian experience.

Are you discovering that that is true in your life? Or do you find that you are far more at odds with God, and in terms with Satan, than the other way round? If that is so, you are going to have to search your heart very carefully to discover how real your spiritual experience is.

Let us think together about this conflict in which we are engaged against sin and the devil. The Apostle Paul tells us three things in this chapter about the conflict in which we are engaged, and I want to think with you briefly about the first two, and at a little more length about the third.

First, he tells us about the *fact* of the conflict. In other words, he teaches us that there is a conflict in which we, as Christians, are engaged. He tells us that this is part of the Christian life—that when we were converted God did not set us out on some kind of easy journey, on flowery beds of ease, to heaven, with nothing ever going wrong and no one ever coming to assail, tempt, and test us. The apostle says, "If you want to know what the Christian life is, here is the description of it: we wrestle—those of us who are Christians. We wrestle." He writes to Timothy, you remember, the young man who was setting out on the Christian life and Christian service, "Timothy, I'll tell you why God has chosen you to be one of His own. He has chosen you to be a soldier."

It seems to me that this is one of the things that young Christian people especially need to learn in these days about the Christian life. There are far too many of us who think that we have been sent out on some kind of release from every kind of trouble in life. I know that by the number of young Christian people who come to me after they have been converted somewhere, and they say, "Do you know, I am quite sure I can't be a Christian." And when I ask them why, they say, "Well, I thought that when I became a Christian everything would be all right, everything would be wonderful, everything would be happy, and every day packed full of lovely joy. But I find that the devil is far more of a nuisance to me now than he ever has been before. I find that I have things troubling and tempting me now, as a Christian, that never came to me before."

I usually say to them, "Well, I am very glad, because that is one of the surest signs that you are a Christian!" You see, one of the things that many Christians—especially, I think, young Christians—have never really learned and believed is that what has happened when they were converted is this: they have been saved by the blood of Jesus Christ from the penalty of sin; that is what God has done. And in our Christian experience He has given us the provision, if we will lay hold on it, for overcoming not only the penalty of sin but also the power of sin.

It is possible, says the Apostle Paul, for sin not to have dominion over us. But there is one thing that we shall not be released from in this life. What is that? I will tell you: it is the presence of sin. If you are expecting, as a Christian, to be released from the presence of sin in this world, then you are expecting here on earth what is going to happen in heaven! There is coming a day, blessed be God, when we are going to be released from sin's very presence, when it will be no more. But while we are here still on earth, we are engaged in a conflict with it and with the personality behind it. You have to remember that, and to distinguish among three things. Being saved from sin's penalty is justification; being saved in your day-to-day life from sin's power is sanctification; and being saved from sin's presence is glorification—and that comes when we go to heaven. Meanwhile here on earth, the Apostle Paul pictures the life of a Christian as lived in a field of conflict.

He speaks not only of the fact of the conflict but also of the *foe* in the conflict. He says,

> My brethren, be strong in the Lord, and in the power of his might. Put on the whole armor of God, that ye may be able to stand against the wiles of the devil. For we wrestle [we Christians] not against flesh and blood [in other words, our battle is not against ordinary enemies], but against principalities, against powers, against the rulers of the darkness of this world, against spiritual wickedness in high places (vv. 10-12).

In other words, says Paul, our conflict—our warfare—is against a supernatural enemy. We have an enemy who is as real in his supernatural being as God is in His. Tell me, is the devil as real to you as he was to the Apostle Paul, or do you think of him in that amusing figure with horns and a spiky tail? He loves that, you know, and he is pulling the wool over your eyes and bringing you down into defeat when you have that kind of picture about him. The Apostle Paul was not such a fool. He says that those of us who have been born again into the family of God, and have been made at peace with God, have a foe who is supernatural in his power and in his cunning. He speaks of the "wiles" of the devil.

If you are not alive and awake to the fact that behind sin and the actions that you see in the world—the foul stains of sin's presence in the world—there is a personality, then you have not begun to be awake to the nature of the conflict in which you are engaged. Satan—the foe in the conflict—is as a roaring lion going about seeking whom he may devour.

It is not, of course, that the devil does not sometimes clothe himself in flesh and blood. The apostle does not mean that; he tells us elsewhere that that is sometimes how Satan works. Our conflict is not against flesh and blood, but there are occasions when Satan clothes himself in flesh and blood to do his work.

You remember Simon Peter, a man who was a disciple of Jesus, one of those who was closest to Him. Yet there came a day when Jesus had to look into the eyes of Simon Peter—when he would keep Him back from the cross—and say to him, "Get thee behind me, *Peter*"? That is not what I read in my Bible. He said, "Get thee behind me, Satan!" But He was talking to Peter.

I suppose there is no thought that ought to make us tremble more as Christians than the thought that we should so drift from God that the devil will be able to use us as the clothing he takes on to do his work. I wonder if, in the fellowship to which you belong, in the place in which you have a position in Christian things, you could be the devil's agent. Why? Because, like Peter, through disobedience you have drifted away from Jesus.

Then finally, I want us to think about *failure* in the conflict. Paul is writing to these Ephesian Christians so that there might be no failure in their lives in the conflict. He is telling them how they may avoid it, and by doing so, he diagnoses for us where failure begins in the conflict—for that, maybe, is the most important truth about this whole matter for many of us. We know what it is to be failures and to have left behind us as the story of our Christian experience—maybe over months, maybe over years—a trail of constant defeat.

Why is there failure in our battle? What causes defeat in the Christian battle? Well, Paul says that it can, first of all, be *failure to flee*. As General Haffenden once told me, a "strategic withdrawal" is sometimes a vital part of battle strategy. And Paul has something to say about that. He says that there is a time in the life—especially of the young Christian, because it is to Timothy that he writes it (2 Tim. 2)—when the thing to do when you are confronted with all the hordes of hell, their temptations, and their foul devices is to run!

The apostle says, "Timothy, there is a time when what I want you to do is not to stand and look at it, and say, 'Now, is this a good thing, or a bad thing? What should I do about this? Let's see! Let's look at it, and examine it, and go through it, and then decide whether we'll have it or not!' " He says, "Timothy, I tell you there are occasions in your spiritual conflict when, if you do not flee, you are going to fail. Timothy, flee youthful lusts. Flee these things." He comes again and again to certain things that are especially going to break in upon the life of the young Christian, and he says, "Timothy, leave them alone."

I wonder if part of the reason for the failure in your spiritual life is because you have been playing around with the kind of fire that the New Testament says you have got to let alone. You know how we teach the young children about the places where God's truth gets in, about "eye gate" and "ear gate." But you know, of course, that the devil gets in the same way, does he not? Oh, yes, we all know that! Well then, what kind of things do you read? What kind of things do you let your eyes look upon? Are you allowing the devil to make his foul devices real in your heart because you are not leaving alone things that God says you have got to flee from?

Perhaps this applies especially, if I may say so, to the thing that the apostle connected it with as he wrote to Timothy. "Timothy, flee youthful lusts. Let them alone!" I want to say to you that our God is a God who demands of His disciples that they walk straight down the center of the moral line. You are bound for failure and defeat all along the way if the devil is getting in there. In the name of God, let them alone.

But there is a second kind of failure that the apostle speaks about in this passage, and that is *failure to stand*. The second kind of military action, I am told, is the action known as a defensive action, where you stand still and wield the armor that the apostle is speaking about. Have you noticed how many times he speaks about standing? He cites these various pieces of equipment by which we are to stand "in the evil day" (Eph. 6:13). They are all pieces of equipment which are used for fighting a defensive action, until you come to the sword of the Spirit, which is an offensive weapon. But I wonder if some of us have been knowing the onslaughts of the devil and the temptations of the world, the flesh, and the devil and we have not been standing. Well, why is that?

The apostle says it is because we have not got the right armor. That is why. It is because we have not been laying hold, first of all, of the truth of God, which is the first part of the armor. "Stand, therefore, having your loins girt about with truth" (v. 14). Do you remember how Jesus in the wilderness, as the devil came to Him constantly, as every foul suggestion that he made came into the soul of the Master, stood against it? Why? Because He was plying him with the truth of God; He was equipped with it.

I wonder if you have been failing to stand against the enemy because the truth of God has but a back seat in your life, because you are a Christian who has never taken the trouble to lay hold upon the Word of God and examine, study, and make it part of the fiber of your being. Are you a Christian in whose life the Bible—the truth of God— has a back place? I want to tell you that you are a Christian who is bound for defeat.

But there is another kind of failure, and that, thirdly, is *failure to advance*. Neither the secular soldier nor the Christian warrior may safely remain static, and it is entirely consistent with what we have just been saying to add now that the New Testament insists upon advance in the Christian pilgrimage and conflict—moving on into enemy ground and gaining victory over him. Robert Murray M'Cheyne used to say, "There are only two things that can happen in the Christian life: you will either go on, or you will go back." This is what the apostle is pleading for earlier in this epistle: "That we henceforth be no more children, tossed to and fro, and carried about with every wind of doctrine… but … may grow up into him in all things" (Eph. 4:14-15). In other words, God's great purpose for His people is not that they should remain spiritual babies, attracted to and tickled by the things that belong to the babies' world, but that they should grow up into effective soldiers—moving out into new ground and gaining triumphs in the strength of their Captain and seeing the enemy retire in confusion. "Resist the devil, and he will flee from you" (James 4:7).

But this is soldiers' work, not children's. Maybe one of the things many of us will have to ask ourselves if we are to get to the root cause of our defeat is just this: "What has been the direction of my spiritual life since I was converted? Where have I been going? Or has it just been a kind of aimless drifting, like the driftwood that is tossed about by the tide?" You will have heard of the little boy who explained his falling out of bed to his mother: "I think I must have gone to sleep too near where I got in." I wonder if that is not a description of many Christian lives—gone to sleep spiritually where you got in.

Notice that the great weapon of offense in this list of Paul's in Ephesians 6 is the "sword of the Spirit, which is the word of God" (v. 17). This is the means of our advance, as it is also described in the epistles as the means of our growth. So we come back to the question which seems to be the most central issue: Where is the Word of God in your life? But before you are too hasty in answering that, may I ask you, has it all been merely in your head? You see, the sword of God's Spirit is primarily for plunging into the heart, to deal with pride and disobedience and rebellion there, to cast out the demon of hypocrisy and unreality and unwillingness, and to make us no more children but soldiers. Hear the prayer of Thomas Hughes:

> Then, God of truth for whom we long,
> Thou who wilt hear our prayer,
> Do Thine own battle in our hearts,
> And slay the falsehood there.
> So, tried in Thy refining fire,
> From every lie set free,
> In us Thy perfect truth shall dwell,
> And we may fight for Thee.[23]

May God give us grace to hear whatever He has to say to us.

---

23 From Thomas Hughes's hymn, "O God of Truth, Whose Living Word."

Chapter 12
Three Causes of Spiritual Defeat

Indeed I have sinned against the LORD God of Israel.
— Joshua 7:20 —

Joshua 7 records the story of Israel's defeat at Ai and the disclosure of Achan and the kind of man he really was. May I remind you that these areas of the Old Testament, of which the Book of Joshua is part, are not merely meant to be historical accounts to the people of God, but they are given to us by God in His wisdom as a pattern of the deep things of God with His own people—as a pattern of the progress of the people of God in their spiritual pilgrimage. They are an example of the kind of things that are liable to hinder them on their pilgrimage and the kind of things that will give them victory over their enemies. It may well be that as we meditate together on the experience of God's people in this particular passage you may find your own experience being mirrored and described.

There is one basic fact which lies behind this chapter and the teaching that God has set down here for us about His people and their spiritual condition and pilgrimage: that this is the pattern of a people who were given by God a land as their rightful inheritance. They were given a possession by God, in His grace and in His love, because He had taken them and chosen them to be His people.

It is, secondly, a pattern of a people who were sent in to possess this land which had been made over to them by Him. I want you to notice, especially, as the background to all that we shall be saying, the method of their possession. I discover through all these historical sections of the Bible that the method by which the people of God went in and possessed their possessions was the method characterized by conflict. They discovered that they were people locked in battle with an enemy who was intent upon their destruction. Every progress that they made, every movement in the direction of God's bidding, was made through conflict with the enemy.

Remember that immediately as they came across the Jordan into the land of Canaan, they were met with conflict at Jericho. And as they went on and went through, at God's bidding, they discovered that they were a people who had an enemy to encounter. This is not merely the history of the people of Israel, but it is the pattern of the life of the people of God in every generation.

It is the pattern described for us, of course, by the Apostle Paul when he writes to the Ephesians. What is the life that we Christians live? What do we do as Christians? Paul's answer is that we wrestle. That is the character of our life. "For we wrestle not against flesh and blood, but against principalities, against powers" (6:12)—against supernatural agencies. We are engaged in this kind of mortal conflict.

Paul wants Timothy to view his ministry in that way. In effect, Paul asks, "Why has He chosen you, my son Timothy?" And Paul answers, "You are a man who has been chosen to be a soldier." And when he comes to the end of his own life, that greatest of apostles says, "What have I done? I have fought a good fight. That has been the character of my life."

You will have noticed, going through the Gospels, that the character of the life of our blessed Lord Himself is perhaps marked out most by this same thing: that in every new movement of His life toward the fulfilling of the very purposes of God, He meets with conflict. He enters into battle with Satan and all his hosts, and this, the New Testament tells us as well as this Old Testament historical section, is the pattern for God's people.

We in our day must be encouraged by this—to understand that if we find ourselves engaged in some of the desperate, secret battles of the soul, then we are following the pattern that God has prescribed for us.

But when we come to Joshua 7 with that as the background, there is something upon which God focuses our attention, and that is the condition of the combatants. That is always the vital thing for us to notice in the battle: the condition of the combatants and the outcome of the battle. You see, there is all the difference in the world between being involved in a conflict and knowing what it is to have victory in the midst of it, and being involved in a conflict, as the people of Israel were in Joshua 7, and knowing the ignominy and the tragedy of a shameful defeat and confusion at the hands of the enemy. The story of Achan and Ai is the story of defeat. And I wonder if there are not many of us who find our own experience mirrored in this section of God's Word.

The victory at Jericho, in chapter 6, is such a different story. I suppose that is why it is so much more popular than this of Ai and Achan. It is a story that we sing a great deal about—the Joshua who fought the battle of Jericho. But, oh, when we come into Joshua 7, we discover that there is a different atmosphere altogether, and a different outcome. The great question which must occupy us is this: Why this defeat? Why is it that the people of God, who had such a history, who had such a background, when they come into this seventh chapter, are in defeat and in hopeless despair—men and women who find that they have no hope and no power to meet the enemy? They are paralyzed people, whether they be the people of God or not.

That was the question Joshua asked of God in verse 7—rather strangely, perhaps, because it almost seemed as if he were blaming God. I wonder if you see your own situation mirrored here. He says,

Alas, O LORD God, wherefore hast thou at all brought this people over Jordan, to deliver us into the hands of the Amorites, to destroy us? would to God we had been content, and dwelt on the other side Jordan!

In other words, "O God, why have You done it? Why did You leave us in this hour?" He says, "The situation is simply this: that God has let us down." I do not doubt that many pastors have had people come to them in hours of defeat and spiritual calamity, who re-echo the sentiment of Joshua's prayer: "God has let me down. It doesn't work. Something's gone wrong somewhere in the heavenly councils!"

Notice how God replies: He begins the diagnosis of the trouble. This is where we all must begin with God: with the diagnosis of what is wrong. May it be that as we examine it together, we may be willing before God to let Him by His Spirit make the diagnosis and apply it to our own experience. God says in verse 10, "Joshua, Get thee up; wherefore liest thou thus upon thy face?" In other words, face the truth about the situation, which is that Israel has sinned (v. 11). Oh, yes, the particulars of it are to be hunted out and made very clear to Joshua and to all the people of Israel—the particulars as they were found in the life of Achan, as God revealed to Joshua the real cause of their defeat and of their condition as the people of God in powerlessness.

THE SIN OF ISRAEL

First, there is the general character of the trouble. God describes it in verse 11: "Israel hath sinned." Notice the general character of Israel's sin which is the background, the general savor of the condition of the people of God. You know, when a Christian is living in defeat and outside the will of God, there is something about the very savor of his life, the general character of it, which has a spirit of being out of touch with God about it. That is the kind of thing you see in this story of the people of God who have sinned.

The general character of Israel's sin was the sin of presumption. They imagined that certain things could be taken for granted about themselves and about God which could not be taken for granted and which were in fact not true. Why, they had the blessing of Jericho behind them and that experience to look back to! How blessed and wonderful these days had been at Jericho, days of the right hand of the Most High. Had not God shown His grace and His mercy to them? Had not He seemed to have His hand upon them in blessing? Were they not a peculiar people, a favored people? What blessing there had been in Jericho! But notice that they found what so many of the people of God have been finding ever since: that the blessing they had experienced in a former day was now absent in the conflict in which they were engaged.

They went to Ai, blithely harking back to what belonged to their spiritual history. I suppose they would have gladly given their testimony on what God had done, what God had been to them, how they had got on at Jericho, and the blessing they had known there. But the fact about them now was that they were out of touch with God. If we were to use one phrase to describe their condition, we should have to coin a rather ugly phrase: "out-of-touch-ness."

It is the kind of thing that characterizes so much evangelical Christianity in our day and generation: lives which essentially, however they have all the façade of orthodoxy about them, have somewhere deep down—and it is the savor of their life—that out-of-touch-ness with God marking their lives. The people of Israel discovered themselves in the same experience as Samson: they "wist [knew] not that the LORD was departed from" them (Judg. 16:20). Like the manna that they had once tried to keep over for another day, they found that their experience, and the blessing that they had been holding on to, was beginning to rot.

I wonder if that is your condition, your situation. You have been a Christian for many years, and you have what we like to call, in the evangelical world, a testimony. But if the truth were uncovered by God (as it is always uncovered by Him when He comes into the midst of His people in power), the fact is that your testimony is about something that happened years ago, and the truth about your life today is that you are out of touch with God.

You remember how the Apostle Paul points out the thing that really matters about the Christian life and about spiritual experience. He says, "The life which I now live…" (Gal. 2:20). That is the thing that counts! It is not the life you lived twenty years ago that matters. It is not the experience you had of God fifteen years ago, or five; it is the life that you now live. Is it a life like that of the people of God in this passage— out of touch with God?

Notice how they went about the battle in the same way. They had the same general method as they had before but went up with a kind of fleshly mathematics: "Let not all the people go up; but let about two or three thousand men go up and smite Ai" (v. 3). The characteristic of the whole of chapter 7, and their preparation for the next move-on, is the characteristic of a people who had no communion.

So that is the sin of Israel, the general savor of their life. I wonder if the general impact of your life is like that—if the general savor that you are conveying to people outside of Christ, and in your own community, is of a life that is out of touch.

THE SIN OF ACHAN

But then God begins to particularize the diagnosis of Israel's defeat, and He comes, secondly, to the sin of Achan—for God is not just content with generalizations. God is not content with the kind of thing that we are so often content with: diatribes against sin—everybody else's sin, of course, except our own. He wants a life that is ready for His probing work, for His searching Spirit to go beyond the surface into the deep realities. He wants to go down, and go deep, to discover the Achan in the camp. So the voice of God who searches out the truth about men begins to go through the camp of Israel, from tribe to tribe, from family to family, from individual to individual, saying, "Where is the Achan in the camp?"

When the sin was uncovered, notice the nature of it. It had three basic characteristics. I wonder, as God begins to particularize His diagnosis, if you find yourself mirrored here. Achan tells us himself what it was, as it becomes uncovered, in verse 21. There are three things that he says he has done: "When I saw among the spoils a goodly Babylonish garment, and two hundred shekels of silver, and a wedge of gold of fifty shekels weight, then I coveted them, and took them, and, behold, they are hid."

Notice that his first sin is *covetousness*. This was the first thing which, in particularizing, God showed them had brought about the defeat in the life of His people. Achan's sin, the battle that he lost himself before Ai was ever reached, was the sin of falling before the great mammon of materialism. This was the thing that ate the heart out of Achan's life. He says, "I saw ... then I coveted them, and took them." There came the great test, you see, in Achan's life. What things matter to you most, Achan? Does it matter more to you to listen to the Word of God and stake your life upon it, or do *things* matter more to you than the word that God has spoken? Achan coveted the "goodly Babylonish garment, and two hundred shekels of silver, and a wedge of gold."

I was greatly shaken, quite recently, when a man who travels widely said to me—a man whose opinion I respect—"You know, there is one thing that seems to me to be eating the very vitals out of the evangelical church in our day: it is the sin of materialism. It is the tragedy of Christian men and women to whom things seem to matter far more than God." Achan's sin was the sin, first, of covetousness.

Secondly, he tells us that his sin was the sin of *disobedience*. "I coveted them, and took them." It was not that Achan was not acquainted with the word that God had spoken about Jericho and what was to happen there. "And ye, in any wise keep yourselves from the accursed thing, lest ye make yourselves accursed, when ye take of the accursed thing, and make the camp of Israel a curse, and trouble it" (6:18). And in the face of the very word that God had spoken, Achan arose and walked across the line, right out of the will of God.

I suppose we do not need to do anything more than ask ourselves, as we are before God, "Does that mirror my condition?" Even as you read this here, you may find yourself to be an Achan, knowing deep in your heart that the true condition, beyond anything that other men may see, is that you are living in sheer disobedience to the word that God has spoken to you. I do not know what that word is; it may be a word that will change the whole future of your life, and you have been unwilling for it. It may be a word that will be costly to obey. But I want to say this: there will never be another hour of victory in your life until what God has called the accursed thing is acknowledged, confessed, and rooted out. "I coveted, and I took."

But I do not want to leave the story of Ai and Achan without noticing the last thing that marks out Achan's sin. "I coveted them, and took them; and, behold, they are hid." It was, first, the sin of covetousness and, secondly, the sin of disobedience; and finally, the sin of *hypocrisy*. Notice that is what God is charging them with. In verse 11: "They have taken of the accursed thing, and have also stolen [robbed God of what was His right and His due] and dissembled also." The word, I am told, which is used in the Greek of the Old Testament for "dissemble" is the same word that is used of Ananias and Sapphira, who lied to the Holy Ghost about the kind of life that they were living.

This is what had happened in Achan's experience. He had come through Jericho and faced Ai, and as he went out into it he seemed to all the other people to be exactly the same. His disobedience and his covetousness were something which he had taken, and from the eyes of other men he had buried and hidden. But oh, the day was to come when before God and in the spiritual experience, not just of Achan "for none of us liveth to himself" (Rom. 14:7) but of us all, he was to discover that what man has hidden, God is going to uncover!

You remember how it happened in exactly the same way with Ananias and Sapphira. Their sin was not that they did not give everything they had to God but that they went out before the apostles, before the church of God, and pretended to have a kind of spiritual consecration of themselves which was untrue, and their lives were a lie. Deep down in their hearts they were living something that was an untruth.

Oh, men and women, I wonder if this is the picture that God wants you to see of yourself—a life that is a lie! Will it all have to be brought out into the open and uncovered before God—the "accursed thing" uprooted—before the blessing can come? Our God is still the God who judges the secrets of men by Christ Jesus. This very day He goes through every gathering joined together, with the cry upon His lips of a searching God who takes sin, disobedience, and pretense seriously, and cries, "Where is the Achan, in your life?" In your life would God root it out, bring it into the open, and deal with it, that the life of defeat might become a life of victory under the One who giveth us the victory over every such thing, even our Lord Jesus Christ. May He do so for His name's sake.

Chapter 13

The Christian's Enemy

And I will put enmity between thee and the woman,
and between thy seed and her seed;
it shall bruise thy head, and thou shalt bruise his heel.
— Genesis 3:15 —

We are deeply concerned not to stay where we begin in the Christian life, not to be like the little boy who said to his mother when he had fallen out of bed, "I'm sorry, Mummy, but I went to sleep too near where I got in!" We are concerned that we may continue in our Christian experience—not just to enter a relationship with God but to grow up into fellowship with Him.

Many of us discover, as we are honest with ourselves, that we are not getting on in the Christian life. We are not growing up; we are not coming to know God better; we are not becoming more obedient to Him daily. Somehow or other there is a stagnation in our spiritual experience. So the first facts that we have to recognize are facts about the Christian's enemy. There is an enemy bent not only upon keeping us from being converted but also upon keeping us from growing in our Christian lives.

There are two things that are true about a Christian. First, he is *at peace with God*. Previously I was an enemy of God; my life was at war with Him. But when I enter into the blessing of the saving grace of God in Jesus Christ, I am at peace with God. That is what Paul is talking about in the Epistle to the Ephesians: "He has made peace," and that is the wonderful thing about us as Christians.

The other thing that is equally true is that we are *at war with Satan*. We discover that not only are we reconciled to God, but in the same act we are also antagonized to Satan. And this second truth is one that the New Testament bids us to remember and recognize.

I want us to look in Genesis 3 at certain things God has taught concerning the person and nature of the enemy. This chapter speaks, first, of the *strategy of Satan*; secondly, of the *essence of sin*; and thirdly, of the *effects of sin*.

THE STRATEGY OF SATAN

The *strategy of Satan* is concerned, first, with his *person* and, secondly, with his *work*. There is a doctrine in the Bible not only about the Person and work of Jesus Christ but also about the person and work of the enemy of Jesus Christ and of all His people, who is called Satan and the devil. One of his master strokes is to concentrate all the attention of Christians upon the first of these things and leave them to ignore the second, and this always leads to fatal results.

First, the *person* of Satan—because, you see, when we speak about failure in the Christian life, the majority of Christians think the reason for this is what they call "sin." This is the Christian's great problem—my sin, my own weakness, the peculiarities of my personality that make me prone to certain sins in my life. People have come to those of us who are in the Christian ministry and said, "My problem is that my nature is so weak; I am prone to so many kinds of temptations that fellow Christians are never tempted in. This is my problem."

But the Bible says this is not your problem, for it is vital for us to grasp the threefold distinction that the Bible makes between "sins," which are the individual acts of trespass in my life as a Christian, and "sin," which is not just the singular of that first word but the principle and power which lies behind the open acts of trespass. And the principle of sin is something different from the practice of sin.

In the New Testament, and especially in the Epistle to the Romans, sin is spoken of as having dominion over people. It is a power which exercises control over the lives of men and women. It is spoken as "reigning." In Romans 6:16 sin is described as a tyrannical master who exercises a rule and an influence over the lives of Christians as well as non-Christians.

Behind sins and sin there is not just the practice and the principle but the personality who lies behind it all. You remember how Jesus, when Simon Peter sought to divert Him from His pathway of strict obedience to the will of God and said, "Be this far from thee, Lord," Jesus did not reply, "Get that nasty idea out of your head, Peter," but He said, "Get thee behind me, Satan" (Matt. 16:23). In other words, Jesus unmasked the personality behind the idea.

We find this happening again and again. In the parable of the tares, Jesus put into the mouth of the farmer not "this is an unfortunate incident that has happened" but "an enemy hath done this" (Matt. 13:28). In Acts 5, when Ananias and Sapphira lied to the Holy Ghost and to the apostles, Peter said, "Why has Satan filled thine heart to lie to the Holy Ghost?" Do you remember how Peter—probably remembering the words of Jesus to him—speaks of "your adversary the devil" (1 Pet. 5:8)?

The enemy we face in our Christian experience is a supernatural personality. Just as God is the author of all that is good, high, and noble in our lives, so that from Him "every virtue we possess, and every victory won"[24] derives, so, on the other hand, the author of all that is base, evil, foul, and horrid is none other than Satan, the archenemy of God and God's people. And it is of fundamental importance for us, in living the Christian life, that we should neither be ignorant of him nor of his devices.

This does not mean that we are going to excuse ourselves for our own disobedience. We recognize the author of sin, but so often we are the executors of sin; we are the people who carry out the will of Satan rather than the will of God. But very often in the lives of Christians there is a kind of self-flagellation, a self-punishment that we seem to indulge, for thoughts that come into our minds—ideas that possess us—which really ought to be traced back to the devil.

Have you heard that in the New Testament the devil is called "the accuser of our brethren" (Rev. 12:10)? Part of his work is to come to the child of God, to the back door of your mind, and in there he pops one of his foul suggestions and diabolical thoughts, and then he whips round to the front door of your mind and says, "Excuse me, what are you doing with a thought like that in your mind if you are a Christian? Can you really be a Christian with things like that going on in your mind?" And you say, "Dear me, it is quite true; perhaps I'm not, after all." And what you don't hear is that he has gone off chuckling with Beelzebub glee.

This is something that could set many of us at liberty from the self-punishment in which we indulge, when we ought all the time to be tracing back so many of these things to Satan and deal with them as Jesus does: "Get thee behind me." Rebuke him! Resist him in the name of the Lord and say, "Get back to hell where you belong! I'm trusting and resting in Jesus Christ and living for Him in obedience to His command." That is the importance of recognizing the personality of Satan.

---

24   From Harriet Auber's hymn, "Our Blest Redeemer, Ere He Breathed."

Notice also his *work*, in Genesis 3. He comes in the form of a serpent, "more subtil than any beast of the field" (v. 1). Of course, we think today of the serpent as being a snake which crawls along and comes to Eve, and we wonder how ever she could be mesmerized by someone like this. But the Hebrew word for a serpent can be translated, some very able Hebrew scholars tell us, as "a shining one." That is a significant thing, because in 2 Corinthians 11:14 Paul tells us that sometimes Satan transforms himself into an angel of light. He does not come with all the accoutrements that we have plastered on to him: horns and a spiky tail. He comes to us in the most disguised form, and no doubt he came to Eve in this way.

My purpose is not to go into all the details of how Satan came to Adam and Eve but to draw out the principles from it. Undoubtedly this is satanic temptation; and there are three things that Satan is concerned to do. His work in Eve and Adam is to bring about disobedience to the Word of God. Adam and Eve, you see, had received the Word of God for living their life (Gen. 2:16-17). The only counsel they had to go by was the Word that God had given: "Of every tree of the garden thou mayest freely eat: But of the tree of the knowledge of good and evil, thou shalt not eat of it: for in the day that thou eatest thereof thou shalt surely die." That was the Word of God to them.

You will notice that Satan's purpose is to bring them to open disobedience to the Word of God, and he begins by tempting Eve to doubt it. "And he said unto the woman, Yea, hath God said?" (v. 1)— that is, Satan begins by seeking to undermine the confidence of Eve in the God-given Word. It ought to have been sufficient for her, of course, that this was the Word that God had spoken; but what Satan is saying is very simply this: "God doesn't really mean what He says. Are you really sure that this is God's Word? Is it the kind of thing you would expect God to do: to cramp your style like this in the garden and to keep you away from all these wonderful things that you see there? This isn't like God; this can't be what God means. He must mean something altogether different." He is beginning to get a foothold into her mind. She begins to sit in judgment upon the Word of God and to doubt the Word that God has spoken.

I studied theology for almost seven years, and I remember that the one thing the devil does in the life of a young man who is an ordinand for the church is this: he begins by attacking the confidence of that man in the Word of God. He begins to delude you into thinking that this isn't anything to do with your spiritual life; this is just an intellectual exercise. "A man of your erudition can't possibly believe that God means all this kind of thing!" You cannot accept it. You sit in judgment on it, and he begins to get a foothold in your mind, and you begin to think, "Why, this is simply not being intellectually honest. It's not as if I'm going to disobey the Word of God; this doesn't enter into my spiritual life."

May I say, in the name of God, don't you believe it! The design of the devil, whenever this kind of temptation begins to come into your life, is to lead you from doubt to denial and then to disobedience. His intention and purpose is to blast, blight, and ruin your ministry, and there are many young men and women whose ministry has been blighted because Satan has entered in to destroy their confidence in the Word of God.

Secondly, having gained entrance into Eve's mind, he proceeds to invite her to an open denial: "Ye shall not surely die" (v. 4). Yet that is precisely what God had said would happen: "In the day that thou eatest thereof thou shalt surely die" (2:17). What Satan is doing is bringing Eve on equal terms before God, asking her to judge the situation with God and reject His command—reject His Word. And this eventually she did, so that doubting the Word of God led to denial of it, and then to disobedience. We read that "she took of the fruit thereof, and did eat, and gave also unto her husband with her; and he did eat" (v. 6).

This is precisely what happened in Jesus's temptation in the wilderness. God had said from the heavens, "This is my beloved Son, in whom I am well pleased," and Satan comes: "If thou be the Son of God, command that these stones be made bread" (Matt. 4:3). In other words, "God would never cramp you like this. Listen to me: 'If thou be the Son of God...' Are you sure you are? Is it really true?" You see the diabolical content in this doubt of the Word of God. That is the person and the work of Satan.

THE ESSENCE OF SIN

Let us look briefly at the *essence of sin* in this chapter. The essence of sin is twofold. It is, first, *pride*. To what did Satan appeal in verse 5? "God doth know that in the day ye eat thereof, then your eyes shall be opened, and ye shall be as gods, knowing good and evil." In that sentence Satan has touched upon the very quick of man's life.

The great question that hung over man's life in this conflict in the garden of Eden, and the question that hangs over the life of every man and woman is, Whom will he worship? Man is an incurably religious creature; he will always worship someone, and the question is whether it will be God or self. And man fell in the garden of Eden. This is the whole message of this chapter; never lose the message in being concerned about the details. Man fell to the devil's device of holding before him the temptation to pride and self-worship and self-centeredness in his life.

It may have been this that the Apostle Paul was talking about when he described sin in Romans 1:25. He says there are those "who have changed the truth of God into a lie, and worshipped and served the creature more than the Creator." That is the essence of sin: the worship of self.

You remember how it is illustrated in Luke 18 in the Pharisee who came with the publican up to the temple one day. Jesus paints the picture of these two men, and He puts it like this: "The Pharisee began to pray thus with himself, God, I thank thee." Do you notice the position of these words, "prayed thus with himself, God,…"? The truth about that man's life was that his god was himself. Notice that through the rest of the parable, he says, "I thank thee, that I am not as other men are.… I give tithes [I do this, I do that]." His life is one great long catalogue of "I's," and that is the very darkness of hell. When a man's life is centered on himself, every sin can be explained in these terms.

You remember David and Bathsheba, when he looked upon her and lusted in his heart the sin that brought out that great psalm, "Against thee, thee only, have I sinned" (51:4). Do you remember what happened? I imagine that David probably went to Bathsheba with the language on his lips that we so often use today and said, "I love you, Bathsheba." But the Bible says that really what he was saying was "I love me, and I want you."

There is all the difference between heaven and hell—between God and the devil—in these two things. Watch that like the very devil himself! In this wicked and perverted generation, watch it. When you say to someone you love them, make doubly sure before God that you are not saying, "I love me, and I want you."

The essence of sin is pride and self, and, secondly, it is *rebellion*, for this is what Satan was calling for with Adam and Eve—mutiny against God and His Word. This is what Isaiah says of it: "We have turned every one to his own way" (53:6), and Adam gives evidence of this immediately afterwards in the explanation of the events. When God comes to him and says, "Where art thou?" and asks him what had happened, in verse 12, he says, "The woman whom thou gavest to be with me, she gave me of the tree, and I did eat." In other words, Adam is rebelling against

God—blaming the thing on Him, standing against Him. "You gave me the woman," he says. And this is what David discovers in Psalm 51: "Against thee, thee only have I sinned." That was not true on the face of it; it was against Bathsheba and Uriah, but David has seen the blackness of sin in that it is always rebellion against God.

THE EFFECTS OF SIN

Finally, we see the *effects of sin*. We must recognize that there are effects. Sin is said in the Bible to have wages, and the wages are always paid out. There is never a sin committed but the wages of it follow, and the effects are very clear here.

They are, first, *guilt*. Notice the tremendous and terrible change that sin wrought in Adam and Eve. They hid themselves from God—from Him whom previously they had regarded as all their joy. And the reason? "I was ashamed," says Adam.

Secondly, you have *disillusionment*. This is one of the bitterest things about sin. The promises that the devil makes are always found out to be lies. "Ye shall be as gods." And here they were as poor, frightened, worm-like creatures, running away from God, going out into a life of slavery. No wonder Jesus said that the devil is not only a liar, but he is "the father of lies" (John 8:44, RSV); and they became disillusioned.

I have just seen a little of the terrible disillusionment that sin can bring in the lives of men and women. I have seen the faces of young people who are aged long before their time when sin has soured them. You know that it operates on the law that the economists call "the law of diminishing returns." It takes more, and more, and more of the same thing to produce less, and less, and less satisfaction. And Adam and Eve were discovering the disillusionment of it.

Thirdly, *estrangement*: banished from God. They were cast out of the garden.

Finally, *enslavement*. They discovered that the devil's devices were precisely the same as they were with Jesus. "Fall down and worship me" (Matt. 4:9). Oh, this is what the devil is out for in your life: to draw you away from obedience and service to the best of masters and to bring you into his foul bondage! There is only one answer, and that is a life that is utterly yielded. As Paul says in Romans 6:18, "Being then made free from sin, ye became the servants of righteousness"— servants of Christ, not servants of sin, because you have to serve one or the other. May our prayer be, "Make me a captive, Lord, and then I shall be free."

Chapter 14

Lord, Is It I?

And they were exceeding sorrowful,
and began every one of them to say unto him, Lord, is it I?
— Matthew 26:22 —

We have seen how Peter failed in his Christian life when he rebuked Jesus for speaking of His need to suffer and die. Peter also failed on the night of Jesus's arrest when three times he denied that he even knew the Lord. We can identify with Peter, for we also fail in our own Christian lives. But we are encouraged because Peter was restored and came to the end of his days in a blaze of glory, a light that shone and burned for Christ.

But I want now to turn to the other disciple whose life is in so many strange ways intertwined with Simon Peter's but who found no place of restoration and ends his days, in the New Testament record, in a pall of unspeakable darkness. Wherever he goes in the Gospels, Judas Iscariot drags after him the stigma which seems to be inseparable from his name—"Judas Iscariot, which also betrayed him"—and he never seems to be able to shake it off. It follows him and hounds him all the way through the pages of the Gospels.

There is another man in the Old Testament who, like him, has a weight that drags after his name. Do you know him? "Jeroboam the son of Nebat, which made Israel to sin" (2 Kings 3:3)—and he never got rid of that title. The solemn thing about Judas and about his Old Testament counterpart is that this is the thing by which they are remembered. It solemnizes my heart to pause for a moment and ask, "What is the thing, when this brief and fleeting life is done, that I am going to be remembered for by those who knew me best?"

The solemnity of Judas's life, you see, is that it is an account of the progressive stages in the hardening of a man's heart against God. In this sense he provides a terrible illustration of some of the things we began to think about previously. The beginning seems so full of promise; and in a sense there are two poles between which Judas's life moves—the beginning, when he is called and chosen by Jesus into the intimate circle of His disciples and into all the privileges of His service, and the end, when the same Christ who called him to Himself dismisses him from His presence: "That thou doest, do quickly.... He went immediately out: and it was night" (John 13:27, 30).

It will not do, it seems to me, to evade the warning of this man's life by saying he was never really converted—that this was his problem—the implication being, when we look at him, "I am converted, and he wasn't, so his life has nothing to say to me." You see, the really disturbing thing about Judas Iscariot is that he is so often described as "one of the twelve." It comes almost as commonly as "who also betrayed him." Judas Iscariot, one of the twelve. You will remember that when Peter was assuring the Lord that there was no place else to go to, save to Him—when others had been turning back from Him, and Jesus said, "Will you also go away?" and Peter said, "To whom else can we go? Thou hast the words of everlasting life,"—Jesus said, "Have I not chosen you twelve, and one of you has a devil?"

I suggest to you that the only true response to the warning of Judas's life is "Lord, is it I?" That ripple that went round the disciple band, is it not a ripple that ought to go round to us as well? "Let him that thinketh he standeth take heed lest he fall" (1 Cor. 10:12).

For instance, I think we need to face afresh the fact of the service in which Judas was involved. It is quite certain, you see, that in the earlier days Judas was deeply committed to all the work of the kingdom, characterized by preaching and healing. One wonders even if he was not among that company who came back to Jesus thrilled at what they had experienced and saying to him, "Lord, even the devils are subject unto us through thy name" (Luke 10:17). There is no question that Judas Iscariot occupied a position of trust and responsibility, and there is a warning here which I do not think I can afford to ignore, and that is that *usefulness in God's service is not always a guarantee of holiness in God's sight.*

Do you remember the words of Jesus at the end of the Sermon on the Mount, when He is speaking about the Day of Judgment, when all appearances will have passed away, and nothing but stark reality will remain? He describes those who will come to Him saying,

Lord, Lord, have we not prophesied in thy name? and in thy name have cast out devils? and in thy name done many wonderful works? And then will I profess unto them, I never knew you: depart from me, ye that work iniquity (Matt. 7:22-23).

We need, then, to probe below the surface of the service in which Judas was involved to the secret behind which he hid. You see, it becomes apparent from Judas's life that as time went on, there were two processes at work together in his experience. One was *an increasing involvement in the Master's service,* but behind this, and unseen to the eyes of men, there is *an increasing detachment from the Master's deepest purposes for his own life and for the world.* I tell you, there is nothing deadlier in the whole world than this spirit of detachment, with its clinical propriety, orthodoxy, and cold metallic touch.

The place where this is thrown into starkest relief is in John 12, where Judas is silhouetted against the story of the extravagant love and devotion of Mary of Bethany, who brought to Jesus—not, I think, with a premeditated purpose but with that glad spontaneity which is the mark of true devotion to Christ—the alabaster box and broke it over Him. Do you remember how the effect of the sheer burning reality of Mary's costly and sacrificial giving of herself to the Lord is to embarrass and embitter Judas? It is true universally, here and now as well as there and then, that a life like hers always turns sour and cynical a life like his. Beloved, I tell you, we need to be on our guard before God about this cynical, sour, and embittered spirit.

As a blind for his bitterness, Judas indulges in a bit of pious talk. "Would it not have been more spiritual," he asks, "to sell this and give the money to the poor?" John incisively comments, "not that he cared for the poor," for the fact is that in the deepest sense Judas Iscariot cared for neither the rich nor the poor. The only man in the world that he really cared for deeply was himself. "This he said, not that he cared for the poor; but because he was a thief, and had the bag" (v. 6).

Here, I suggest to you, we are coming to the core of Judas's problem as the New Testament, line by line and bit by bit, exposes the diabolical reality of the heart of the man. His problem, you see, is not merely that his life has been corroded and his soul destroyed for the love of money, although the love of money does do this. But in Judas's case, as in every other, that is only the symptom. The disease was that he was in love with himself. And he is facing, here in Bethany, in the home of Mary and Martha and Lazarus, the challenge—the crux of the gospel. As Jesus says in Matthew's account, "Verily I say unto you, Wheresoever this gospel shall be preached in the whole world, there shall also this, that this woman hath done, be told for a memorial of her" (26:13). The point of that comment is that this is what the gospel leads to. This is what the gospel does in a man's heart. "This," says Jesus, pointing to Mary, "not that."

Do you remember how Paul expounds in 2 Corinthians 5:15 the driving purpose of the death of Christ? "He died for all, that they which live should not henceforth live unto themselves, but unto him." This is something of the dimension of the salvation that God longs to bring to us in all its fullness—not merely a salvation from something but a salvation into something. "And this," says Jesus, pointing to Mary, "is what the gospel leads to." You see, the opposite of the love with which Judas is confronted at Bethany is not hatred, but it is self-love; and that is always the opposite of New Testament love. This is the thing that lies at the root of this tragic life: an uncrucified self.

You get it coming out in the very language of his approach to the chief priest: "How much will you give me?" That is always the language of a man into whose heart the Spirit of God has never really come to break down the citadel of himself.

It is the language of the prodigal son, you will remember, who went over that hill caring nothing that he had left a father with a broken heart. He was only caring for himself. He had come to his father: "Father, give me…"

You get it also in the respectable Pharisee: "God, I thank thee, that I am not as other men.… I fast.… I give tithes [I do this, I, I, I]." And Jesus puts the whole thing in a nutshell for that man when he juxtaposes two words: "He prayed thus with himself, God,…" That was the man's problem, and that was Judas's problem, and this is the root of all sin: his god was himself.

Now this is not an amiable weakness, Christian men and women, but this is something that has the marks of the pit upon it. Listen to these words of the prophet,

How art thou fallen from heaven, O Lucifer, son of the morning! how art thou cut down to the ground.... For thou hast said in thine heart, I will ascend into heaven, I will exalt my throne above the stars of God: I will sit upon the mount of the congregation.... I will ascend above the heights of the clouds; I will be like the most High (Isa. 14:12-14).

There is nothing blacker than this. And it is the same voice that speaks in the garden of Eden: "Ye shall be as gods, [not as men]" (Gen. 3:5). This is the quintessence of sin.

Do you know these words of Archbishop Temple? "A great deal too much attention has been given to sins, as compared with sin."[25] And so, if it happens that I cannot think of a particular wrong I have done, or any particular good thing I might have done and have neglected, yet I must still cry to God, "Be merciful to me, a sinner," for I make myself in a host of ways the center of the world. That is the root of the matter. You see, Satan is perfectly happy if a man is delivered from lust and even from debauchery and all the outward trappings of sin, if he can confirm that man in a life of secret self-absorption and chronic self-centeredness. There is something very solemn to me about the fact that increasingly for Judas Iscariot, the service of Christ was a means of feeding and fostering his own purposes. Have you noticed that? He was deeply involved, but it was to foster his own ends.

That was not the last time that the service of Christ has been used for such a purpose. How frightsome, and how frightening! You see, you cannot isolate this spirit. It touches everything. In that Upper Room in Bethany, meeting under the very shadow of the cross, ultimately it was the cross that Judas refused. He had heard Jesus say, "If any *man* will

---

25 William Temple, "Current Religious Thought: Volume 1" (United States: n.p., 1941), 11.

come after me, let him deny himself, and take up his cross, and follow me" (Matt. 16:24). And "He that loveth his life shall lose it, and he that hateth his life … shall keep it unto life eternal (John 12:25).

And as he came from that room that day, Judas Iscariot had refused to let the Savior lay the cross over his proud heart.

In the light of all this, is it not the more amazing to think of the indescribable love of Jesus? Oh, the folly of men who turn away from a love like this! Can you think of the scene as they meet in Jerusalem for the washing of the disciples' feet? Judas is there, and his was one of the places where the Savior stopped and stooped. One can see the picture so clearly in the words of the hymn:

For Thou hast stooped to ask of me
The love of my poor heart.[26]

Jesus received from Judas nothing but a cold stare. The darkness gathers quickly, and soon he is identified by the bread Jesus dips in the dish. And then these dreadful words afterward: "Satan entered into him. "

You see, Judas Iscariot's last foolish act was still to come. His final folly was that when he saw his sin, he went to the wrong place with it, and so he found remorse but not repentance. Of course he should have gone to Jesus with it. God never brings us to the place where He shows us all our hearts to send us away in despair. He shows us all the truth about ourselves that He might drive us to Himself—that we might find what Judas would have found if he had gone there even in that eleventh hour. With his heart broken he would have found, however the world might have despised him, that "a broken and a contrite heart, O God, thou wilt not despise" (Ps. 51:17).

---

26   From Frederick Faber's hymn, "My God, How Wonderful Thou Art."

I think that was the ultimate difference between Judas and Peter. Peter, with all his blundering folly and weakness, sin and failure, was ready to come to Jesus with it. What a meeting that must have been by the lakeside after the Resurrection! "Go and tell my disciples, and Peter." Even though he knew the love of Christ in all the humiliation of that encounter, he was ready to go and to discover that He searches.

> Search all my thoughts, the secret springs,
> The motives that control;
> The chambers where polluted things
> Hold empire o'er the soul.
>
> Search, till Thy fiery glance has cast
> Its holy light through all,
> And I by grace am brought at last
> Before Thy face to fall.
>
> Thus prostrate I shall learn of Thee,
> What now I feebly prove,
> That God alone in Christ can be
> Unutterable love.[27]

With all our hearts' need, therefore, let us quietly come to Him, ready and willing to say, "Lord, is this man me?"

---

27   From Francis Bottome's hymn, "Search Me, O God, My Actions Try."

Provisions for the Journey

Chapter 15
THE SOURCE AND CONDITIONS OF BLESSING

In the last day, that great day of the feast, Jesus stood and cried, saying, If
any man thirst, let him come unto me, and drink.
— John 7:37 —

It was the last day of the great Feast of Tabernacles. Jesus was surrounded by religious men, many who had walked with Him for days. They had been talking a great deal about Him and expressing their views concerning Him. Then on the last great day of the feast, Jesus took the unusual course of standing in their midst, for it was the habit of the teacher to sit. We read,

> Jesus stood and cried, saying, If any man thirst, let him come unto me, and drink. He that believeth on me, as the scripture hath said, out of his belly [inmost being] shall flow rivers of living water (But this spake he of the Spirit, which they that believe on him should receive: for the Holy Ghost was not yet given; because that Jesus was not yet glorified.) (John 7:37-39).

Jesus came to the end of these days of the great feast with a heart greatly burdened, and with a heavy concern weighing on His soul, that

He might bring the people to the pathway of true blessing—to the place where they were really going to have dealings with Him.

Might this be the hunger of your own heart? Having come from a life where you felt you had lost the way, having come from a background which was parched and dry, having walked along a wilderness journey, you wanted to get on to the pathway of blessing. Jesus seeks to lead the people there. And there are three things which He has to say in these three verses concerning the blessing He longs that they might discover.

THE CONDITION OF THIS BLESSING

Jesus begins, you will notice, by being explicitly clear about the kind of man for whom God is looking. He tells us that there is a *condition of this blessing* He longs to bring them. There is a certain kind of man for whom God the Lord is looking and waiting. He stands in the midst of the people on that last, great day of the feast and cries, "If any man thirst, let him come unto me." You see, Jesus is declaring that God takes the trouble to discern and reveal whether or not we are absolutely serious in the things we are asking Him and in the request we are making. That is the first thing that God wants to know, and it is the condition of blessing. Are you serious about the things you profess to want from God? I tell you, on the authority of the Word of God, that our God only deals with those who are in earnest.

I have seldom been so completely taken aback as I was some time ago when speaking with a man I know. It happens to be my lot to meet often with those in religious circles who do not share my convictions and do not stand on the same ground theologically as that on which I stand. One such man said to me, "I have met with, and spoken with, and got to know many evangelical Christians, and I have been in many kinds of evangelical meetings. The one impression which I have taken away from them all is that the vast majority of those who go under the name of 'evangelicals,' far from being warriors in the kingdom of God, are playing at Christian soldiers." I speak for myself, but I do not think there is a man or woman who can afford to get away from shouldering that indictment. Did you know that we are giving to the religious world outside the impression that we are play-acting—that we are not really in earnest with God? Jesus said, "Oh, be sure that the man who is coming to me is in earnest with God."

I believe with all my heart that one of the things that we are needing to learn, perhaps more than many others, is that the blessing of God is not a cheap commodity, lightly dispensed. "If any man thirst, let him come."

We say so often, "O God, I do so want to know Thy blessing in my life; I want to be the kind of man in whom Thou canst delight." But the answer of God to that kind of prayer should be something like this: "Very well, but that is going to mean something very painful in your life. If you are to become the kind of man in whom I delight, there will be an awful lot of old furniture taken out of the dwelling place of your heart and life and smashed up and thrown out." What is the answer of your heart to a God who means business like that?

Beloved, it is well to be sure that we are in earnest with God. You know the kind of thing we pray for so often: "O God, I long to know the living touch of Thy Spirit in my church, in my fellowship. I want to see the Spirit of God working, and unconverted men and women being saved and brought into the joy of the Lord." But what if the answer of heaven to that prayer is, "Very well, but that means that you have to get under the burden and become the kind of man who shares the load in bringing this to pass"? What then? Are you as thirsty as that? If it means that you have to become the kind of person who is at the prayer meeting week by week, bearing the burden with God, what then? Are you then in earnest with God? Oh, how we cheapen the faith so often by imagining that there is some kind of magic formula which we bring into operation and, presto, the deed is done! Not so do I read of God in my Bible, nor of the ways of God with His people. "If any man thirst, let him come." Here is the condition to the pathway of blessing.

THE SOURCE OF THE BLESSING

Jesus goes on to say that those who would know the riches that He has to give to His children must look to the right place for blessing: "Let him [who is at thirst] come unto me." Jesus says that every blessing that God has for us is bound up in Himself. He is the *source of the blessing*, and He goes on to tell us in what way He is the source of the blessing.

The believing man, He says, will discover that "out of his [inmost being] shall flow rivers of living water." And the Evangelist adds, "This spake he of the Spirit." The source of blessing is not in an experience, and it is not in a theory; but the source of blessing for the believer, says Jesus, lies entirely in the Holy Spirit of God who dwells now within the heart of every believing man and woman. That, says Jesus, is where the blessing will come from. It is not found in seeking for some kind of mystic experience, but it is found in the Holy Spirit who dwells within the believer.

I suppose there are few subjects on which there is so much muddled thinking and so much confusion as the subject of the Holy Spirit and the ministry of the Holy Spirit in the life of the believer. It seems to me that there is one great reason for that being so: and that is that believing men and women ignore the fact—which Jesus makes so clear—that in the life of every Christian, God by His Holy Spirit dwells already in His totality. Paul says, "If any man have not the Spirit of Christ, he is none of his" (Rom. 8:9). "Know ye not," says the apostle, "that your body is the temple [a dwelling place] of the Holy Ghost [who dwells within every believer]?" (1 Cor. 6:19).

Jesus says that the living water flows from that source alone. That is the well within the soul of every believing man and woman from which the living water flows. And it is the living water that we are needing so desperately! God knows that we have just about had enough in our churches and in our fellowships of the lifeless water of a spiritual stagnation which has tried to work up something that is not really from the Spirit of God who dwells within us.

You remember how the psalmist discovered this truth: that the place of power was not the place of some new technique or new idea; it was not the place of some emotional experience which he had managed to work himself into. He said, "God hath spoken once; twice have I heard this; that power belongeth unto God" (Ps. 62:11). Jesus says that, if you are a Christian, that same Lord by the Spirit dwells in your heart. "Not by might, nor by power" shall these things be done for which we long, "but by my spirit, saith the LORD of hosts" (Zech. 4:6).

Paul was trying to teach the Corinthians this very fact. In the third chapter of his first epistle, he begins to speak to them about their preoccupation with themselves, with their preacher, and with their program. He says Paul may plant, and Apollos may water, but planting and watering are not the efficient causes of vegetation. It is "God that giveth the increase" (1 Cor 3:7). Oh, beloved, it is the increase that we are desperately needing! Jesus says that the source of blessing is within.

THE HINDRANCES TO BLESSING

There is, however, something else we must take into account.

I recall once speaking to a man at a conference who told me that things had been going all wrong, and he had been making a mess of the Christian life. He added quite simply, "I have come to this conference so that I might discover the thing that God has not given me that He seems to have given to so many others." He seemed to think that he had had rather a raw deal from the Almighty. I had to take him graciously and humbly to the Word of God, to show him that in Jesus Christ there is everything that the believer requires; and that Jesus Christ dwells in every heart. "Out of [him] shall flow rivers of living water."

I can almost hear someone asking a difficult question about that matter: "If that is so—if the Holy Spirit of God in all His totality dwells within my soul—why is it that this Spirit is not doing in my life, in my experience, in my fellowship, and in my work the kind of things that He is said to be able and willing to do? Why is it that I am not experiencing the effects of the Holy Spirit if He really dwells within?" Well, I think our passage has the answer to such a question: "This spake he of the Spirit, which they that believe on him should receive: for the Holy Ghost was not yet given; because that Jesus was not yet glorified." What does the Scripture mean by "the Holy Ghost was not yet given"? Not yet evident, "because that Jesus was not yet glorified."

My friends, I believe that we have within these words the eternally ordained pattern for the activity of the Spirit of God in the life of a believer and in the life of the Christian church. The Spirit was not yet evident because "Jesus was not yet glorified." There is set down the pathway by which the Spirit of God is able to work in a man and through a man. It is all involved in this word "glorified." Do you remember the next time that this word occurs in John's Gospel? It is in 12:23, when Jesus, having come in triumphal entry into the city, spoke these words to His disciples: "The hour is come that the Son of man should be glorified." What will that involve? "Verily, verily, I say unto you, Except a corn of wheat fall into the ground and die, it abideth alone: but if it die, it bringeth forth much fruit" (v. 24). Very simply—for the truth is simple—what Jesus is saying is this: that the pathway to a fruitful experience of the power of the Holy Spirit, the pathway to a Pentecost, always lies through Calvary. "Father,… glorify thy Son" (John 17:1).

What was the immediate answer to that prayer? It was the harrowing agony of the cross. And Calvary ever comes before Pentecost. The reason why the Holy Spirit of God is not being evidenced in so many of our lives and in so much of our ministry is not that there is a gift that we have been unfortunate to miss. It is not that there is a technique we have been unable to adopt, but it is that there is a death we have been unwilling to die. Jesus tells the disciples that the pathway to glory lies through the seed going into the ground to a death that the fruit may abound. And this is precisely the pattern which the New Testament declares in every book: the way to Pentecost lies through Calvary.

This is the last thing which you and I are ready to face. You see, an uncrucified self will allow a man to profess anything, to go anywhere, or to gain any kind of reputation if that be the price of survival. I tell you that the way by which God would lead men and women who are seeking earnestly for the pathway of blessing is for self and pride and that great, ugly specter of the "I" in my life to be crushed, smashed, broken, and cast out, that the Spirit of Jesus may fill the temple.

Jesus says that the water that will flow out of such a man is living water. How does it become living water? The Apostle Paul knew that. He says this is the principle: "Death worketh in us, but life in you" (2 Cor. 4:12). *Death* worketh! That is, of course, what George Matheson wrote of in his hymn:

I lay in dust life's glory dead
And from the ground there blossoms red
Life that shall endless be.[28]

What is holding back the blessing? The more I read my New Testament the more I am driven to this conclusion: it is an unwillingness for the cross. Once a man has been willing for God to take his ambition—

---

28 From George Matheson's hymn, "O Love That Wilt Not Let Me Go."

his reputation, all that he holds dear, the pride of his life—and break it, I tell you that Spirit who dwells within you will begin to be evident in an outflow of living water. It may not stop at the place from which you come but may reach and bring life to some of the far corners of the earth. Death worketh!

The Lord Jesus says,

If any man thirst, let him come unto me, and drink. He that believeth on me, as the scripture hath said, out of his [inmost being] shall flow rivers of living water....

The man God is looking for is the man who is in earnest. That man will go forth to be the man in whom God delights and whom God uses.

Chapter 16

THE WORK OF THE HOLY SPIRIT IN OUR HEARTS

For which cause we faint not; but though our outward man perish,
yet the inward man is renewed day by day.
— 2 Corinthians 4:16 —

I wonder if you would agree with me that it would scarcely be true to say today that the Holy Spirit is the neglected Person of the Godhead, as has been said in previous times to our own. In our own day Christians all over the world have been much exercised in their thinking on this great theme, and we thank God for this. But what is indisputably true is that there are multitudes of us within the evangelical Christian church who are far from clear in our minds concerning the nature of the work of the Holy Spirit in our hearts as the children of God.

If we are to understand the New Testament's teaching on the Holy Spirit, we shall find ourselves concentrating on the teaching of Jesus in the Gospels and on the systematic exposition in the epistles rather than on the narrative in the Book of Acts. A great deal of confusion in our thinking has been derived from a feeling that the experience of many people as described in the Book of Acts ought necessarily to be our own. We have to remember that the narratives in the Book of Acts are primarily historical and not doctrinal treatises. For this reason I want to try to gather together some of the teaching of St. John's Gospel on the ministry of the Holy Spirit. And out of all the riches that are there I want us to focus our attention upon four descriptions or titles given to the Holy Spirit.

THE SPIRIT OF REGENERATION

The first of these takes us nearer the beginning of the Gospel where in chapter 3 we find Jesus teaching that the Holy Spirit is primarily the *Spirit of regeneration.* Jesus said in His interview with Nicodemus,

> Except a man be born of water and of the Spirit, he cannot enter into the kingdom of God. That which is born of the flesh is flesh; and that which is born of the Spirit is spirit. Marvel not that I said unto thee, Ye must be born again (vv. 5-7).

The point of this is clear. It is that the Holy Spirit's primary ministry is as the author of spiritual life in man. That is where His work begins in our hearts. It is this that Paul has in view in Romans 8:10 when he equates the two and speaks of the Spirit being life.

The implications of this for us in our own spiritual thinking are of great importance. It means that the blessing of the Holy Spirit is a primary and initial blessing for the believer—that the gift of the Holy Spirit is a gift that God gives to the believer with the beginnings of his spiritual life and is not a subsequent and secondary gift. The evidence of the indwelling of the Holy Spirit, in other words, is quite simply that you are a regenerate child of God, in whose character the marks of what has been called "the life of God in the soul of man"[29] are appearing.

It is through this work of the Holy Spirit that we are identified as the children of God. Paul writes, "If any man have not the Spirit of Christ,

---

29   Henry Scougal, *The Life of God in the Soul of Man* (National Library of Scotland: 1870).

he is none of his" (Rom. 8:9). That means that the man who prays, "Lord, I want to receive the Holy Spirit," is tacitly assuming that he is not converted, for the gift of the Holy Spirit is the initial work of God's grace in our hearts, and nowhere in the New Testament are Christians exhorted to receive this gift. Indeed, it is pointed out in John 1:16 that "of his fulness have all we received," and it is of course because the gift of the Holy Spirit is an initial blessing of Christian experience that the New Testament speaks of a baptism of the Spirit. That baptism, like the concept of baptism throughout the whole of the New Testament, is an initiatory gift of God. May I repeat that it seems to me that clarity in this realm is all-important, for much of the confusion in the thinking of many men and women today finds its roots in this soil.

THE COMFORTER

In the second place, notice that in these chapters of John's Gospel the Spirit is described as the *Comforter*: "I will pray the Father, and he shall give you another Comforter…. The Comforter, which is the Holy Ghost, whom the Father will send in my name, he shall teach you all things" (John 14:16, 26). In this word translated "Comforter" and "Counselor" (RSV) and by various other terms—because it is a difficult term to capture in English—we come to something that is tremendously important in the body of truth in Scripture about the ministry of the Holy Spirit.

As you will readily recognize, the English word "Comforter" in the twentieth century means something very different from what it meant in the seventeenth century when the Authorized Version was written. The true meaning of the word "Comforter" then was not the kind of rather soft term that it suggests to us today, but it was a term that implied strengthening, and this was part of the meaning of the Greek word which is transliterated into English, "Paraclete." Its true meaning is something which combines this idea of a strengthening Spirit with the other way that it is translated in the Authorized Version in 1 John 2 as "Advocate."

Together, the idea of an advocate, one who represents me before another, and the idea of a mighty strengthening power full of grace and of might, is the fullness of the meaning of the word "Paraclete." You will notice that in John 14:16, Jesus describes the ministry of the Holy Spirit as "another Paraclete," and the word for "another" means "another of exactly the same kind."

For instance, if we went into a library and asked for another book, we might mean that we wanted one that was different from another kind of book. But if we wanted a book which was identical—another copy, as it were, of the previous one—we would have to use the same word "another." The Greek, however, has two words to express these two different meanings; the word used here means "identical"—another of the same kind.

Notice what Jesus is doing: His primary usage of the word for the Comforter—the Paraclete—is therefore of Himself and not of the Holy Spirit. Jesus is in effect saying, "I will send you another Paraclete, who will be recognized by His identity with me—another of the same kind." The implication is this: that Jesus Himself is a Paraclete—an Advocate or Comforter—as the disciples experienced all through their lives. He was the One called alongside them to care for them—to strengthen them, to heal them, to bless them, to be to them all that they needed. "And now," says Jesus, "when I go to the Father I am going to send you another of exactly the same kind: the Holy Spirit who shall be in you—not only with you but in you."

Do you see the full picture? Jesus was not ceasing to be a Paraclete or Advocate or Comforter. 1 John 2 tells us, indeed, that He is continuing this work; this is precisely His present ministry. In the midst of all the weakness of our flesh through our tribulation and anguish, says the Apostle John, "If any man sin, we have an advocate with the Father, Jesus Christ the righteous" (v. 1). So we have two Paracletes, one in heaven and the other on earth—one at the Father's side above us, and the other in our hearts. The present ministry of Jesus in heaven is to bring us, in all our desperate need and weakness, to God: "an advocate with the Father, Jesus Christ the righteous." The present ministry of the Holy Spirit in the heart of the believer is to bring Christ, in all His riches and grace and might, to us. "He shall testify of me,… for he shall receive of mine, and shall shew it to you" (John 15:26, 16:14).

Do you catch from this something of what ought to be the ministry of the Holy Spirit in the life of the believer? That means, you see, that the evidence of the gracious work of the Holy Spirit of God in my heart will be that I am more and more taken up with the knowledge of Christ. My focus will therefore be primarily not on the Holy Spirit but upon the Christ to whom He has come to testify. And His ministry will be in the truest sense a self-effacing ministry.

He will be bringing into the depths of my own need all the wonderful riches—the unfathomable glories of the Person of Jesus—and ministering the reality of the living Christ to my heart. And I shall find Him, if this ministry is being exercised in my experience, taking me further daily into the depths and the wonders of the character of my blessed Lord and Savior. He will be ministering to me something of the sheer greatness of the Christ, in His Godhead and His manhood.

I shall see Him ministering of Jesus in my experience, to take all the twisted, broken, and crooked things and heal them and set them right by His risen power. I shall see Him, in all the glory of His humanity, coming into the midst of the darkness, discouragement, and tribulation of my own experience and drawing near, even as the disciples found Him doing.

Now, as Jesus is speaking to them, they wonder if they are going to be bereft of this as they found Him coming to them—and oh, the wonder of it!—weeping with those that weep, sitting where they sat, sharing and entering into their agonies, and caring for them in a dimension that defies our fathoming.

This is the ministry of the Holy Spirit of God: to make us men and women who glory in Christ and whose burden and hunger is "that I may know him" (Phil 3:10). Is that ministry taking place in your experience? Or are you the kind of person who talks a great deal about experiences of the Holy Spirit, but it is manifest to the world around that Christ is not meaning more to you day by day? You are not searching into the depths and riches of His grace and wonder. They do not see your character being transformed and touched, habits broken, devils exorcised, and grace and beauty being created there.

THE SPIRIT OF TRUTH

How does the Holy Spirit perform this task? Well, John goes on to tell us, in the words of Jesus, a further description of this Holy Spirit of God who is not only the regenerating Spirit and the Paraclete but also the *Spirit of truth*. "I will pray the Father, and he shall give you another [Paraclete], that he may abide with you for ever; Even the Spirit of truth … the Holy Ghost … shall teach you all things" (14:16-17, 26).

Notice the emphasis on this aspect of the Spirit's ministry: "The Spirit of truth, which proceedeth from the Father … when he, the Spirit of truth, is come, he will guide you into all the truth" (15:26; 16:13). To summarize what we have found so far, the ministry of the Holy Spirit is a ministry which, first of all, regenerates the dead; secondly, glorifies Christ; and, thirdly, instructs the believer.

It is the witness of the Bible that there are two main obstacles to spiritual growth and health. The first is *a lack of knowledge of God and His will*, and the second is *a lack of will to do what God has spoken.* How my heart has been warmed as we have been reminded of this first crying need in the church of God in our time: that we might become the kind of people in whom the Holy Spirit is ministering to instruct us, to bring us to grow up in the knowledge of God! What a blessing it would be if we should carry away with us, and into the various places from which we are gathered together, the kind of blessing that would make us, in the deepest sense, students of the Word of God! That is part of the Holy Spirit's ministry.

I am always somewhat disturbed by the man who says, as if it were something to boast about, "Of course, I'm no theologian." In a sense I know what he can mean, and it is true of us all; our knowledge is so puny. But in another sense, I feel that the answer from the Scriptures to that man is that he ought to be, if he is not. It is the purpose of God to begin the work of sanctification in our minds. "As [a man] thinketh … so is he" (Prov. 23:7).

My dear friends, this is why God has given us this holy Book: in order that we might grow in the knowledge of the Lord and thereby find our whole nature refined. The Bible is not a book from which blessed thoughts are to be gathered by Christians, but it is for our instruction in righteousness—for our increase in the knowledge of God. This, more than anything else, is the way by which increase in righteousness and knowledge comes.

Let me read to you again those words that John Newton wrote in one of his letters:

They who study the Scriptures, in an humble dependence upon Divine teaching, are convinced of their own weakness, are taught to make a true estimate of every thing around them, are gradually formed into a spirit of submission to the will of

God.... The word of God dwells richly in them, is a preservative from error, a light to their feet, and a spring of strength and consolation. By treasuring up the doctrines, precepts, promises, examples, and exhortations of Scripture, in their minds, and daily comparing themselves with the rule by which they walk, they grow into an habitual frame of spiritual wisdom, and acquire a gracious taste, which enables them to judge of right and wrong with a degree of readiness and certainty, as a musical ear judges of sounds. And they are seldom mistaken, because they ... [have] regard to the glory of God, which is the great object they have in view.[30]

My dear friends, is the Word of God, over which you are poring with the labor of a student, doing that in your life? That is why the Holy Spirit is described in Isaiah 11:2 as "the spirit of the LORD..., the spirit of wisdom and understanding, the spirit of counsel and might, the spirit of knowledge and of the fear of the LORD."

THE SPIRIT OF HOLINESS

But this knowledge, let it be said clearly, is no mere academic thing. It is a knowledge which is intended to lead us into what the last of these four names and descriptions in John 14:26 speaks of: "The [Paraclete], who is the Holy Ghost," and I think the very wording suggests, the *Spirit of holiness*. If the ministry of the Holy Spirit is a ministry which regenerates the dead, glorifies Christ, and instructs the believer, then it is, fourthly, a ministry which creates conflict with the devil.

Do you remember how Jesus discovered this in His own experience, when at His baptism the Holy Spirit of God came down upon Him, and

---

30 Newton and Cecil, *The Works*, 88.

the people marveled? What an experience this was! But we read just afterwards, "Immediately the Spirit driveth him into the wilderness [to enter into warfare with Satan]" (Mark 1:12). The mark of the Spirit's work in the experience of our Lord and in the lives of believers is that He antagonizes us to unrighteousness.

There are two things I want to say about this. First, for the comfort of the people of God, the evidences of the Holy Spirit's ministry in your heart will be that you will find yourselves in an unspeakable warfare with Satan and with the powers of darkness. Two things become true of a man when he is regenerated by the Holy Spirit: he is reconciled to God, and he is antagonized to Satan. The experience of our Lord, after the Spirit had come upon Him, was that He was engaged in mortal conflict with the powers of darkness; and that is part of the blessing the Holy Spirit brings. The ministry of the Holy Spirit, in other words, is not to extract us from conflict but to send us forth into the midst of it, in the name of Christ, to do battle victoriously.

Secondly, the Holy Spirit not only instructs our minds in the truth of God but also inclines our hearts to the law of God. The whole purpose of God in His grace is that the righteousness of the law might be fulfilled in us who walk not after the flesh but after the Spirit. The indelible and unmistakable mark of walking after the Spirit is that the righteousness of the Lord God will begin to be fulfilled in your life—that just as before you were inclined to depart from God's law, now the Spirit of God will create a new prayer in your heart: "Give me understanding, and I shall keep thy law.… Incline my heart unto thy testimonies" (Ps. 119:34, 36).

One of the most agonizing experiences I have had in recent months was speaking to a man who made great pretenses about some experience he had had of the Holy Spirit of God and talked for most of an hour with me about the Holy Spirit, and I discovered the man was living in immorality. The mark—the only mark of walking after the Spirit, the evidence of your regeneration—is righteousness beginning to be seen in your life. That is how the world will be convicted. Speaking of the Spirit, Jesus says, "And when he is come, he will reprove the world of sin, and of righteousness, and of judgment" (John 16:8). How? Through righteous, holy lives. May God make us obedient to the ministering and moving of His Spirit in our hearts, and may God have His way in the hearts of us all, for His name's sake.

Chapter 17

Inner Renewal by the Spirit

He that hath ears to hear, let him hear.
— Mark 4:9 —

In Paul's second letter to the Corinthians, we are given one of the most personal insights into some of the peculiar stresses and strains, burdens and problems which the apostle faced in his life and ministry. It becomes very clear, even from a cursory reading of the letter, that this great man of God is laboring and living in the midst of tremendous pressures which face him with perplexity and trouble his mind. He is not afraid to acknowledge it clearly: "We are troubled on every side.... We are perplexed,... persecuted,... cast down,... always bearing about in the body the dying of the Lord Jesus" (4:8-10). The Apostle Paul is obviously a man under a great burden. He is surrounded by many kinds of conflict: fightings within and without.

In 1:4, he speaks of being comforted in tribulation and of how the sufferings of Christ abound in him. In 1:8 he speaks of being pressed out of measure, above strength, so that he despaired even of life. And in 7:5 you find him saying, "our flesh had no rest, but we were troubled on every side; without were fightings, within were fears."

There are many of God's people, and especially many of God's servants, who have lived through days when they were glad that the Apostle Paul was sufficiently honest, open, and real to acknowledge the kind of conflict through which he passed. You find nowhere here the kind of unreality of a man who is trying to pretend that the skies of his spiritual life are always blue and that the work to which God has called him is always an unclouded joy. He is going through the mill spiritually; and there are many of God's servants who, like the Apostle Paul, are going through the mill in their Christian living and in their Christian service, for whom the concerted opposition of the world and the flesh and the devil is not mere words, or an idea for a preacher to elaborate upon, but sober reality.

In the midst of such a situation as this, the great danger is that we might lose heart. Isn't that the danger of the servant of God in the pressure of things in the mission field today? Isn't that the danger that is constantly overhanging us in every sphere of Christian service and in the midst of our Christian living? In these days which seem to be beset by peculiar pressures, we are able to understand the apostle's words when he says that we are "troubled on every side,… perplexed,… cast down,… bearing about in the body the dying of the Lord Jesus."

Indeed, it seems as if the Corinthians had almost expected that this is just precisely what would happen to the Apostle Paul, because more than once he takes the trouble to assure them in the words, for example, of 4:1 that "we do not lose heart" (RSV). Contrary to what you might expect from a human point of view, the apostle says in 4:16, "For which cause we [do not lose heart] … but though our outward man perish, yet our inward man is renewed day by day."

Here is this most remarkable picture of this great man of God living in the midst of the most crushing pressures, in which he says, "We are troubled on every side; we know what it is to have the marks of the Lord

Jesus in our body; nonetheless we do not lose heart." There is not an air of pretended buoyancy about him, but there is a quality about his life which enables him to testify to a reality in his spirit. "We do not lose heart, beloved; though we are troubled on every side we are not distressed; though we are perplexed we are not in despair; though we are persecuted we are not forsaken; though we are cast down we are not destroyed."

Of course, the thing that we want to do is to come to the Apostle Paul as he writes this letter and say, "Paul, how can you say that? How is it possible for a man to be in the midst of this kind of perplexity, in the midst of this kind of agonizing experience of the pressures from within and from without, and still to be able not to lose heart?"

It is something of the secret which the apostle unfolds in these verses that I want us to look at. There are two places specifically to which the apostle points for the grounds for this assurance to which he testifies. In both places where he makes this claim, Paul associates this quality of not losing heart and grounds it upon the inward work of the Holy Spirit—what he describes as the *inward renewal which God is accomplishing day by day*. Look at 4:16: "For which cause we [do not lose heart]; but though our outward man perishes, yet the inward man is renewed day by day." Look at 3:18:

> We all, with open face beholding as in a glass the glory of the Lord, are changed into the same image from glory to glory, even as by the Spirit of the Lord. Therefore seeing we have this ministry, as we have received mercy, we [do not lose heart].

I want us to look together at this inner renewal which is the essence of the present work of God in the hearts of His children. Paul speaks of it in many different ways, but one of the most suggestive is in these words of 3:18 wherein he describes this work of inward renewal which is God's characteristic present work in the life of the believer: "We all, with unveiled face, beholding the glory of the Lord, are being changed [present continuous tense] into his likeness from one degree of glory to another; for this comes from the Lord who is the Spirit." I want to try to focus your attention upon several of the characteristics of this inner renewal which is the work that God is designing to do in the here and now of our spiritual experience.

NATURE OF THE INNER RENEWAL

First, notice something of what the apostle has to say about the *nature* of this inner renewal. Earlier in the chapter, Paul has been reminding the Corinthian Christians of the occasion in Exodus 34, when Moses was given the law by God (vv. 7-11). You remember when he went up Mount Sinai and came back down again with his face shining, and God had given him on tablets of stone His holy, inexorable law. Paul is saying that that law written on tablets of stone had a glory about it, a glory which was reflected in Moses's face, so that when he came down to the people he veiled his face. The apostle tells us it was a glory which later was to fade but a glory which resided in the law of God for a very special reason. It was a glory that derived from the fact that the law reflected the very character and purpose of God. This is one of the great underlying facts about the law of God throughout the whole of the Old Testament. It is a *law that is marked by glory* because it reflects the character of God and His purpose. That was in the old covenant.

But now, in the new covenant, God is working again to see the glory of His character reflected not this time in tablets of stone but in what he calls the fleshy tablets of the hearts of His children, so that the glory of the character of God might be seen not in stone tablets but in human hearts and lives.

This was the great promise which was made, you remember, in Jeremiah 31:33: "After those days, saith the LORD, I will put my law in their inward parts, and write it in their hearts." The point of God's work in our inner hearts, a work to which the whole of the Old Testament looks forward, is related to the nature of the law which God gave to Moses, in that the reflection of His character and likeness is to be seen in the design and purpose of God in the lives of His children.

In the old covenant, the place where the character of God was to be seen blazing out in all its glory was the law. That is why Sinai was a place of blazing lightning and thunder; it was the glory of God that was there. Paul, in essence, is asking, "Do you see where God now, in the new covenant, in fulfillment of His promises, is going to have His glory seen? Where? In the hearts of His children who are indwelt by His Holy Spirit."

This is the nature of this inner renewal; this is the work of God in the here and now.

> We all, [now, no longer with veiled faces, but] with open face beholding as in a glass the glory of the Lord, are changed into the same image from glory to glory, even as by the Spirit of the Lord.

So the nature of this inner renewal which is the present work of God through His Holy Spirit is to bring the reflection of His character into the lives and characters of His children.

This is not something which is a kind of "honors degree" stage of Christian living, but this is something which lies at the very roots of God's saving purpose. I believe that we need to remind ourselves in these days that the salvation which God has provided, procured, and proclaimed in the Scriptures through Jesus Christ is not merely a salvation that is designed to change a man's eternal destiny, but it is a salvation which is designed to transform his character into the likeness of Christ. Nothing less than this is New Testament salvation. Listen to the words of John Calvin, for few men have been able to penetrate further into the depths of scriptural teaching. Calvin says, "Salvation is the process whereby God restores in us the divine image which we lost at the fall, and which process will only be completed in the glory."[31]

That is God's saving purpose. This is what it means to be saved. Are you being saved today? Is there this work of inner renewal going on in your hearts, changing you into the image of Christ? Do you remember how in Romans 8:29 Paul points back to God's mighty purposes from before the foundation of the world: "Whom he did foreknow, he also did predestinate to be conformed to the image of his Son, that he might be the firstborn among many brethren"? The point is, you see, that God does not simply meet us in Christ to forgive us our sins and then keep us comfortable until glory, but He is still saving us and changing us, by His grace, into the image of His Son. This is what the apostle means where he encourages the Christians, "Work out your own salvation…. For it is God which worketh in you" (Phil. 2:12). Oh, there is a glorious thought for us: God is working in you, now! And the nature of this inward renewal is to restore in us the image of God.

EXECUTOR OF THE INNER RENEWAL

A word, secondly, about the *executor* of this inner renewal. The apostle makes it clear it is *the Holy Spirit*: "We … are changed into the same image from glory to glory, even as by the Spirit of the Lord." This is something that a man cannot do by himself; he is incapable of executing this transformation. But there is one important fact that we need to realize, and that is that if we are Christians—if we are the redeemed children of God—we do not invite the Holy Spirit to come into our lives to fulfill this ministry, but He is already there.

---

31   John Calvin, *Institutes of the Christian Religion*, Book One, Ch. XV, 4 (United Kingdom: Presbyterian Publishing Corporation, 1960), 189.

One of the things that the apostle emphasizes in this chapter is what we might call the givenness of the Spirit. This is one of the great guarantees, indeed, that he holds on to in the midst of his tribulation and perplexity: that God has not left him alone in the midst of his trials and testing, but He has given us, he says in 1:22, "the earnest ['the guarantee' is the real translation of the word] of the Spirit in our hearts." That is the ground on which Paul is established in Christ. He is given the guarantee of the Spirit.

So we may come a stage further in understanding what the apostle is declaring by saying that this inner ministry, this inner renewal, has as its character our transformation—the same word as is used for the transfiguration of Jesus—into the image of Christ. And the executor of this inner work is the Holy Spirit. This is the essence of His ministry. May I say in passing and purely as an aside that when a man gets taken up with any other ministry of the Holy Spirit which tends to thrust that basic ministry into the background, he is out of line with the emphasis of the New Testament. This is the Spirit's characteristic ministry: to renew in us the image of God.

MEANS OF THE INNER RENEWAL

Thirdly, the *means* of this renewal. How are we thus renewed in the inner man? There are two answers that we might do well to remember. The first is the one which the apostle gives very clearly in 3:18: "We all, with open face beholding as in a glass the glory of the Lord, are changed into the same image from glory to glory." The answer, then, to the question of how we are thus renewed in the inner man—how we are made new by the Spirit—is *by beholding the glory of the Lord.*

What does that mean? According to the biblical commentator Charles Hodge, it means this:

It is not the immediate, beatific vision of the glory of the Lord, which is only enjoyed in heaven, but it is that manifestation of his glory which is made in his word and by his Spirit, whose office it is to glorify Christ by revealing him to us.[32]

It means that the Spirit of God laboring within the heart of the believer is transforming us into the character of God in Christ as we give ourselves to gazing into all the height and length and breadth and wonder of the character of the living God revealed to us in Jesus Christ in the Scriptures. That is the place where we find this vision that we need. It is not by some mystic experience—this is not what the apostle is meaning. It is not what Hodge calls the "beatific vision," but it is the vision of God as He has manifested Himself in the Scriptures and peculiarly in Jesus Christ.

This, my dear Christian friends, is what ought to be occupying the heart of the child of God: that he might come to the Word of God to gaze into it, to come face to face there. That is the only place where he will find Him. That is what the Bible is for. God has not given us His Word, we need to remind ourselves, merely as a depository of blessed thoughts, but it is given to us by God to show us Himself--that we might acquaint ourselves with His purposes, that we might identify ourselves with His interests, and that we might find ourselves being transformed into His likeness.

Have you noticed how, in all its teaching about sanctification, the Bible places such a strong emphasis upon the mind? When the apostle is speaking to the Ephesians about renewal, he speaks about the renewal of "the spirit of your mind" (4:23). And the reason is that as a man "thinketh in his heart, so is he" (Prov. 23:7).

---

32 Charles Hodge, *An Exposition of the Second Epistle to the Corinthians* (New York: Robert Carter & Brothers, 1860), 77.

My dear friends, this is what we need; this is the sphere in which the Spirit of God takes the poor clay of our lives and our characters, with all their twists and with all their inconsistencies, and molds them into the likeness of Jesus.

But within the context of this letter there is another means that God's Holy Spirit uses for our inward renewal. Notice 4:16 where Paul has something to say about this renewal: "The inward man is renewed day by day." He goes on at the beginning of verse 17 to explain how our inward man is renewed day by day. And one of the ways is this: "*Our light affliction*" (italics added). Oh, you can almost see the Corinthians raising their eyebrows when they have been hearing the kind of thing the apostle has been going through, and he refers to it as "our light affliction"! But look what he says his light affliction has done: "Our light affliction, which is but for a moment, worketh for us a far more exceeding and eternal weight of glory."

Here is a glorious thought, my dear Christian friends, to lay hold on: "Our light affliction,… worketh for us." This is one of Paul's great bastions to his faith, in the midst of trial and tribulation: "Tribulation worketh." That is the gospel answer to the trials and testings of our daily living and of our Christian service. It is not that they are incidentals which come to us and that we have got to get rid of. It is not that they are things that are uncharacteristic of Christian experience, but "our light affliction,… worketh for us." And one of the great significances of the inward trials that the people of God experience is that they are the very things that the Spirit of God uses to refine our character into the image of Christ. Are you a child of God who has been passing through trial—you have been going through the mill spiritually, and things have been hard? My dear friend, take courage: "Tribulation worketh." This is the very essence of the work of God in the souls of some of His greatest saints. "For our light affliction,… worketh for us."

The story is told of a man who one day was passing by a little branch of a bush and saw on it what he recognized as the chrysalis of a butterfly, and the chrysalis was being broken open by the emerging butterfly. And as is the character of this operation, there was a tremendous struggling and striving, a breaking forth. Within that chrysalis there was a great trembling and shuddering and struggling going on to get out. The man came up, thinking of course that he was doing some service to the emerging butterfly, and he took his pocket knife and slit the chrysalis up the middle. Immediately the tribulation was gone and the butterfly emerged, but it emerged as a poor, maimed, shrunken creature. The man learned that day that it was the very tribulation that put glory into the thing.

May I quote you again some words of John Newton?

I asked the Lord that I might grow
In faith and love and every grace,
Might more of His salvation know,
And seek more earnestly His face.

I hoped that in some favored hour,
At once he'd answer my request;
And by his love's constraining power,
Subdue my sins, and give me rest.

Instead of this, he made me feel
The hidden evils of my heart;
And let the angry powers of hell
Assault my soul in every part.

Yea more, with his own hand he seemed
Intent to aggravate my woe;

Crossed all the fair designs I schemed,
Blasted my gourds, and laid me low.
Lord, why is this, I trembling cried,
Wilt thou pursue thy worm to death?
"Tis in this way," the Lord replied,
"I answer prayer for grace and faith.

"These inward trials I employ
From self and pride to set thee free;
And break thy schemes of earthly joy,
That thou mayst seek thine all in me."[33]

That is why the psalmist was able to say at the end of an experience like the apostle's, "It is good for me that I have been afflicted" (Ps. 119:71).

MARKS OF THE INNER RENEWAL

We have talked about the nature of the renewal, the executor of the renewal, and the means of the renewal. We now come to the marks of the renewal, which is God's present work in our hearts. And there are two things that the apostle has to say.

First, it is characterized by our *being changed into the same image as the Lord*. "We all,… are being changed into the same image [from one degree of glory to another, RSV]." And that is the second thing: *from one degree of glory to another*. I would like to look at the second thing first.

The marks of this renewal are, first, that we are being changed *from one degree of glory into another*. This means, as you will notice the apostle's language translated thus in the RSV, that this work of inner renewal has stages to it. It is a gradual thing. It is the present continuous tense

---

33   Newton and Cecil, *The Works*, 539.

that the apostle uses. We are being changed from one degree of glory into another. He goes to some trouble to make it clear that this inner renewal, which is the work of the Holy Ghost in our hearts, is not the business of a day, but it is the work of a lifetime. We need to grasp this.

There are always some people who pick up books or go to conferences hoping to find some utopian blessing which is going to extract them from all the trials of Christian living and bring them heaven on earth. Quite frankly, I have been unable to find any place in the Scriptures where we are promised heaven on earth.

Dr. Graham Scroggie once said that we need to remember that in the Christian life, one defeat is not the end of the battle—for which we will no doubt say together, thank God! But one victory does not extract you from the conflict. This is a gradual work of the Spirit of God: we are being changed from one degree of glory into another. And if you look at the lives of the great saints of God in the Bible, you will see that this is the pattern. Of course, there are critical moments in this great ongoing work of God's Spirit. Let us never be afraid of them: crises of repentance, when suddenly God faces us with all the agonizing truth about our own pride and folly—when suddenly some glorious truth dawns upon us. But the ongoing pattern is that this is a gradual transformation, which is begun here below by the same Lord who will complete it in His nearer presence.

The second thing is that we are not only being changed from one degree of glory to another, but we are also being changed *into the same image*. Being changed into the likeness of Jesus will not mean that we are going to become some kind of unnatural and forbidding freak. You know, there sometimes is real truth in the allegation that Christians can be, in the worst possible sense, the Lord's peculiar people! Nor does it mean that you are going to be an inhuman, unnatural kind of person. There are all sorts of distorted ideas about being made into the image of the Savior. You know how the little girl once prayed by her bedside at night, in the hearing of her parents, "Lord, please make all the bad people good, and O Lord, make all the good people nice!"

It is true that in the early church and in the heart and life of our Lord, especially, there was a fire that burned and scorched everything that was alien to His Spirit. But, my dear friends, it was a fire that warmed, too. There was something gloriously attractive about the Lord Jesus and something very wonderfully human. Part of God's gracious purpose, I do believe, is that there might be restored in us a true humanity to make you far more of a man, far more of a woman, than you could ever otherwise have been. You see, this is recalling all the qualities in all their depth and wonder that we have lost through the robbery of sin. Into the life of the man who is being made more like Jesus there will not only come some of the glories of His grace and power, but there will also come some of His sheer human goodness, His love, His joy, His peace, His patience, and His self-control, for that is the fruit of the Spirit of Jesus. And the man who is made most like Him is the man who is least conscious that he bears the image.

May God so go on to do His work in our hearts, employing every means, employing our very trials, employing His Word as, in a new sense, perhaps, we give ourselves to gazing into it, that we may behold Him and find ourselves all taken up with Him. May He use these means to bring in us the image of His Son, so that we shall with all God's saints be satisfied when we awake with His likeness, for His name's sake.

Facing a task unfinished,
That drives us to our knees,
A need that, undiminished,
Rebukes our slothful ease,
We, who rejoice to know Thee,
Renew before Thy throne
The solemn pledge we owe Thee,

To go and make Thee known.

Where other lords beside Thee
Hold their unhindered sway,
Where forces that defied Thee,
Defy Thee still today,
With none to heed their crying
For life, and love, and light,
Unnumbered souls are dying,
And pass into the night.

We bear the torch that, flaming,
Fell from the hands of those
Who gave their lives proclaiming
That Jesus died and rose.
Ours is the same commission,
The same glad message ours,
Fired by the same ambition,
To Thee we yield our powers.

O Father, who sustained them,
O Spirit who inspired,
Savior, whose love constrained them
To toil with zeal untired.
From cowardice defend us,
From lethargy awake!
Forth on Thy errands send us,
To labor for Thy sake.[34]

---

34 Frank Houghton's hymn, "Facing a Task Unfinished."

Chapter 18

The Flesh and the Spirit

Do not be deceived; God is not mocked, for whatever a man sows,
that he will also reap. For he who sows to his own flesh will
from the flesh reap corruption; but he who sows to the Spirit
will from the Spirit reap eternal life.
— Galatians 6:7-8 (RSV)[35] —

What is going to make the real difference in our lives and through our lives, in the world where God has set us? To answer that question, I want to draw your attention to the great biblical principle of sowing and reaping. This principle comes with a warning: "Do not be deceived," or as another translation puts it, "Let no one fool you."

That is a warning you find several times in the epistles. Writing to the Ephesians, Paul says, "Let no one deceive you with empty words" (5:6); and here in Galatians 6:3 you get the same concern in the heart of the apostle that somehow or other believers to whom he is writing may be victims of a great deception. He speaks of it in special regard to pride: "If anyone thinks he is something, when he is nothing, he deceives himself." The Apostle John wonders in 2 John 7 that "many

---

35   Unless otherwise stated, Scripture quotations in this chapter are from THE HOLY BIBLE: REVISED STANDARD VERSION, International Bible Society

deceivers have gone out into the world" and behind them, of course, the Arch-Deceiver, the father of lies.

There is, in other words, a principle which the Apostle Paul is burdened to lay before the believers to whom he has been writing, in this church in Galatia, who have so many things that have apparently gone wrong in their lives. It is a principle about which people often deceive themselves. But, says Paul, it is something about which no man deceives God. "Do not be deceived; God is not mocked, for whatever a man sows, that he will also reap."

That is one of the inexorable laws which has the ring of inevitability about it. It is one of these things that we might wish were different, but from which we cannot get away. It is something that keeps pursuing us, haunting us, and turning up in people's lives in the world of nature as well as in the world of grace. It keeps facing us as something that we cannot get away from. "Do not [let yourselves] be deceived," says the apostle. "Whatever a man sows, that he will also reap."

If in the world of nature you want a certain kind of harvest, you have to do a certain kind of sowing; and both the quality and the quantity of the crop has everything to do with what you sow and where you sow it. What is true in the material order is true also in the moral order. What is true in the natural world is true also in the spiritual world. You reap what you sow.

It is a widespread biblical principle which goes right through Holy Scripture. God presents the principle to Israel in the days of Hosea: "For they sow the wind, and they shall reap the whirlwind" (8:7). Paul presents it to the reluctant Corinthians: "He who sows sparingly, shall also reap sparingly, and he who sows bountifully will also reap bountifully" (2 Cor. 9:6). It is a principle which we can see in society in our own day. It is a principle with which our nation needs to be faced in these days, my Christian friends. It is a principle with which the church of Jesus Christ needs to be faced. It is a principle with which parents need to be faced. It is a principle with which young people, at the beginning of life, need to be faced in these days. "Whatever a man sows, that he will also reap."

What Paul is doing in Galatians 6:8 is presenting us with alternative fields in which we may sow, and they are the flesh or the Spirit. "He who sows to his own flesh will from the flesh reap corruption; but he who sows to the Spirit will from the Spirit reap eternal life." What I want us to do is to ask three questions, very simply and briefly: What are the fields in which we sow, what is the seed we sow into them, and what are the harvests we reap from that sowing?

THE FIELDS IN WHICH WE SOW

Here is the first: *What are the fields in which we sow?* Well, the apostle says there are only two alternatives: either we are sowing *into the flesh* (for that is what the Greek means), or we are sowing *into the Spirit.* These are the fields into which we sow, and these are the competitors, as it were, as harvest fields, calling upon us, "Sow here!" and "Sow here!" The flesh is crying out, "Sow here; invest your seed here!" And the Spirit of God is crying out, "Sow here! Sow here!" They are competitors. But let me point out to you, from the general context of this passage, that they are not friendly competitors, but they are, indeed, implacably opposed to each other.

Indeed, if you look back to 5:17, you will see that the same two—the flesh and the Spirit—are not just competitors in a harvest field, but they are combatants in a battlefield. Paul says, "The desires of the flesh are against the Spirit, and the desires of the Spirit are against the flesh; for these are opposed to each other"—they war against each other. In the Authorized Version: "The flesh lusteth against the Spirit, and the Spirit against the flesh." There is a war going on between these competitors for the harvest field, and they really are combatants in the battlefield.

So this competition between the flesh and the Spirit, as the two fields we sow, is actually a warfare. And the battleground is the heart of the believer.

J. B. Phillips translates "the flesh" as "our lower nature"—that is, our sinful nature, what we are by nature. It is elsewhere described as the old nature or the old man. It is not so much our physical condition and flesh as our fallen condition. It is everything that we are apart from the grace of God.

What is the Spirit? Well, the Spirit is, of course, the Holy Spirit of God who comes to indwell us when we are born again. If you are a new creature in Christ Jesus, then the Holy Spirit of God indwells your heart. "Any one who does not have the Spirit of Christ," says Paul, "does not belong to him" (Rom. 8:9). But when the Holy Spirit of God comes to take up His residence in your heart—to make your body His temple—He does not take you out of the flesh any more than He takes you out of the world.

In the believer's heart and in the believer's experience there are these two competitors who are combatants at war with the believer: the flesh opposing the Spirit, and the Spirit the flesh. But the significant thing about both the flesh and the Spirit, who oppose each other as combatants and compete with each other as harvest fields, is this: that they each have a homing instinct. You know what a homing instinct is. There are certain birds which have a homing instinct. Some people keep homing pigeons, and they have a homing instinct which brings them, without fail, back to the same place all the time. You may let them off anywhere, but wherever you let them free, they will come back to the same place.

The flesh and the Spirit both have a homing instinct, and the flesh homes upon one thing all the time, and that is self and the gratification and the pampering of self. This is the great homing place of the flesh: self-pleasing, self-interest, self-gratification. The Spirit has a homing instinct too, if one may so speak of the Holy Spirit. He homes upon Christ to glorify and honor Him (John 16:14), and to make the believer holy.

THE SEED THAT WE ARE TO SOW

The second question: *What is the seed that we are to sow?* Let me say a word about the *nature* of it. It is, of course, our lives, our faculties, our gifts, our possessions, our time, and our future. The seed that we are to sow, I cannot but conclude from what Paul is saying, is just *our whole being*. It is everything you are. And he is speaking now about the whole of a man's life—about the issue, you see, of what you are going to do with your life. The seed is your whole being. That is the nature of the seed which you sow.

A word about the *manner* in which we sow this seed: How do we sow to the flesh, or to the Spirit? What is it that Paul means when he says, "He who sows to his own flesh … but he who sows to the Spirit"? What is he speaking about? Well, he means the same thing as he speaks of in Romans 8 when he talks about setting your "mind on the flesh" and setting your "mind on the Spirit," or in Galatians 5:16, walking "by the Spirit" as opposed to gratifying the desires "of the flesh." If you are pampering and cultivating the flesh—that is, this old nature that wants to drag you down away from God to live for self, by feeding your mind with the kind of thing the flesh loves—you are sowing to the flesh.

The way we sow is by our thought life and by our actions. When a man is filling his mind and pampering himself with everything that is going to gratify self, and is going to coddle it, he is sowing to the flesh—by certain books that he may read; let me say even by the kind of newspaper he takes; by the things he watches; by the whole manner of his life; by what we call these days his "lifestyle"; by the things he focuses on; by the things he gives himself to, the things that he feeds himself upon. This is how we sow to the flesh. We say, "Sow a thought, reap an action; sow an action, reap a habit; sow a habit, reap a character; sow a character, reap a destiny." It is what you feed your mind on that so often is the key to where you are doing your sowing. We refuse to sow to the flesh by starving it—by mortifying the flesh, as Paul says —by withholding the seed of our thoughts and deeds from that field.

To sow to the Spirit, on the other hand, is, as Paul tells us in Romans 8:6, to "set the mind on the Spirit"; or in Galatians 5, to "walk by the Spirit," to be led by the Spirit—that is, that instead of giving our selves, our mind, and our whole being to gratifying the flesh, pampering and feeding it from all the sources it loves to draw its food from, and which the world is engaged in pampering the flesh with, we are to soak our minds in the Word of truth. We are to give ourselves to the things that are true, honorable, just, pure, and lovely (Phil. 4:8). We are to sow our whole being in the field of the Spirit. That is something we do at every turn of every day. We are either saying, "I choose the flesh," or "I choose Jesus."

You may be able to tell me that you chose Jesus five, ten, or twenty years ago. You may be a new Christian, and you may say, "I have chosen Jesus as my Savior just this last year." But, my friends, the thing that really matters is what you are doing day by day in the everyday situations of life. That is what is going to matter as you live the life to which God has called you—in the things that you do; in the way you pattern your life; in the whole ordering of your time; in the things you read, in the things you will not read and refuse in the name of God to read; in the things you look at; in the things you feed yourself upon. Are you saying then, "I choose Jesus"? That is what matters. "Walk by the Spirit, and do not gratify the desires of the flesh," says Paul.

The nature of this seed which we sow, then, is just our whole being. The manner of it, sowing to the flesh and sowing to the Spirit, is what Paul means by setting our "mind on the flesh" and setting our "mind on the Spirit."

May I say a word about the mystery of this sowing? Sowing, if you think about it, is a strange business. There was a little boy, the son of a friend of mine, who was watching his daddy out in the garden in the early spring sowing some seeds. He was very small; he had never seen this kind of thing before. He had noticed the beautiful packet that came into the house, and he saw some of the seeds, and he thought how interesting they were, and how nice. And then he went out with his daddy, and he was not there very long before he came running back into the house, crying, "Mummy! Mummy! You'll need to stop Daddy. He's throwed all his seeds away!" You see, sowing is like that. To the uninitiated, when you cast seed into the soil it looks as if you are throwing something away. But the fact is, if it is into the right soil, that is the only element in which it is worth anything.

I want to say to you that this sowing of which the apostle speaks is precisely like this, and your life is like this. Let me illustrate. I know a young woman who, when she was a medical student, was a brilliant girl. She carried off every medal in the medical faculty where she studied. She was set for a great career, and everything seemed to lie at her feet. Her professors had mapped out a certain course for her, and it seemed as if there was nothing she could not have gotten. Her fellow students looked at her enviously, and they began to think of the kind of pattern that her life was going to take. But during her university days she came to a glorious and blessed knowledge of the Lord Jesus Christ, and her life was utterly transformed.

On the day after her graduation, when her friends said to her, "Now, where are you going? What are you going to do? Which of these offers are you going to take up?" she announced to them, "I am going to India!" And she is there still. They all turned upon her and said, "That's a life thrown away!" It was the talk of the whole faculty: "There's a life thrown away!" You see, her life was seed. If you hold seed back to yourself and put it in the wrong soil, it will go rotten. It is only when you put it to the element for which it is created that it is ever of use and comes to anything.

I want to say to you that your life is like that. The Holy Spirit of God is the element for your life. This is where you belong: in the very center of the will of God, who is able to possess you by His Holy Spirit and bring forth the glories in your life and character that the world is waiting to see, of that holiness which is observable, durable, and attractive.

THE HARVEST THAT WE ARE PROMISED

That leads me to the last thing: *What is the harvest that we are promised?* You will notice in 6:8 that the harvest of the flesh is *corruption*: "He who sows to his own flesh will from the flesh reap corruption," that is, decay. It will be a degenerating process. It sometimes takes decay and degeneration a while to work out; it sometimes takes a generation for degeneration. But that is the end of it; that is the result of it, whether at a personal or at a national level. You sow to the flesh, and the harvest is corruption.

The harvest of the Spirit, says Paul, is *eternal life*, which is knowing God and becoming like Him and is spelled out in 5:22 in these words that are so familiar to us: "The fruit of the Spirit is love, joy, peace, patience, kindness, goodness, faithfulness, gentleness, self-control." Notice that this harvest is fruit: it grows out from within. If you are ready to do the sowing, you can leave the harvest to God. He will see to the fruit, and you will be the last to notice it.

One last word: there is an urgency about this sowing. You see, the fruit of the Holy Spirit is something that grows out by the work of the

Holy Spirit in a man's life. It grows out from within; and it grows out gradually; and it grows out naturally. It is the natural production of the sowing to the Spirit. But there is an urgency about this sowing. There is what the Bible calls a "seed time," isn't there? My friends, I believe that these seed times are very real in many of our lives.

I have been in the ministry for something in the region of fifteen years, and I have observed over that time that there are such things as seasons of grace in a person's life. There is such a thing as a day of grace, as we are accustomed to saying when somebody is converted; there are seasons of grace, too. Let me say this to you: Life is very brief, is it not? I am just about the age now when I am conscious of how life is passing so swiftly—how the days and the years are melting away into nothing. And it is so easy to fritter it all away. I sometimes long, as I go to universities here and there, to come to some of these young people and say to them, "Oh, in God's name, don't fritter your life away, as a child of God, on trivialities! Sow to the Spirit!"

My friend, Tom Rees, who died unexpectedly many years ago, had his ashes buried in Kenneth Prior's churchyard in Sevenoaks. It was Tom Rees's desire to have there, on the stone, this epitaph:

Only one life, 'twill soon be past;
Only what's done for Jesus will last.

My friends, the time is short. Life is swift and passing, and the world is very sick. It is high time for many of us to awaken out of sleep, to give ourselves to sowing to the Spirit, and to live to God before it be too late. May God enable us to do so, for His name's sake.

Chapter 19

Therapy for Troubled Disciples

Let not your hearts be troubled; believe in God, believe also in me.
— John 14:1 (RSV)[36] —

It is a great privilege to study John 14 to 17, four wonderful chapters from the fourth Gospel. I am not a little conscious, as you may guess, that it is also a great responsibility. That consciousness was heightened when I read that Bishop Ryle—who himself has three volumes on St. John's Gospel— said that the Gospel of John is so full of such refined truth that for any man to attempt to expound it at all is a peculiarly serious undertaking. It is obviously going to be impossible for us to dig into the depths of every part of these great chapters of the Bible; but I cherish the hope that our study together may stimulate you to go back to the Word of God for yourself, and to get down to some serious study of these wonderful words of our Lord.

Bishop Ryle is right, of course, when he speaks of the profound depths of John's Gospel. But Dr. Leon Morris, who likewise wrote on John's Gospel, is also right when he points out that there is a combination in the Gospel of John of great profundity and great simplicity.[37] There

---

36 Unless otherwise stated, Scripture quotations in this chapter are from THE HOLY BIBLE: REVISED STANDARD VERSION, International Bible Society.

37 Leon Morris, *The Gospel According to John, Revised* (Grand Rapids, MI: William B. Eerdmans Publishing Company, 1995, rev. ed.), 66.

are riches here, in other words, for the mature Christian, and there is enough here to stretch the largest mind; but there is an abundance here for the newest believer from the hand of the Lord whose delight it is to make wise the simple.

The Gospel of John devotes almost half of its chapters, 13 to 21, to the last week in the earthly life of Jesus. Indeed, many people divide the Gospel into two books: the Book of the Signs (chapters 1 to 12), and the Book of the Passion (chapters 13 to 21). It is a remarkable thing that almost half of the Gospel is devoted to the last week in Jesus's life.

What we have in John 14 to 17 are the last words that Jesus spoke on the very last night of His life. While from the cross He spoke a few final sentences, these chapters represent the last sustained period of teaching, all given within twenty-four hours of the time when He was to hang upon the cross of Calvary. And the fact that almost one-fifth of the Gospel of John is devoted to these last words of Jesus invests them with a very special significance.

We are being permitted here to listen to our Lord's most intimate words to His disciples, spoken under the very shadow of the cross, and above all to overhear Him open His heart to His Father in the great High Priestly Prayer. It is not surprising, therefore, that so often these chapters in John have been described by Christian people as "the holy of holies" of the New Testament, the inner sanctuary of the Bible. It is obvious that something enters your spirit as you come here to read these chapters with a believing heart. You are conscious that you are treading on holy ground. There is a sense in which, when one begins to expound them, one almost has the feeling of treading with clumsy feet over this kind of territory.

The occasion which provides the context of these chapters is, of course, the impending departure of Jesus from the world, and particularly from His disciples, by means of the suffering and sin-bearing of the cross. The prospect of Jesus departing from them, and in this manner, is something so different from everything that the disciples had expected and planned. That His departure is to be associated with suffering, shame, and agony—that He is to be the object of ridicule and mockery and spitting by the Jews—filled their hearts with a great sense of heaviness, foreboding, and sorrow.

I wonder if we can grasp just how shattering an experience this must have been and what kind of men these were whom Jesus is originally addressing. These men who, as they said, had left everything to follow Him—who had staked everything upon Jesus—are now discovering that He is going to leave them. The whole world seems to be collapsing around them, and they are filled with sorrow.

The teaching of John 14 to 16 and the intercession of chapter 17 are really the caring ministry of Jesus for such weak, fearful, and discouraged disciples. What is the whole content of these chapters? It is as though the Lord was standing above the storm which is about to break in all its fullness upon the disciples, and He is saying to them, "Let not your hearts be troubled."

This trouble of heart of which Jesus speaks in 14:1 is neither an uncommon nor an unworthy thing in the experience of the believer. Bishop Ryle says, "Even the best of Christians have many bitter cups to drink between grace and glory,"[38] and that is true. This trouble of heart is neither an uncommon nor an unworthy thing. Indeed, our Lord Himself uses this same word in 12:27 about His own feeling and His own heart condition: "Now is my soul troubled," He said. "And what shall I say? 'Father, save me from this hour'? No, for this purpose I have come to this hour." But he says, "My heart is troubled." The Lord Jesus knew what it was to have a troubled heart.

---

38   J.C. Ryle, *Expository Thoughts on the Gospels*, Volume 7: John Part 3 - Chapters 13-21 (Edinburgh, UK: The Banner of Truth Trust, 2012), 37.

If you look a little more closely at these chapters, you will see that the troubles of the disciples really derive from the three classical sources of *the world, the flesh,* and *the devil*—the three areas from which we ourselves discover some of these pressures. These troubles pour in upon our lives as believers, an inevitable part of our spiritual experience. The disciples' distress came, of course, from this special situation when the Lord was going to leave them—when the world was collapsing around them—but if you analyze it, the trouble came from these three great classical sources.

Look at 15:18-19, and you will see the beginning of the account of the troubles that they are going to experience from a hostile world:

If the world hates you, know that it has hated me before it hated you. If you were of the world, the world would love its own; but because you are not of the world, but I chose you out of the world, therefore the world hates you.

What is going to be one source of their agony and their trouble? It is going to be the world—a world which is hostile to God, a world which is implacably opposed to the Lord Jesus Christ.

If you read through chapter 14, you will have noticed that in the first eleven verses, and, indeed, further back from 13:36, there is an abundant illustration of the weakness and limitations of the flesh from which their troubles were deriving, too. It is the very fact that they were men—that they were saints and not angels, that they were still in the world and still in the flesh. When a man is brought to the Lord he is no more taken out of the flesh than he is taken out of the world, and we experience the pressures and tensions that arise from being in the flesh. These men are full of the kind of questionings that derive from these limitations in their understanding and their ability. They are asking questions of Jesus.

"Lord," they say, "where are you going?"

Peter says, "Lord, why cannot I follow you?"

They say, "Lord, when will you reveal yourself? Lord, how can we know the way?"

All this questioning derives from their weakness and limitations of the flesh. "Lord, why? Lord, where? Lord, how can we?"

We know this kind of thing ourselves, don't we? It is this that our Lord Jesus put His finger on in the Garden of Gethsemane, when He was looking into the hearts of these men. He said, "The spirit truly is willing, but the flesh is weak." The weakness of the flesh is one source of their troubled hearts.

But in 14:30 we are introduced for the first time in these chapters to the ultimate source of their troubles: the personal malevolence of the evil one. "The ruler of this world is coming," says Jesus. "He has no power over me." He recognizes that one of the fundamental factors in this situation to which He is addressing Himself, the troubled heart of the believer, is that there is a personal foe; there is an enemy of the souls of men. And the great conflict both for the disciples and for Jesus is with the evil one.

In 17:15 our Lord specifically prays about this dimension in their trouble: "Keep them from the evil one." Beloved, I think perhaps many of us do not think enough about this. I know that it is possible to be more Satan-conscious than God-conscious, and that is a bad thing. We have got to be more God-conscious than Satan-conscious. But some of us have not obeyed the apostolic injunction that we should beware of the devil as a roaring lion. Behind the disciples' troubled hearts is the subtle attack of the evil one, seeking to dismay them, to discourage them, to engender distrust in the Lord Jesus Christ. Whenever you find that happening in your experience—when that is one of the elements in your trouble—then behind it lies the personal malevolence of the devil who is out to discourage you, to dislodge your trust in the Lord Jesus Christ, and to bring circumstances with all their clouds to be the great issue that you are seeing. Jesus warns the disciples about it and prays against it.

We live our Christian lives, beloved, in the midst of the same foes. I am sure there are many servants of God who know what it is to be living in the midst of these kinds of pressures. You know what it is to have this kind of trouble of heart in a different context, and the teaching of Jesus has a timeless relevance for us as we seek renewal.

In the first four verses of John 14, then, the Lord Jesus provides the disciples with the divine therapy for this condition of heart. He is dealing with human frailty and failure. There are at least four elements in this therapy which Jesus brings to the troubled hearts of the disciples.

THE SELFLESS LOVE OF JESUS

The first is this, and it is really implicit within the whole: *the amazingly selfless love of the Lord Jesus Christ*. As I was studying these chapters, this is the thing that came home to me again and again. You see, the really striking thing about it all is that Jesus Himself was filled with heaviness and sorrow of a depth and dimension unknown to men, because it was the sorrow of bearing the world's sins and the Father's wrath. "Behold, and see," we sing in the *Messiah*, "if there be any sorrow like unto His sorrow." Yet throughout the whole of His experience of bearing this kind of sorrow, and knowing that in front of Him as He left the Upper Room there was this cup that was waiting for Him to drink—the cup of the judgment of God on sin, the cup of all the agonies of the sins of men—and yet facing all this He is apparently quite thoughtless of His own sorrow and only taken up with theirs. They are unable to enter into His affliction, and there was no man in the world who could enter into His sorrows. But "in all their affliction he was afflicted" (Isa. 63:9).

That is why the great text for this whole ministry of Jesus is in 13:1: "Having loved his own who were in the world, he loved them to the end." You know, beloved, there is nothing in the whole world, no treasure that the whole Bank of England can give to us, like the love of Jesus for His own—the amazing, the selfless love of the Lord.

THE GRACIOUS REALISM OF THE LORD

Secondly, the *gracious realism of the Lord*. Notice that immediately before chapter 14, in 13:37, Peter has been protesting that whatever happens, the Lord can count on him; he will remain faithful, even unto death. Simon Peter says to Him, "Lord, why can I not follow you now? I will lay down my life for you." Peter has turned, in other parts of the Gospels, upon his fellow disciples, because he has a very unrealistic assessment of himself. It is one of the characteristics of the man. He looks at these other men when Jesus is saying, "I will strike the shepherd, and the sheep will be scattered" (Mark 14:27), and he says, "Lord, I don't know about these others; I don't think you can trust them. But you can count on me!"

You see, in 13:38 Jesus faces Peter with the stark realities about himself. And that is very like Him; that is part of His therapy. "Will you lay down your life for me?" he says. "Truly I say to you, the cock will not crow till you have denied me three times." You see, the Lord's therapy is not to retreat into a world of make-believe but to face us with reality. That is what He does when He draws us to His heart of love. It is not to cover over the truth about us; it is not to bring us to the place where we are hiding from the facts—hiding from our true selves. The glorious thing about the Lord Jesus Christ is that He draws the real truth right out into the open, and He loves us still.

It is a very blessed thing when you are in the company of somebody with whom you do not need to pretend, isn't it? We all have a great tendency to be actors in one form or another. Isn't that true? And it is a glorious thing to be able to rest and relax and not need to pretend to be something different from what you are. That is the background to the third element in the Lord's ministry to the disciples' troubled hearts. That is a great step forward when a man has come to terms with himself; and that is what Jesus is seeking to do with Peter: seeking to bring him face to face with the things that are naturally true of him, in his background, his temperament, his personality, and everything else.

I have found that there are many young people today who are running away from their background. It is a wonderful thing to let Jesus face you with the truth about yourself and tell you that it is you, just as you are, that He is able to deal with, heal, bless, and save.

THE TRUSTWORTHINESS OF GOD

Jesus's teaching at the end of 13:38 continues in chapter 14. This leads us into the third element, *the trustworthiness of God*. The last phrase of chapter 13 is "The cock will not crow, till you have denied me three times. Let not your hearts be troubled; believe in God, believe also in me."

Do you see what Jesus is doing? Here He is, faced with the frailty and fickleness and weakness of these men like Simon Peter, and He says, "Here is the truth about you. But let not your hearts be troubled; believe in God, believe also in me." Incidentally, these words should be, as in the Revised Standard Version, both imperatives. If you have an Authorized Version you will notice it is "Ye believe in God"—which is the indicative mood. And then "Believe also in me"—which is in the imperative mood. I take them to be both imperatives, so that it should be "Let not your hearts be troubled; believe in God, believe also in me."

The point is, you see, that the disciples may be fickle and faithless, but the Lord is so utterly trustworthy that He urges the disciples to rest their confidence on Him. Where are they going to look for a rock to rest on? Where are they going to find an anchor to hold them as the storm is about to break upon them?

You know the kind of question that arises when you are in this kind of situation, and it seems as if the gathering clouds are everywhere, and the storm is about to break. Well, Peter says, "Lord, you can rely on me."

And Jesus says to him, "Ah, no! The source of cure for the troubled heart is this: believe in God, believe also in me. My child, rest everything you are on what I am—what God is. It's everything in the Godhead that is your anchor."

Notice the particular realm to which Jesus points the disciples. He urges them to rest their confidence on the Father and the Son in three ways. First of all, *on the wisdom of God*: "In my Father's house are many rooms" (v. 2). In other words, He is speaking to them about what is happening as He goes from them, and Jesus says He has wisdom and understanding about where He is going. He knows what they do not know: He is going to His Father's house. And the disciples are exercised about this; they do not know. But now Jesus says to them, "Let not your hearts be troubled; believe in God, believe also in me. The place I'm going to is my Father's house, and I'll tell you about it, because I know about this." He has the wisdom which they do not have.

You will perhaps have noticed in 16:30 how the disciples have moved on to rest in this kind of wisdom. This is the resting place for the believer. The disciples say to Jesus in 16:30 *not* "now we know everything" but these wonderful words: "Now we know that you know." That is enough for the believer. That is resting on the wisdom of God, beloved, and there is nothing more blessedly secure than this: "We know that you know." He says, "In my Father's house are many rooms. Trust me to know about where I am going and what I am doing."

The disciples are to rest not only on the wisdom of God but, secondly, *on the Word of God*. I prefer the Authorized Version translation of this: "If it were not so, I would have told you. I go to prepare a place for you." If you have the Revised Standard Version you will notice it says, "If it were not so, would I have told you that I go to prepare a place for you?" I think the Authorized Version is better: "If it were not so, I would have told you."

There is a great testimony to the absolute sufficiency of the Lord's word for the Lord's people. Do you see what Jesus is saying? "Believe in God, believe in me." He says, "If it were not so, I would have told you. I wouldn't have left you without a word about that." There is not an area in the believer's life for which the Lord has not provided a word. And he says, "I want you to rest in My wisdom, that I know what you don't know; and rest in My word, for I would have told you if you needed to know about this." So He says, "I want you to rest in My word. I would have spoken a word to you about it."

Thirdly, their faith is to rest *in the work of Christ*: "I go to prepare a place for you." That phrase does not primarily mean, I believe, that Jesus is preparing a special corner in heaven for each of us. That may well be a lovely truth, but I do not think that is what the Lord is teaching here. What He is saying here is this: that what He is about to do by His death, resurrection, and return is to accomplish a full salvation for all these men who have troubled hearts. "I go to prepare a place for you" speaks of His death and resurrection, His ascension into glory, and His coming again. He goes on to say, "When I go…, I will come and will take you to myself, that where I am you may be also." It is His finished work that the Lord Jesus is speaking of in all its fullness. "Now," He says, "you are to rest on this."

Do you see? In other words, "What seems to you to be an agonizing sorrow, what seems to the world to be a great tragedy of a life cut off in early manhood, is in fact the eternal plan of God for the salvation of His people. That's what I'm going for." So He says, "You are to rest on the wisdom of God. You are to rest on the Word of God. And you are to rest on the work of the Savior." Beloved, if you are resting there, you are resting indeed.

Our faith and confidence, says Jesus, are to be specific. They are to rest on His boundless wisdom, on His infallible Word, and on His saving work.

THE SURE HOPE OF GLORY

That leads me to the fourth of these elements in our Lord's therapy for His troubled disciples. It is not only the amazingly selfless love of the Lord Jesus Christ, the fact that He was graciously realistic in all His dealings with His disciples, and that God is trustworthy in His wisdom, His Word, and His work. The fourth element, you will notice, is *the sure hope of glory*: "When I go and prepare a place for you, I will come again and will take you to myself, that where I am you may be also." That "coming again" of which Jesus speaks has many references in John's Gospel, even within these chapters. I think you will readily see, as you look at verse 3, that the significance of the "coming" is the ultimate coming, the Second Coming as we say, of our Lord Jesus Christ: His return to consummate history, to wind up the affairs of this bankrupt world, to hold His last assize, and to take all His children—the living and the dead—into the glory of His presence, ransomed and redeemed and resurrected in their bodies. That is the coming of which John speaks here.

It seems to me a very significant thing that when Jesus wants to deal with the distress and perplexity of His disciples, He lifts their minds up to heaven and links His coming departure with their ultimate destiny. It may be that there is a secondary reference in the coming of Jesus at death—to take the believer to Himself, to be "with Christ, for that is far better" (Phil. 1:23). That is why this passage is so often read as a glorious word from God at funerals of Christian people. But notice this: what Jesus is implying is that one of the great answers to the troubled mind is the heavenly mind.

There is a rather foolish gibe, which is common parlance among even Christian people, about some folks being so "heavenly minded that they are of no earthly use." Of course we know what people sometimes mean by that. If they mean he is unrealistic and not facing the facts of life as they are—well, that is fair enough. But if they mean what the Bible means by "heavenly minded," beloved, this is not a problem that I have come across too often, quite honestly! It is a consistent biblical theme, you see, that heavenly mindedness is the key to earthly usefulness.

Think of Paul writing to the Corinthians about his ministry in days of pressure and perplexity. "We do not lose heart," he says. Why? "Because we look not to the things that are seen, but to the things that are unseen" (2 Cor. 4:16, 18). Or to the Romans about perseverance in Christian discipleship through suffering. What does he say is the answer to it? He lifts up their minds to heaven when he says, "The sufferings of this present time are not worth comparing with the glory that is to be revealed to us" (Rom. 8:18).

This is what it means to trust the Father and the Son. What is the characteristic of the men of faith in Hebrews 11—that great catalogue of the men who displayed trust in the Father and the Son? Let me read it to you:

> For people who speak thus make it clear that they are seeking
> a homeland. If they had been thinking of that land from which
> they had gone out, they would have had opportunity to return.
> But as it is, they desire a better country, that is, a heavenly one.

Therefore God is not ashamed to be called their God, for he has prepared for them a city (Heb. 11:14-16).

Beloved, I say to you, heavenly mindedness is the key to earthly usefulness, and we need to remind ourselves that there is a dimension in our salvation which is much neglected in evangelical circles. It is this: we are not only saved by grace, through faith, but we are also saved in hope.

It was said of godly Samuel Rutherford, that great Scottish pastor of the seventeenth century, that he had his feet on the ground, his hands to the plough, and his heart in heaven. Peter learned this great lesson, didn't he? He was listening to our Lord speaking these words. In 1 Peter 1:3-4 he says,

Blessed be the God and Father of our Lord Jesus Christ! By his great mercy we have been born anew to a living hope …, and to an inheritance which is imperishable, undefiled, and unfading, kept in heaven for you.

In verses 5 to 11, Jesus goes on to elaborate the sense in which they are to trust Him, and He does so in answer to two questions—one from Thomas: "How can we know the way?" in verse 5, and one from Philip in verse 8: "How can we see the Father?" It is important to see that the answer to both these questions is, *in Christ*. The answer to the question, "How can we know the way?" is "I am the way," says Jesus (v. 6). The answer to the question, "How can we see the Father?" is "He who has seen me has seen the Father" (v. 9). The central point of these verses (vv. 6-11) is that everything in Christian salvation is found in Christ. And if we are found in Him, then there is no need for our hearts to be troubled. That, in summary, is what Jesus is saying. It is of great significance that Jesus is not only the destination of the believer ("I will take you to myself") and the guide on the journey ("I will come again and take you"), but He is also the way we travel ("I am the way").

In all these great personal claims that Jesus makes, between verse 6 and verse 11, the dominant idea seems clearly to be of Jesus as the way to the Father. He is speaking about Himself, the great Mediator who reveals God to men and brings men to God. This is how they are to understand both His going and His coming. Look at these familiar words in verse 6, in which Jesus is speaking in answer to Thomas: "I am the way, and the truth, and the life; no one comes to the Father, but by me." The first claim seems really to be expounded in the other two, and I want to look at them briefly in that way.

He is the way in the sense that He reveals God to us as the truth and takes away our spiritual blindness, so that to know Him is to know God; to see Jesus is to see God (v. 9); and to hear Jesus is to hear God (v. 10). "Do you not believe that I am in the Father and the Father in me? The words that I say to you I do not speak on my own authority; but the Father who dwells in me..." Now, you would expect "speaks the words," but it is actually "does his works." The reason is that very often in John's Gospel the deeds of God are His words and the signs by which He speaks. So He is the way in the sense that He reveals God to us as the truth.

When they are seeking the way to the Father and wondering what this way is, Jesus says, "I am the way" in the same sense that He reveals the Father to them. There is the Christian answer; and it is Christ as the answer to man's first great problem as he seeks to come to know God—the problem of his ignorance and blindness. God has spoken in Jesus to dispel our darkness.

It is in this same area that Philip touches in his question, "Show us the Father" (v. 8). We are still in the realm of revelation. He is saying,

"Show us the Father; we do not see God!" The place where God is to be known is in Jesus.

Jesus says to him, "Have I been with you so long, and yet you do not know me, Philip? He who has seen me has seen the Father" (v. 9). The place where God is to be known—in other words, where truth is to be found about God—is in Jesus Christ. The place where God is to be seen is in Jesus Christ. "The light of the knowledge of the glory of God" (2 Cor. 4:6) is to be found in the face of Jesus.

So Jesus appeals to Philip to trust Him as the revealer of the Father, and you will notice that this is a trust that Jesus makes exclusively His own. When men want to know God and see what He is like, we have only one reliable place to come, and that is to Jesus.

But there is another need which man has, and it is his deeper problem, not just that he is ignorant of God, confused, and needing to be sorted out. It is a great mistake when we make the Christian gospel restricted to that—that men are searching for God and they cannot find Him; they are confused and distorted in their thinking. Certainly modern man is, and the gospel of Christ comes and sorts out his thinking and leads him into the truth. And we convince men of the truth as it is in Christ. But there is something infinitely deeper. Man is not just ignorant of God and confused, but his deepest problem is that he is dead in trespasses and sins. His need is not just to be sorted out but to be resurrected. So Jesus is the way to the Father in this second sense—not only as the truth-revealing God but also as the life who brings men resurrection into everlasting life. He gives them eternal life, as He says in John 17.

Now, let us summarize these first eleven verses. They are sandwiched between appeals, in verse 1 and verse 11, for faith in the Father and the Son. Notice again in verse 11: "Believe me that I am in the Father and the Father in me; or else believe me for the sake of the works themselves." We are to trust Him, therefore, in His going to be our Sin-Bearer and Mediator; in His coming to lead us to heaven; and between His going and coming to provide us in His Word and wisdom with everything needful to salvation.

In verses 12 to 20, Jesus turns from Himself, as the object of the believer's faith, to the disciples, to show them how this trusting and believing in Him will affect their lives. It will do so in three ways, described in three sets of three verses. They are almost paragraphed out this way in the Revised Standard Version.

In verses 12 to 14, this trusting in the Lord which Jesus encourages in verses 1 to 11 will produce in them the *work of faith*: "Truly, truly, I say to you, he who believes in me will also do the works that I do; and greater works than these."

In verses 15 to 17, it will produce the *labor of love*: "If you love me, you will keep my commandments."

And in verses 18 to 20, it will produce the *patience of hope*: "I will not leave you desolate; I will come to you. Yet a little while, and the world will see me no more, but you will see me; … In that day you will know." Let us briefly look at this part.

THE WORK OF FAITH

First, the *work of faith* (vv. 12-14). Jesus is saying, "If you are ready to trust me," and this must have been a wonderful thing for these beleaguered disciples to hear. "It is not just that I have got a comforting word for your spirits, to hold you up and anchor you in the midst of the storm, but I have a ministry for you," said Jesus. Do you grasp this? He says, "He who believes in me will also do the works that I do; and greater works than these will he do, because I go to the Father." His going to the Father, far from being the end of the ministry, is just the beginning of it. He says, "You will do greater works than these."

Oh, that is a wonderful thing—for somebody who knows his weakness and weariness, his sin and his failure, a sense of bewilderment, and the awful experience of life seeming to tumble in upon him—for the Lord to come, and not just say, "My child, I'll hold you up, even though you're weak, down, and weary, even though you are failing, even though you are going to deny me." It's not just that He will hold you, but "I've got a ministry for you." Oh, that the Lord Jesus would say that into your heart! In John 21, as He drew Peter back to Himself at the lakeside, He said to him not only "Peter, do you love me?" but also "Peter, I've got a ministry for you. Feed my lambs. Feed my sheep." Beloved, that is what the Lord is like.

This blessed and astonishing promise was fulfilled in the Book of Acts. It is not that the disciples performed more dramatic miracles than Jesus; that is not what He is speaking about. The greater works refer, according to Bishop Ryle, to the spiritual work of conversion. That is the greater work, when on that day of Pentecost thousands of men and women were swept into the kingdom of God, and the Holy Spirit came down and worked the greater work in the hearts of men. The greater works are the spiritual work of conversion. In other words, Jesus, by His very going, is doing that work which will make the powerful preaching of the Word and the conversion of men possible. James Denny says, "Jesus came not primarily to preach a gospel but that there might be a gospel to preach."

In verses 13 and 14 Jesus calls their attention to the source of this power that He is promising them for their greater works. "Whatever you ask in my name, I will do it, that the Father may be glorified in the Son; if you ask anything in my name, I will do it." So the mighty works that He forecast have two characteristics.

One, they will be *His works*. It is not that the disciples are going to be more gifted than the Lord Jesus, but it is that the Lord Jesus, by

His ascension and by His coming again in the Holy Spirit, is going to continue to do greater things in the world. That is what Luke declares at the beginning of Acts. He says, "The former treatise have I made, O Theophilus, of all that Jesus began both to do and to teach" (1:1, AV). He began it in the Gospels; he continues it in greater glory in the Acts. That is what Jesus is referring to here, and that is the first thing about these greater works: they will be performed by the Lord.

The second thing is that they will be performed by the Lord *in answer to the prayers of the Lord's people*. The greatest ministry that He is going to give them is the ministry of prayer. Someone may be saying, "It's all right for him to talk about people to whom the Lord is going to give a ministry. But that's not me at my age, in my situation, at my time of life or with my inadequacies." Beloved, here is the greatest ministry of all. This is the ministry that matters—the real work of faith. We have our language all wrong, haven't we, when we talk about somebody who is "praying for the work"? You know, beloved, prayer *is* the work. Prayer is the real work; and that is why there are so few people ready to give themselves to it.

THE LABOR OF LOVE

Second is the *labor of love* (vv. 15-17). "If you love me," says Jesus, "you will keep my commandments." What is the labor of love which believing in Jesus will produce? Well, the answer Jesus gives is this: "You will keep my commandments." The disciples' sorrow and distress at Jesus's departure, you will remember, is an evidence of their love for Him. Sorrow and distress when someone is leaving is an evidence of love. They grieve most who love most. But now Jesus asks, "What is the real evidence of love?" It is not emotion, beloved. Great as emotion ought to be in the life of the child of God, it is not emotion that is the evidence of love. There is a moral and ethical content in the evidence of love, and it is this: "If you love me, you will keep my commandments."

There is a further amplification of this where Jesus says,

> He who has my commandments and keeps them, he it is who
> loves me; and he who loves me will be loved by my Father, and
> I will love him and manifest myself to him…. If a man loves me,
> he will keep my word, and my Father will love him, and we will
> come to him and make our home with him. He who does not
> love me does not keep my words (vv. 21, 23-24).

So the evidence of love for Jesus is obedience.

We need to stay with this truth for a moment, for it has something vital to teach us, both about our personal experience and about our personal evangelism. What is the secret of a real experience of the love of God and the reality of His presence? Jesus says, "If a man loves me, he will keep my word," and the result will be that "my Father will love him, and we will come to him and make our home with him."

Now, "home" is the same word that Jesus uses for the Father's home in heaven. He says, "If a man obeys my word, my Father will love him." That is what will draw down the love of God—and the smile of God—upon our life. It is obedience to His Word that does it. And the heart of such a believer will become heaven upon earth. No wonder Bishop Ryle says there is more of heaven and earth to be attained than most Christians are aware of.[39]

But this has something to say not only about our personal experience but also about our personal evangelism, because "Judas (not Iscariot) said to him, 'Lord, how is it that you will manifest yourself to us, and not to the world?' " (v. 22). In other words, "Surely we are not going to

---

39   J.C. Ryle, *Holiness: Its Nature, Hindrances, Difficulties and Roots* (Edinburgh, UK: The Banner of Truth Trust, 2014), xxiii.

ignore the world and end up a private little coterie?" Verse 23 says that Jesus answered him, but it looks as if Jesus didn't answer him at all. And yet He does most powerfully answer him.

How is Christ manifested in the world? Well, the answer is, *in the lives of obedient believers*: "We will come to him and make our home with him." Jesus says, "What about the world, then, Judas? Well, here is the way that we are going to reveal ourselves—the Father and I— to the world. We will come and make our home in the hearts of the obedient believer, and he will be sent out into the world." And as he is sent out into the world, he will be a tabernacle, as it were, for the Lord. "The world in its rebelliousness," Jesus is saying, "cannot know me and cannot know my Father. But it can know you, and it can see you."

Martin Luther, preaching on this passage, remarks, "The Christlike heart is the chariot of God, by which He comes to the world in grace and conviction." That is an element in the problem of communication which we do not take seriously enough, my Christian friends. Let me say simply that it is a dreadful waste of time to think about the problems of communication with the world divorced from the need of sanctification in the church.

When a man takes seriously these words about obedience being the evidence of love and the key to deep spiritual experience and true personal evangelism, he finds that there are two great problems in seeking to obey the Lord. One is *discovering His will*; and the other is *doing it*. Jesus says in verses 16 and 17, "I have provided for that, too." And in this context we have the first of many references in the Upper Room discourse to the Holy Spirit.

Notice, first, how the whole Godhead works together to enable the believer to live a life of consistent obedience. The Son prays to the Father; the Father sends the Spirit; and the Spirit's ministry here is to meet the believer's need of a lack of knowledge and a lack of will to do the will of God. So, He will instruct you as "the Spirit of truth" (v. 17) and indwell you as the Spirit of power.

The word Jesus uses of the Holy Spirit is the Greek word *parakletos*, sometimes transliterated in translation as "Paraclete," which means "Advocate," "Comforter," or "Counselor." Dr. Leon Morris says it is impossible to find one English word which will cover all that *parakletos* means. He is the One called alongside to help; He is the One who draws near to us and who, Jesus says, will not only dwell with us but also be *in* us.

It is very significant that our Lord speaks of sending "another Comforter," or Counselor, or Paraclete. In 1 John 2:1 the word is used of Jesus Himself, and now He promises to send another Paraclete. The word means "another of the same kind." So the Holy Spirit who is going to come to indwell us and instruct us is going to be another Jesus—as someone has said, "Jesus's other self."

THE PATIENCE OF HOPE

In verses 18 to 20, Jesus says that the third fruit of confidence and faith in Him will be the *patience of hope*: "I will not leave you desolate; I will come to you. Yet a little while, and the world will see me no more." It seems as if this, too, is a reference to the coming of the Holy Spirit. The disciples will see Jesus in a spiritual sense; and because He lives, they will have the life of God by the indwelling Spirit.

Then, in verses 25 to 31, Jesus seeks to turn the disciples' fear and doubt into peace and confidence, and He provides them with three particular buttresses for their faith.

First, in verses 25 and 26, the *Spirit of Christ*, and we shall come back to this in John 15 and 16.

Secondly, in verses 27 to 29, the *peace of Christ*—that peace which is Jesus's own peace, the natural outcome of all that He has been teaching them, that peace which comes of being "stayed upon Jehovah / hearts are fully blest, / finding as He promised, / perfect peace and rest."[40] Can you think of it? The poise that the Lord Jesus had, even in this hour. He says, "I will give my peace to you."

And lastly, in verses 30 and 31, the *triumph of Christ*. Notice it is not men and human conflict that Jesus sees approaching, in verse 30. He recognizes that Calvary is to be a battleground with the ancient prince of hell. But He says, "He has nothing in me," that is, "He has no power over me, no foothold in my life." So Jesus triumphs over him. Do you see how Jesus gets victory over the devil for Himself and for believers? "I do as the Father has commanded me." In other words, it is His obedience, even unto death, which produces His triumph.

Professor C. H. Dodd says that the closing words of the chapter, "Rise, let us go," are not an invitation to go out from the Upper Room to someplace else. Dodd says very suggestively that these are really military words, and they imply in normal Greek usage, "Let us go to meet the advancing enemy."[41] It is a stirring battle cry, in other words. May we take the Lord's teaching and the Lord's words in these verses to our hearts, as we go out into the world—as we face the world, the flesh, and the devil—and hear His voice saying to us, "Rise, let us go to meet him." And we may say, "We rest on Thee, and in Thy Name we go."[42]

40　From Frances Havergal's hymn, "Like a River Glorious."

41　C. H. Dodd, *Engaging with C.H. Dodd on the Gospel of John: Sixty Years of Tradition and Interpretation* (Cambridge: Cambridge University Press, 2013), 41.

42　From Edith G. Cherry's hymn, "We Rest on Thee, Our Shield and Our Defender."

Chapter 20

THE CHRISTIAN'S RELATIONSHIPS

This is my commandment, that you love one another
as I have loved you.
— John 15:12 (RSV)[43] —

At John 15:8, our Lord seems to me to turn to a subject which is taken on into chapter 16. In chapter 15 our Lord Jesus Christ is still exercising His gracious caring ministry for His disciples as they face with fear and trembling the prospect of His departure. On this last night of His earthly life, He is coming to them with a heart that is overflowing to them. "Having loved his own who were in the world, he loved them to the end" (John 13:1), and here is His ministry of love and care for them. But in the wider context, our Lord's words are His ministry to believers who are under pressure, knowing what it is to go through the same kind of tribulation— the pressures of the world, the flesh, and the devil—in the whole period between His going to the Father and His return in glory.

If the great appeal in chapter 14 is for faith ("Believe in me" is Jesus's repeated appeal to the disciples), the great appeal of chapter 15

---

43   Unless otherwise stated, Scripture quotations in this chapter are from THE HOLY BIBLE: REVISED STANDARD VERSION, International Bible Society.

is for *fellowship* ("Abide in me" is the repeated appeal of this chapter). It is a threefold appeal.

First, it is an appeal for fellowship *with the Lord Jesus Christ* through our vital union with Him: "I am the vine, you are the branches. He who abides in me, and I in him, he it is that bears much fruit" (v. 5).

Secondly, it is a fellowship *with the Father* through His careful and faithful husbandry in our lives: "I am the true vine, and my Father is the vinedresser" (v. 1). There is a fellowship with the Father to which Christ draws us.

Thirdly, it is a fellowship *with one another* through our mutual love in Christ and our obedience to His commandments: "This is my commandment, that you love one another as I have loved you" (v. 12). Verses 1 to 11 are concerned with the first two elements in that fellowship, and verses 12 to 17 are concerned largely with the third.

Now, if our Lord Jesus has an overriding aim in this passage in John 15, it seems to me that it is not so much the urging upon us of our duty to abide in Christ, but it is rather to show the disciples what abundant provision God has made for them in His Son. He does this by emphasizing this truth: that the Lord Jesus Christ is not just a friend who has the transforming effect upon the believer that many friendships have. You know how friendships can produce in us a sense of security. They can produce in us a stimulus to a different kind of life. But what Jesus is saying in John 15 is not just that He has come to be a friend, but that He is an abode for the believer. He is a home richly furnished with all the fullness of the blessing of God and with all the wealth of heaven.

He shows us this by revealing something of the glorious teaching that derives from that great and blessed truth of which the Apostle Paul makes so much in his epistles: the doctrine of our union with Christ. You remember how Paul sees the Christian fundamentally in these terms: the Christian is a man "in Christ." In 2 Corinthians 5:17: "Therefore if any one is in Christ, he is a new creation." In Ephesians 1:3: "God … hath blessed us with all spiritual blessings … in Christ." That is our position if we are Christians. If you are a child of God, this is a fundamental truth about you. Above everything else you are a man, a woman, in Christ Jesus. At one time you were outside of Christ, separated from Him; but now grace has brought you to be in Christ Jesus. And all the resources the believer needs in this world are in Christ.

The New Testament teaches us about our union with Christ by using various metaphors with which you will be familiar. Sometimes we are limbs in a body; sometimes we are living stones in a building. But here our Lord's metaphor is that of believers being branches in the vine: "I am the vine, you are the branches" (v. 5).

The background of this metaphor in verse 1 is not so much the possible existence of a vine near the Upper Room with its tendrils trailing down over the window, as may well have been the case, but rather the body of teaching in the Old Testament where God's vine is the nation of Israel (Ps. 80:8-16; Jer. 2:21; Ez. 15, 19; Hosea 10). In so many places throughout the Old Testament you get the picture of Israel as God's vine. Perhaps the best known is Isaiah 5:1-7: "The vineyard of the LORD of hosts is the house of Israel" (v. 7). So the vine is a symbol of Israel, and the picture that it presents is that salvation is to be found in being incorporated into this nation. Israel is God's chosen people. He has chosen a people for Himself, and as He draws people to Himself He incorporates them into this nation. Israel is God's vine, and He means to produce His fruit in the world through this vine.

But the vine means something more than this in the Old Testament. It is not only a symbol of Israel—"The vineyard of the LORD of hosts is the house of Israel, and the men of Judah are his pleasant planting"—but it is also in the Old Testament a symbol of failure. Not God's failure, because God asks the question, "What more could I have done with my vineyard than I have done with it?" He tells us everything that He has done. He has lavished His care upon it; He has poured out His attention upon it; He has done everything that could be done for the vineyard. Yet the vine is the symbol of failure, and the failure is the failure of Israel. Isaiah 5:4: "When I looked for it to yield grapes, why did it yield wild grapes?" Jeremiah 2:21: "I planted you a choice vine…. How then have you turned degenerate and become a wild vine?" There is God's lamentation over His vine, as He has lavished His care upon it, as He has planted it, as He has walked to and fro. He says, "It has become a wild vine. It is degenerate." And in Ezekiel 19:12: "The vine was plucked up in fury, cast down to the ground; the east wind dried it up; its fruit was stripped off."

It is against that background of Israel's failure as the false vine that Jesus stands in John 15:1 and says, "I am the true vine"—not the true as opposed to the untrue but the true as opposed to the false. The Greek word means "the one which is spurious"—the degenerate vine, the failed vine. He is standing here over against the whole background of Israel, God's chosen vine, and He says, in the light of that failure, "I am the true vine, and salvation now means being incorporated into me."

This metaphor of the vine tells us how we can share in the life and abundance which is in the Lord Jesus Christ. May we pause for a moment and see how we can do so, in two ways.

The first is by *derivation*. That is how the branch, as you will know, obtains its life from the vine. It has no life of its own; it derives all life—all its potential for fruitfulness, everything that it has of life, strength, vigor, and reality—from the vine. If you sever the branch from the vine, it will be lifeless and useless. So it is with the believer. Says Jesus in verse 5, "Apart from me you can do nothing." Every spiritual grace, and every evidence of spiritual life in us, is derived from our union with Christ.

It is not only by derivation, but it is also by *identification*. While Jesus says He is the vine and we are the branches, there is another sense in which branches and vine are identified with each other. By this metaphor Jesus is describing that union of which He spoke in John 14:20, where He says that "in that day you will know that I am in my Father, and you in me, and I in you." This is that gracious identification whereby all the riches that are Christ's by nature become ours by identification with Him. So there is the picture of the man who is "joined to the Lord," to use Paul's lovely phrase in 1 Corinthians 6:17, and engrafted into Christ. He derives all that he is, all his potential, and everything of good within him, from the vine. All the riches of God and of glory that are in Christ Jesus by nature we obtain from Him by identification.

Now we must ask what the great purpose of this union with Christ is, which has been effected in us by God's grace. When you turn to John 15, there is no mistaking the answer to this: it is *fruit*. In verse 2: "Every branch that does bear fruit he prunes, that it may bear more fruit." And in verse 5: "He who abides in me, and I in him, he it is that bears much fruit." The great purpose for which we are united with Christ, and engrafted as branches into the vine, is that we might bear fruit.

Of course, the image of the vine is uniquely suitable for drawing out this teaching. The vine is useful for nothing else but fruit. This is what it is for, and this is why this is such an appropriate metaphor. It is not for wood; the wood of the vine is classically useless. It is not for foliage; it is not for flower. The great purpose of the vine is to produce fruit; that is what it is for. And that is what Christians who are joined to the Lord are for: they are for the production of fruit. This is the great burden of our Lord's ministry in these verses.

It is a very vital thing, my Christian friends, for us to discover exactly what it is that we are for in the world. It is an appalling and dangerous thing that so many Christian people drift through so many years of their lives without stopping to ask what it is that they are for in the world. That is why you get this lack of a real sense of focus and purpose in Christian living. Have you yet discovered what you are for? Well, here is the answer: like the branches of the vine, you are for the production of fruit. This is what Christian salvation is all about.

Although it is common to interpret this fruit-bearing in terms of service and witness, I have come to the conclusion that bearing fruit does not primarily mean winning souls. We speak about somebody who has had "a very fruitful ministry." It is true that that is a wonderful thing to see God doing through you, and we ought to covet and pray for that kind of fruit. But the weight of biblical teaching seems to me to be that fruit is not so much that kind of success but holiness of life and character and Christlikeness in our daily living. That is what Jesus is concerned about. He says, "The Father is to prune you, and you are to abide in me, in order to bear fruit."

This is certainly how the Old Testament uses this language. In Isaiah 5 God comes to look for fruit on His vine. What is the fruit that He looks for? Isaiah says, "He looked for justice, but behold, bloodshed; for righteousness, but behold, a cry!" In other words, they were moral qualities of godly character that God was looking for, and it was the absence of that fruit that breaks the heart of God. And He says, "What more could I have done?" but the fruit was not there.

Not only the Old Testament but John the Baptist also uses this metaphor in this way in Matthew 3:8, where he pleads, "Bear fruit that befits repentance." John's great concern was for the evidence of a change of character. Jesus uses the word in this way, too, in the Sermon on the Mount in Matthew 7:20. He is speaking about a lack of righteousness in the Pharisees—about the false shepherds who appear to be on the outside what they are not, in fact, on the inside.

He goes on to speak about this kind of godly character for which He looks, penetrating behind all disguises. He says, "By their fruits ye shall know them." The Apostle Paul also uses it in this way in Romans

6:22: "Ye have your fruit unto holiness" (AV), and in Galatians 5:22: "The fruit of the Spirit is love, joy, peace…" It seems to me, therefore, that Dr. Leon Morris is right when he says that, although this fruit is not defined, he has no doubt that it is qualities of Christian character which are in mind.[44]

The pressing question is, How can we bear this kind of fruit? If this is why God has incorporated us into Christ, if this is His great saving design in our lives, beloved—and it is—the issue is, How can I bear this kind of fruit? How can I become this kind of man? What is the secret of becoming a branch in the vine that is really bearing fruit to the glory of God?

BELONGING TO THE VINE

Well, in these early verses of John 15 Jesus describes three things on which fruitfulness depends. It depends, first, on our *belonging to the vine*. In verse 2 the Father distinguishes between branches which belong to the vine and those who are merely intertwined in it and associated with it: "Every branch of mine that bears no fruit, he takes away, and every branch that does bear fruit he prunes, that it may bear more fruit." And in verse 6 you have an amplification of this negative side of the Father's distinguishing: "If a man does not abide in me, he is cast forth as a branch and withers; and the branches are gathered, thrown into the fire and burned."

I suggest to you that the basic teaching of that part of the chapter is that our fruit-bearing depends upon our belonging to the vine. The first kind of branch which belongs is *pruned*; the second kind of branch which does not belong is *cast out*. The illustration of the first would be the disciples; the illustration of the second would be Judas Iscariot. That illustration would still be vivid in the minds of the disciples as

---

44   Leon Morris, *Jesus Is the Christ: Studies in the Theology of John* (Grand Rapids, MI: Wm. B. Eerdmans Publishing Company, 1989).

they remembered how our Lord had not just seen him slink out of the door but had dismissed him ("What you are going to do, do quickly!"), and he is taken out—cast out. Then there is the appalling story of the end of Judas Iscariot.

There may be some questions about how Jesus could speak of someone being "in the vine" and next taken away and burned. Let us not bypass such a question as that. How is it that someone can be said to be "in the vine," or "a branch of mine," and yet to be taken away and "cast forth as a branch," withered, and then burned in the fire? Well, let me say one or two things about this. First, this is one of these cases where one must never press the details of an analogy like this too far, and particularly to make it contradict other Scriptures. That is a very important principle in interpreting the Bible: that we are never to build our doctrine upon truth drawn by analogy from this kind of metaphor, and particularly to make it conflict with other parts of the Scripture.

In other words, let us go no further away than John 10:28, to the question that people are asking when they are concerned about this kind of thing. Is it possible for somebody to be a believer, incorporated into the vine, and yet to be taken out and cast out and burned? Here is what Jesus says about that question, in John 10:27-29:

My sheep hear my voice,… and they follow me; and I give them eternal life, and they shall never perish, and no one shall snatch them out of my hand. My Father, who has given them to me, is greater than all, and no one is able to snatch them out of the Father's hand.

Where are you as a believer? You are in the hand of the Great Shepherd of the sheep, and nobody can snatch you out of His hand. "Ah, but more," says Jesus, "you are in the hand of My Father. I and My

Father are one. And you cannot be snatched out of such a great, mighty grasp as this." So our Lord Jesus Christ is not, a few chapters later on, teaching the reverse of what He taught in chapter 10.

Secondly, this specific personal example of what Jesus is here speaking about, namely Judas Iscariot, perhaps gives us the key to what our Lord is meaning. He was the man who appeared to share everything with the other disciples; who appeared to share the mind and purpose of the Master; who was even given a position in the company. He kept the bag; he was the treasurer. And yet the time came when it was recognized that every appearance had been false, and that he did not really belong. It is belonging that matters, you see.

Listen to the words of John Calvin: "It may be asked whether anyone engrafted in Christ can be fruitless. I reply that many are reckoned by men's opinions to be in the vine who in fact have no root in the vine."[45] The whole point of the analogy here is that the production of fruit is ultimately the only reliable evidence of belonging to the vine—that is, the only reliable evidence that a man is in Christ is the evidence of the beginnings, at least, of a godly character.

May we pause in our thinking to ask, How then do we come to belong to the vine? Well, one answer would be, *by faith*. When we speak about believing, in the New Testament, it is believing into the Lord Jesus Christ. That is the great significance of this word *pisteuo*: "believing into the Lord Jesus Christ." By faith we are united into the Lord Jesus Christ. It is therefore a faith-union. When you believed on the Lord Jesus Christ, this is what happened: you were believing into Him; you were being brought into this faith-union with Him. Belonging to the Lord Jesus Christ is by personal, saving faith.

____

45   John Calvin, *Calvin's Commentaries: The Gospel according to ST. JOHN 11-21 and the First Epistle of John*, trans. T.H.L. Parker (Grand Rapids, MI: Wm. B. Eerdmans Publishing Company, 1974), 94.

It would be possible, secondly, to answer that question of how we belong by saying that we are united to Christ *by the work of the Holy Spirit*. In 1 Corinthians 12:13: "For by one Spirit we were all baptized into one body." How do we become limbs in the body? We are baptized by the Holy Spirit. This is His work: to incorporate us into Christ as the body, and we are the limbs.

If you wanted an even fuller answer than that, it is not only by faith and by the Holy Spirit, but we are in Christ, my dear Christian brothers and sisters, also supremely *by the Lord's gracious choice*. That is what Jesus is saying at the end of this passage: "You did not choose me, but I chose you" (v. 16). Well, of course we chose Him, but the vital thing is that He chose us. The Apostle Paul, when he is speaking about our union with Christ, says we were chosen "in him before the foundation of the world" (Eph. 1:4). This union is not only a faith-union and a spiritual union, but it is also an eternal union. It depends upon belonging.

PRUNING BY THE FATHER

Notice, secondly, it depends upon *pruning by the Father*. John Stott says, in his comment upon verse 2, that God the Father is pictured here "as an indefatigable gardener,"[46] and that is a very good description of what God the Father is. He is an indefatigable gardener, out for fruitfulness in the branches. He is not, in other words, content to leave them to themselves. He is constant and thorough in His care and concern for fruit.

Now, I know what an indefatigable gardener is, because one used to live next door to us. From the crack of dawn until last thing at night, there he was, looking over his garden, and he would pluck out something here, and cut back something there. It is the picture of a man

---

46   John Stott, *Christ the Liberator* (Downers Grove, IL: InterVarsity Press, 1971), 52.

who, wherever he sees evidences of growth, begins to set about dealing with the plant, because he longs to see a harvest; he longs to see fruit. So it is that whenever God the Father sees evidence of life, He takes His pruning knife to husband the resources of that life for fruit.

Notice in verse 3 that God is not satisfied when we are justified. It is to justification that verse 3 refers: "You are already made clean by the word which I have spoken to you." That is the initial cleansing to which Jesus refers in John 13. But Jesus says that is only the beginning. "My dear children," He says to His disciples, "this is only the beginning of what the Lord is to do for you; it is not the end. It is not a terminus, but it is the starting point." He is the indefatigable gardener who sets about pruning the vine that it may produce fruit.

The great principle is apparently, according to our Lord, that the fruitfulness of the vine depends upon the faithfulness of the pruning. Otherwise, you see, the possibility is that the life of the vine may be diverted into something other and less than fruit-bearing. Bishop Westcott says in his commentary on John, "Everything is removed from the branch which tends to divert the vital power from the production of fruit."[47]

Do you see how Jesus is putting the tribulations and trials of the disciples into a different light? Remember that He is still ministering to these heart-weary, broken disciples who are going through the mill spiritually. I do not doubt that there are many servants of God who are going through the mill this very moment. See how this puts it in a different context altogether and sheds light on our adversity and tribulation? He is describing it as the gracious, purposeful work of the Father's pruning. When He comes with this knife that seems so harsh and sharp and painful and applies it to the life, and when these men are smarting under the blow, Jesus says, "Oh, you can trust my Father,

---

47 B. F. Westcott, *The Gospel According to St. John: The Authorised Version with Introduction and Notes* (London: John Murray, 1889), 217.

because He is the husbandman; and He has a great purpose in view, and it is fruit for His glory."

Remember those words of Amy Carmichael, that godly woman with the beautiful mind? She went out as a missionary to India from the Keswick Convention, and her life was shot through and through with suffering of many kinds. She is writing about pruning, and she says this:

"Rid me, good Lord, of every diverting thing." What prodigal waste it appears to be, to see scattered on the floor the bright green leaves, and the bare stem, bleeding in a hundred places from the sharp steel. But with a tried and trusted husbandman, there is not a random stroke in it all; nothing cut away which it would not have been loss to keep, and gain to lose.[48]

"Not a random stroke in it all." That is a great prayer, is it not? "Rid me, good Lord, of every diverting thing."

I think it was W. P. Nicholson, that great rough-hewn man of God in Ireland, who said one night, "If the devil can't keep you from being converted, he'll bend all his powers to get you diverted." Beloved, I tell you, as a pastor who cares for men and women, one of the most heartbreaking things in the whole world is to see a man or woman whose life has begun to show signs of promise, in whose heart there have begun to be evidences of grace, and then they have been diverted. I wonder if the story of your life is like that. It may be through a relationship or through something that came to you at a time when God was telling you to do this or that, and you refused it, and you have been diverted. The Father's pruning work is the counterpart of this. Is this not why Paul so often speaks of tribulation working for us "a far more exceeding and eternal weight of glory" (2 Cor. 4:17)? "Our light

---

48   Ferguson, *Maturity*.

affliction," he says, "worketh for us." Do you see what this is? God the Father is putting our tribulations to work; He is employing them in His service. And it is the tribulation, so often, which is the pruning knife of the Father to bring glory into your life.

You may remember the story I told earlier of the missionary who went out still wondering about so much that had happened in his life and so many things that God had been doing to him that seemed so mysterious. When he got out to the mission field, he was walking one day along a pathway and came to a little bush. He saw there hanging the chrysalis of a butterfly. The butterfly was just about to emerge, and he saw in the chrysalis that tremendous struggle that does go on before the butterfly emerges. He saw the striving and the struggling and the tribulation. He put his hand in his pocket and he took out a penknife and began carefully to slit open the shell of the chrysalis. And the butterfly emerged. All the tribulations were past, and all the agonies were done. And he looked at it and discovered that it came out a poor, deformed creature. He learned that day that it was the tribulation that put glory into the thing.

That is how we are to see the conflicts and trials of our lives, beloved. They are the very fabric of the Father's greatest work.

ABIDING IN CHRIST

Fruitfulness depends on belonging to the vine, pruning by the Father, and, thirdly, on *abiding in Christ*: "Abide in me, and I in you" (v. 4). Fruitfulness is conditional on abiding, and if the emphasis of belonging to the vine is on union with Christ, the emphasis of abiding in the vine is on communion with Christ.

Notice that there are two sides to it: "Abide in me, and I in you." There is our abiding in Christ and Christ's abiding in us. He abides in us as the God who is at work in us "to will and to work for his good pleasure," as Paul tells us in Philippians 2; and we are to recognize that truth and to glory in it. We abide in Him when we cultivate a communion of heart and mind and will with Him, which is deepening every day. This is to be the great business of our life: "Abide in me."

Now this whole idea of abiding in Christ has been distorted—partly, I think, because of some hymns which have misused the word as though it meant "lolling, relaxing." When I was a young Christian we used to sing hymns about constantly abiding, and I always had the picture in my mind of a man strung up between two trees in a hammock on a calm summer's day with a "Do Not Disturb" notice over his life! This was what it meant to me to be "constantly abiding." You probably have not had that idea at all, but this was the idea that I had.

Abiding in Christ is not a passive thing like that, but it is an active thing. It is pressing on into Christ against all the tendencies of the world, the flesh, and the devil. It is the great pursuit of the Apostle Paul: "That I may know him, and the power of his resurrection, and the fellowship of his sufferings, being made conformable unto his death" (Phil. 3:10, AV). It is focusing the life. It is, in Paul's words, "this one thing I do,… I press toward the mark" (3:13-14, AV). That is what it is to abide in Christ, beloved. Bishop Westcott says, "Whatever leads to this is good. Whatever hinders this is bad. Whatever does not bear on this is futile." And this is what Jesus is calling us to: it is pressing into Him with all our being, that we might know the fullness that is in Christ as an abode for the believer.

How, then, are we to abide in Christ? Are there some guidelines Jesus gives us? Well, in verses 7 and 10 there are two equations which give us some help. Verse 7: "If you abide in me, and my words abide in you, ask whatever you will, and it shall be done for you." Verse 10: "If you keep my commandments, you will abide in my love, just as I have kept my Father's commandments and abide in his love."

In verse 7, a parallel is drawn between our abiding in Christ and *His words abiding in us*: "If you abide in me, and my words abide in you." Sir Edwyn Hoskyns, one of the great commentators on the fourth Gospel, says, "The phrase *abide in me* is expanded and defined as the abiding of the words of the Lord in the disciple."[49] So that abiding in Christ is to let God's Word sink into the very depths of your being, to feed upon it, to let it become part of the fibre of your life. When Spurgeon was urging this upon his students one day, he said, "Brethren, this is the thing that makes the minister of God. Get into the Word; soak it up, lap it up, drink it up. Get your heart and mind and body into it, until your very blood becomes Bibline." That is great! How do we abide in Christ? By letting His Word abide in us.

In verse 10, He equates abiding in His love with *keeping His commandments*: "If you keep my commandments, you will abide in my love." The Lord Jesus's communion with the Father, as we see so often in John, is the pattern. Hoskyns again says, "To abide in His love and to keep His commandments are therefore but two modes of saying the same thing."[50]

Now notice, beloved, as we put the two truths of verses 7 and 10 together. We may say that we abide in Christ by making His Word our earnest study and by making His commandments our daily delight. Therefore, abiding in Christ is really a moral rather than a mystical matter. May I quote Bishop Ryle to you again? "Our Lord," he says, "guards us against supposing that a mere indolent abiding in Him, with a dreamy, mystical kind of religion, is what He means. His words must be burning like fire within us, and constantly activating

---

49   Edwyn Clement Hoskyns, *The Fourth Gospel* (London: Faber and Faber Limited, 1950), 476.

50   Hoskyns, *The Fourth Gospel*, 477.

our characters."[51] So abiding—fruitfulness, Christian holiness—is the outgrowth of a life which obeys the commandment of Jesus. Let me say this: there is no more a shortcut to that kind of biblical holiness than there is a shortcut to growing grapes on a vine.

It is a significant thing that the Bible always speaks of Christian holiness in horticultural terms, never in mechanical terms. It is never the pulling of a lever or the pressing of a button; it is a growth "in the grace and knowledge of our Lord and Savior Jesus Christ" (2 Pet. 3:18). Beloved, we need to beware of this, because we live in an age of instant things. Some of them are a great blessing—like instant coffee. But some of them are a great error—like instant holiness. Oh, there is no way to fruitfulness of the kind that impresses God but by abiding in the vine!

PRIVILEGES FOR THE BELIEVER

Now, from verses 7 to 11, the Lord goes on to speak of four privileges inherited by the believer who is abiding in Christ. And they are all four the sharing of privileges which are already Christ's.

First, the privilege *of answered prayer* (v. 7). Of course, that privilege is our Lord's already: "I knew that thou hearest me always," He says to the Father in John 11:42. Now He says to His disciples, "If you abide in me, and my words abide in you, ask whatever you will, and it shall be done for you."

What is the connection between abiding in Christ and answered prayer? There are two things. First, prayer depends not so much on the words I speak as on the man I am. The fruitful life, which is abiding in Christ, is the real secret of authority and power in prayer. That is why you cannot compartmentalize a man's life and speak about his prayer life dissociated from the rest of his life.

---

51   Ryle, *Expository Thoughts on the Gospels*, volume 7, 81.

The second thing is that, as His words abide in us, our minds are schooled and our wills are molded to His mind and His will, so that we desire and ask what pleases Him. That is the key to this apparently dangerous promise that Jesus makes. Do you notice the daring of the Lord Jesus, when He says to the disciples, "If you abide in me, and my words abide in you, ask whatever you will, and it shall be done"? But you see, if His words abide in them, then their minds are conformed and their wills are bent to the will and the mind of the Lord, and the things that they ask and the things they desire are the things that please Him. That is the key to the privilege of answered prayer.

Secondly, the privilege *of glorifying the Father*: "By this my Father is glorified, that you bear much fruit, and so prove to be my disciples" (v. 8). There is a blessed privilege indeed. Jesus says in 13:31 that God is glorified in His Son. That is a privilege enjoyed by the Lord Jesus: God the Father is glorified in His Son. But now He is also said to be glorified in fruitful believers; and the reason is that we shall be, as we abide in Him, gradually "changed into his likeness from one degree of glory to another; for this comes from the Lord who is the Spirit" (2 Cor. 3:18).

In verses 9-10, we see the privileges *of a family love*: "As the Father has loved me, so have I loved you.… If you keep my commandments, you will abide in my love, just as I have kept my Father's commandments and abide in his love." You know, we skip over verses like that, don't we? What love the Father has for the Son our poor minds just cannot comprehend! That is something outside of our ethos altogether. But it is a love, we at least know, which takes an infinite delight in the Son; and this is the love of Christ for us.

"Now," says Jesus, "that love will be your abode." This will be the abode of the believer; it will be the element in which he lives. And that is a wonderfully healing thing. That is what these men were so greatly needing to know. In all the wounds that were gradually being exposed in their hearts, they were needing to know that their dwelling place was in the love of Jesus, which was like the love of the Father for the Son.

Fourthly, the privilege *of sharing Christ's joy*: "These things I have spoken to you [that is, the things about belonging to the vine, being pruned by the Father, and abiding in Christ—He has spoken them all with this great aim in view], that my joy may be in you, and that your joy may be full" (v. 11). This is what Jesus had in view. This is His aim all along. It is for the glory of the Father; it is for the blessing of the church of God; it is for the need of a stricken, tired, needy, and perverted world; but it is for your joy, too, you see. George Matheson writes in his great hymn of that "Joy that seekest me through pain."[52] Beloved, we need to be convinced of this.

What is Christ's joy? Well, Christ's joy is not a frothy, effervescent kind of thing. There are many Christian people who misunderstand what Christian joy is, and the Lord Jesus says, "I have a joy to give you; and my aim and end in all my dealings with you is joy." I say again, we need to be convinced of this, because the devil is constantly at work seeking to convince us of the reverse. As he did with Adam and Eve in the garden of Eden, he is out to cramp your life. He is out to impoverish you; he is out to filch away all the happiness and fullness that life can bring. The Lord Jesus says it is a lie from hell: "My great burden is to bring you joy." That is why you bow yourself with a glad abandon to the will of God.

We talk about the will of God in such a strange way as Christians. Some frightfully appalling thing comes, and we say, "Ah, well, it's another disaster, but it must be the will of God." Or we say, "We accept it as the will of God." Of course, one knows what people mean when

---

52 From George Matheson's hymn, "O Love That Wilt Not Let Me Go."

they are going through dark days, but the will of God is good and perfect and acceptable to His children because it is the road to joy.

FELLOWSHIP WITH EACH OTHER

Now in verses 12 to 17, Jesus is turning to the fellowship they are to have with each other. He has been speaking about fulfilling His commandment. What is the commandment? "This is my commandment, that you love one another as I have loved you." Each individual branch must have a certain relationship with the vine; but since all the branches belong to the same vine, they inevitably have a relationship with each other.

The same is true with all these metaphors of our union with Christ. If we are sheep in a flock, then, beloved, if you have a shepherd standing in the middle of a field, and the sheep are all over the field, as you bring the sheep nearer to the shepherd, they come nearer to one another. If you have limbs in a body, when the limbs start working against each other and not coordinating, that is a mark of sickness in the body. The limbs are intended to work together for the satisfaction of the head.

We have already seen that abiding in Christ can be equated with keeping His commandments. And one of His commandments is this: that we love one another. This paragraph (vv. 12-17) begins and ends with the same commandment, as you will notice in the Revised Standard Version: "This is my commandment, that you love one another." Bishop Ryle comments on that:

He would have us to know that we can never think too highly of love, attach too much weight to it, labor too much to practice it. Truths which our Master thinks it needful to enforce on us by repetition, must be of first-class importance.[53]

---

53   Ryle, *Expository Thoughts on the Gospels*, volume 7, 83.

There are two things that Jesus has to say about this love. Firstly, it is *commanded by the Lord Jesus Himself*. In other words, love among brethren is not an optional luxury for those who are blessed with a nice nature, but it is a divine obligation. The reason we find it difficult to see how love can be commanded is an evidence of how much we misunderstand the nature of Christian love. We think of it as something which has its origin in the person we are loving and arouses this emotion, therefore, in us. But you see, Christian love is not stimulated by the one who is loved but by the one loving. It is not, to use John Stott's excellent phrase, "the victim of our emotions, but the servant of our will."[54] That is what God's love is like: it has no cause in its object but in itself. And one vital mark of the person who is in Christ is that he loves like that.

Secondly, it is *revealed in Jesus Himself*: "Love one another as I have loved you. Greater love has no man than this, that a man lay down his life for his friends." Jesus says that His love has this character, as He describes it in verse 13. And this leads us to the very heart of the matter, doesn't it? The nature of love is self-giving. That means that the opposite of Christian love is not hatred but self-love. That is the reason why so many of us find it so very difficult to love. It has nothing to do with our temperament; it is that we are so much in love with ourselves that we are unable to love others.

Finally, in verses 14 to 16, Jesus gives the disciples two gracious words of assurance. First, the assurance of *His friendship*. He longs to draw them nearer to Him. He says, "No longer do I call you servants," because He wants to bring them to a more intimate place than the servant's. He is drawing them in, you see: "I have called you friends" (v. 15). But notice that this is a friendship of a different sort from the friendship that we

---

54 Stott, *Christ the Liberator*, 59.

have with others. It is a friendship which involves obedience. The lesser title of servant is included in the greater title of friend.

The second is the assurance of *His election*: "You did not choose me, but I chose you and appointed you that you should go and bear fruit and that your fruit should abide" (v. 16). And that, beloved, is our anchor and our stay: that we go out as those on whom the hand of the Lord our God has been laid—mystery of mysteries!—from before the foundation of the world. That is what gives us our eternal security and the ethical energy to go and be fruitful men and women in a world that has never been so needy, to the glory of His great name.

BOOK FIVE

Obedience and Consecration

Chapter 21

Obedience in the Christian Life

I beseech you therefore, brethren, by the mercies of God,
that ye present your bodies a living sacrifice,
holy, acceptable unto God, which is your reasonable service.
— Romans 12:1 —

We turn now to the life of obedience which we are called as Christians to live. This is going to be a practical subject for many of us. There are things that we will discover, no doubt, about which we have been disobedient to God. Before we get anywhere in the Christian life, we may discover there are certain things we have to put right. We may discover that we have not been taking God seriously—that we have been playing at churches and playing at being Christians—and that there are some things which God wants to speak very seriously to us about.

We have observed several times over that it is a most necessary thing that Christians should be clear about what they believe and that we all should give ourselves to see what the Bible teaches about all the things that God has done for us in Jesus Christ—about what He is like and about what He demands of His children.

When we turn to Romans 12, we come to the place where the Apostle Paul has just finished laying that kind of foundation. He has been telling the Romans that they must give their attention to understand all that God has really done in Christ: "You say Christ died for you. What do you mean by that? What does it mean in your experience, in your life, and in your future that Christ has died for you?" The apostle goes into great detail in this Epistle to the Romans to tell them what it means that God has done all this for them.

But then he goes on in the second part to say, "I want to tell you how you ought to behave if that is what you believe," because belief and behavior are always married together in the New Testament. The Bible knows nothing about the kind of person who says, "I believe all this that God has done for me, and I believe the whole range of evangelical truth," and yet in their lives they are behaving exactly the same way as people who believe nothing of the kind.

That is why the apostle begins so many of these central parts of his epistles with the word "therefore." When you come to this word "therefore," you should always ask yourself the question, Wherefore the therefore? Why is there a "therefore" here? Well, what does the "therefore" mean? It is a word like a signpost, you see, as somebody has said—a signpost that points first back, and then forward. It looks back to the things that the apostle has been saying, and it points you forward to where you go, and the kind of path you tread, if that is the thing you believe.

The apostle does exactly the same thing in the Epistle to the Ephesians. In the first three chapters, Paul has been speaking at great length about all that God has done in Christ to break down the middle wall of partition that separated us from Him. He has made peace between us and Himself in the cross. We were formerly aliens, he has told us; we were enemies of God, we lived as enemies of God, and God was against us. The wrath of God was against us because we were His enemies. Now, says Paul, in Jesus Christ this has been dealt with, and

God has made peace possible. He has reconciled those who were at enmity with each other: you and God.

Then he says in chapter 4 (for his readers might be saying, "That is very good. We are glad to hear that this has been done."), "I therefore, the prisoner of the Lord, beseech you that ye walk worthy of the vocation wherewith ye are called." In other words, says Paul, "This is what you believe; you, therefore, have to walk as a Christian in the light of all that you have been saying you believe."

We have been saying a lot about doctrine so far. We have been saying that it is very necessary for Christians to lay hold of the great doctrines of the faith and to study them. I hope that those who have never done it may read their Bibles and other helps to study the doctrines of our evangelical faith and become students of the great facts of the faith. But, says the Apostle Paul, if you have all these things at your fingertips and you only know them with your mind and it does not affect your behavior, there is something very seriously wrong with your life. Why? Because the Christian life is a life that not only deals with creed, but it also deals with conduct; it is concerned not only with doctrine but also with discipleship; and true doctrine always gives rise to a certain quality of discipleship. The right kind of belief always produces the right kind of behavior.

That is what the Apostle Paul has come to in Romans 12, and, using this signpost word "therefore," he says, "Look back on all that I have been saying. What have I been saying?" Well, he gives us the summary of all that he has been saying in three words in the first verse: the "mercies of God." This is the ground on which he beseeches them to be entirely different from everybody else because they believe these things. It is the mercies of God that he points back to.

The mercies of God are the things that send the Apostle Paul away from ordinary descriptions to wonderful language of praise. He sometimes breaks out into the doxology when he is speaking about what God has done for him in Christ: the amazing wonder of the fact, and it thrills the apostle—I wonder if it thrills you—that God has left His glory and come down in His Son Jesus Christ to take hold of sinful, rebellious man and pour out all His love upon him, to the extent of giving up His only begotten Son, in order that He might save him from the peril in which he was living!

The Apostle Paul finds this an amazing and wonderful thing. In Romans 5 he can hardly find words to express it. He finds that in human life it is scarcely possible that for another man who is a friend will some die. For a good man, a man who is greatly to be admired, "some would even dare to die." But he says that God commends His kind of love toward us in that while we were sinners—while we were the most unattractive of people, while we were rebels against God—God sent His Son into the world to be our Savior. "Now," says the apostle, "as I have been telling you all about what God has done to save us from sin's penalty and from sin's power, I want to tell you what the result of that ought to be in your life."

What do you think the result of that ought to be? I think that for many people the answer to that question is that they will go to heaven instead of hell. That is one result, but that is not the thing that the Apostle Paul says ought to be your primary concern here and now. That is something that has been dealt with and is fixed and decided if you are a Christian. But if that is the only thing that has concerned you, the apostle says there is something wrong with your belief—with your life as a Christian—and you have got to get right back down to the roots and re-examine everything because it ought to do something infinitely more than this. He says it ought to issue in a life of obedience. What is the obedience to which we are called? "I beseech you therefore, brethren, by the mercies of God." What are we to do? What is the obedience to which we are called as Christians, on account of all that God has done?

Notice the language that he is using has the word "sacrifice" in it, and this may be a key to what the apostle is speaking about (v. 1). Do you remember how, in the Old Testament, there were, generally speaking, two kinds of sacrifice? There was, first, the sacrifice that was offered *for sin's remission,* in order that sin might be taken away. One example of that is the trespass offering. But there is another kind of sacrifice in the Old Testament offered after the sin offering has been offered up, when sin has been dealt with. That is the offering which is offered up as a result of the taking away of sin; we might loosely call it an offering *of thanksgiving.* One of these was the whole burnt offering, the peace offering. And the Apostle Paul is using this kind of language. He says, "I have been speaking to you," when he talks about the mercies of God, about the sacrifice that God has offered up in Christ. He has given Himself for us.

"Now," he says, "I want to speak about the other kind of sacrifice which ought to be producing in your life, if you really believe this." There is a sense in which the test of whether you believe it is whether you obey the kind of thing the apostle is talking about here. You see, Jesus had no time for the kind of person who said, "Yes, I'm a Christian. I believe this. I'm following You," but he had nothing of obedience in his day-to-day life to prove it. Jesus says, "I want some proof of the fact that you really believe"—in other words, that you are really a Christian.

What is the proof of your really being a Christian? What does Jesus say? Is it that you have a decision card that you can show from some time when you made your decision for Christ? Jesus says that is not it. He says, "I will tell you how you will know my disciples: by their fruits," and the kind of fruit of which the Apostle Paul is speaking in this chapter is the fruit of an obedient life that is offered up to God.

The picture he is giving us is the picture that the hymn writer was using in the hymn,

> My spirit, soul, and body,
> Jesus, I give to thee…
> My all is on the altar…[55]

In other words, it is the giving back of yourself—your whole self—to God, as His right and His due, because of what He has done for you.

That is the picture that the apostle is using, and he is speaking about the sacrifice that we are to offer to God. What kind of sacrifice is it? Well, I think we ought to notice, as a background to what we are saying, that it is an entire sacrifice. It is without exception and without qualification. "I beseech you therefore, brethren, by the mercies of God, that ye present your bodies a living sacrifice, holy, acceptable unto God, which is your reasonable service." In other words, it is your all that God is demanding, and the obedience which is the central part of the Christian life goes out into every part of your being. It is in every section of your life that God demands that He be absolute Lord and Master. And if you think you can become a Christian, receiving Jesus Christ as the Savior of your sins, and go out and live as you would had it never happened, and not have Him as the Lord and sovereign Master over every section of your being, then I tell you that the Bible says you are living under a delusion. It is an entire sacrifice; it is everything.

Do you remember how Ananias and Sapphira tried a partial obedience—tried to pretend that offering part of themselves to God and being obedient to God in one section of their lives would do, rather than the whole? You remember how the seriousness of that kind of

---

55   From Mary D. James's hymn, "My Spirit, Soul, and Body."

attitude was shown up, and the judgment of God came out against them. I think there are many Christians who are trying with God exactly the same game that Ananias and Sapphira tried, and I want to say to you that it does not work, but it leads to disaster. It is an entire sacrifice that the Lord demands.

LIVING SACRIFICE

I want to say three things briefly about this sacrifice. It is, first, *a living sacrifice*: "I beseech you therefore, brethren, by the mercies of God [on account of all that God has done], that ye present your bodies [that you offer yourselves] a living sacrifice." The word that is used here for "sacrifice" is the word "victim"—in other words, that you give yourself to God, having renounced every right that you have to yourself. That is the Christian life, you see—a life in which I have renounced every right to myself to live as I want to, and I give myself to God. But the sacrifices that the apostle is referring to as he looks back into the Old Testament were all sacrifices that were dead.

He says that, in contrast, God is waiting for you to give Him a living body, so that through the rest of your days God may work and God may move through every faculty of your whole life. You are to hand over in obedience every part of your body and your life to Him, so that it may be a living sacrifice. That will mean that in every day, from this day on, the motto of your life will be obedience to what God has said. It is a living sacrifice.

LASTING SACRIFICE

Secondly, it is a *lasting sacrifice*. Paul is not speaking about something that he is asking them to do once, and then they never need to do it again. This is not some kind of emotional crisis that he is trying to work the Roman Christians up into, saying, "This is something that you have got to do at the end of some great meeting or occasion. Offer yourself to God, and be obedient to what God is saying to you; give yourself wholly to Him." No. This is something which the apostle tells us in a thousand other places must happen every day of your life. It is a lasting thing, and if you have picked up this book thinking that you are going to do something or get something which is going to do you for the rest of your life and make you an obedient Christian, I want to say to you that you have done so in vain. Discipleship in the New Testament is something that demands a daily discipline—a daily offering up of myself to God.

Bishop Taylor Smith was once asked what the secret of his consistent spiritual life was, and this was his answer:

> Every day when I waken, I do something before ever I rise. I lift up my heart to my Lord, and I say "Blessed Lord, this bed is the altar, this body is the sacrifice, and gladly I offer myself up to Thee, so that for these next twenty-four hours I may be Thine alone, for Thy pleasure and for Thy service."

And so must it be for each one of us: a lasting sacrifice.

LOGICAL SACRIFICE

But notice that the apostle insists that this will also be a *logical sacrifice*. The word in the Greek of verse 1 translated in the Authorized Version "reasonable" is the word *logiken*—and you can see of course that that is where we get our word "logical." So the apostle's argument is that, in the light of all that Christians say they believe (which he has set down in the previous chapters), there is only one logical and consistent way for them to live: as a willing, living sacrifice to God, as glad bondslaves of the Savior.

That means that any other life is utterly inconsistent and illogical in the light of what we believe. This is not the life of the spiritual elite of which Paul is speaking, but this is basic Christian living. In the light of all that, and of the fact that we are not our own but bought with a price, be quiet before God this moment and ask yourself very seriously, "Is the life I am living really Christian? Or am I robbing God of what is simply His rightful possession?" That is the nature of the sacrifice: a life utterly and consistently at His disposal in every part, and simply because it is the logical outcome of what I believe.

Now the *implications* of this sacrifice, as they are described in verse 2. They are both negative and positive. Negatively it will involve that your life is not conformed to the standards, values, and criteria of the world around you which does not believe what you believe. It means that your life will be influencing rather than influenced—not that you will become different because you are in the world but that the world will become different because you are in it.

Positively it implies that there is a transforming work to be accomplished in such a life, which Paul describes by using the word that is used of our Lord being transfigured. His purpose is that we should be changed into the very likeness of Jesus. Notice that the means by which it is to be accomplished is the "renewing of your mind" (v. 2). That is the New Testament's teaching on sanctification. It is in our Lord's own prayer for His disciples in John 17:17: "Sanctify them through thy truth: thy word is truth." Robert Murray M'Cheyne used to say that the Christian life is just being made daily more like Jesus, and the instrument the Spirit uses to fashion us after Jesus's likeness is His Word. That is why a diligent application of ourselves to the Scripture is so utterly vital.

That is the life of obedience: it is a life offered up and a life transformed. The apostle concludes the whole matter by telling us that it is the only life which will ever really know what it is to be in the will of God. I wonder if some of you have problems about guidance, and all the time you have been ignoring the very basis of being in the will of God—"that ye may prove what is that good, and acceptable, and perfect, will of God." These things are the roots from which a life in the will of God will grow.

> I beseech you therefore, brethren, by the mercies of God, that ye present your bodies a living sacrifice, holy, acceptable unto God, which is your reasonable service. And be not conformed to this world: but be ye transformed by the renewing of your mind, that ye may prove what is that good, and acceptable, and perfect, will of God.

> Whatsoever He saith unto you, do it.

Chapter 22
The Life of Obedience

By faith Moses, when he was come to years,
refused to be called the son of Pharaoh's daughter.
— Hebrews 11:24 —

Previously, we were thinking of the meaning of faith. We said that there are two main ideas to be found in the New Testament's teaching about faith: that it had a concentration on its object rather than on itself, and that it is essentially a committed obedience to the One to whom we have entrusted ourselves. Obedience and faith are so closely linked together in the Bible that the New Testament finds it quite natural to speak of the obedience of faith. These two characteristics of faith are illustrated in the life of Abraham, of whom it is said that he looked for a "city that hath foundations, whose builder and maker is God" (Heb 11:10).His eyes were on the object of his faith. Abraham, when he was called, obeyed. "He went out, not knowing whither he went" (v.8) but committed himself by the decisive fact of obedience to the word that God had spoken to him.

I want to now take up this second word, "obedience," and to try with you to understand further the Bible's teaching about it. I want to look for this purpose at the life of Moses, as we find the inspired commentary on it in Hebrews 11:24-26. Here again you find faith and obedience linked together in this man's life, as in all these great men of God in Hebrews 11:

> By faith Moses, when he was come to years, refused to be called the son of Pharaoh's daughter; Choosing rather to suffer affliction with the people of God, than to enjoy the pleasures of sin for a season; Esteeming [or considering, accounting] the reproach of Christ greater riches than the treasures in Egypt: for he had respect unto [and that might be translated "he had his eyes upon"] the recompence of the reward.

Of course, no true Christian who has read the account of Moses's life in the Bible and discovered some of its fullness and fruitfulness can possibly avoid a desire to have the same quality of life and character which marked this man. Both in Hebrews 11 and in the fuller history in the Old Testament, there is a clear order in the record of Moses's life. Notice the preoccupation of this passage, and this brings out a principle of immense importance for Moses, for Abraham, for Paul, for every other man of God in the Bible, and for every single one of us: the kind of man I am determines the service I render—the kind of work I do for God.

I am persuaded that a great part of the reason for the pathetic condition of evangelical life and witness in our time is that we have neglected this fundamental concentration in the Scripture upon character. We have put our concentration upon what is supplemental and not on what is fundamental. We have neglected the building of our spiritual characters—what we are. All too often we have focused all our interest upon what we do—our service.

I well remember the first time that I read in E. M. Bounds's book *Power Through Prayer* the words, "Men are God's method. The church is looking for better methods; God is looking for better men."[56] This could be summarized by saying that the work that God does in man is always primary to the work that God does through him.

You find this illustrated again and again. Here, for instance, is a man like Saul of Tarsus, arrested by the Holy Spirit on the Damascus road and converted. What happens to him, first of all? Well, he is sent away for a number of years into Arabia, and I am persuaded that what the Apostle Paul was doing in these years was laying the foundations for the mighty life of service and power for God which was the remainder of his career. Do you remember how Elijah heard two words from God as he was set in the midst of a crooked and perverse generation to witness for God in the world? He first heard the word, "Elijah, hide thyself," and then, "Elijah, show thyself." The hiding, in a very real sense, determines the nature of the show. In other words, the secret work God does in me determines the public work God does through me. That is what the man meant who first said, "The secret of failure is very often failure in secret."

One thing I long to see is a great company of Christian people being thrust into God's work. But I want to say at the same time that far too many of us are in too much of a hurry to get immersed in Christian activity. I believe that God's primary work is something that demands the discipline of our allowing Him to build our character.

Look at three marks of the work God did in Moses. The first concerns Moses's *refusing*: "Moses, when he was come to years, refused by faith to be called the son of Pharaoh's daughter" (v. 24). Second, Moses's *choosing*: "Choosing rather to suffer affliction with the people of God" (v. 25). Thirdly, Moses's *esteeming*: "Esteeming the reproach of Christ greater riches than the treasures in Egypt" (v. 26).

---

56   E.M. Bounds, *Power Through Prayer* (Grand Rapids, MI: Zondervan Publishing House, 1962), 11.

MOSES'S REFUSING

Look with me at Moses's *refusing*. It is quite obvious that there was a negative side to the work that was done in Moses by the Spirit of God. This consecration of Moses, described step by step in these verses, has a negative side to it. First, he refused to be called the son of Pharaoh's daughter. I wonder if you realize what this means. From his earliest days, Moses was clearly destined for fame and fortune—for eminence and authority in the land. He was the son of the daughter of Pharaoh, and from the worldly point of view his prospects were very bright. But Moses heard the call of God and knew that he had come to the place where he was either to listen to the word of God and turn his back upon the allurement of Egypt, or he had to part company with his conscience and with his soul and turn his back on the word of God.

I believe that the challenge that Moses faced in those days to make a decisive refusal of all the calls and claims of position, wealth, authority, and ease is a challenge which faces us in these days. We are living in a generation which is marked by what the title of a recent book called "the cult of softness," and we have to recognize, although it is unpopular in many circles, that there is a refusal that we have to make. You will remember that it was not atheism that crucified the Lord Jesus Christ, but it was worldly religion.

I am certain that if there is one thing that is crippling and ruining the lives of so many people who begin as converted evangelical Christians, it is this whole issue of the claims of things—the spirit of worldliness. Worldliness, of course, is not a round of things that some people do or do not do, but worldliness is a spirit which enters into a man's life and seduces him away from the prior claim which Jesus holds upon him.

This is why Jesus brought together these two sides, both negative and positive, in Matthew 6 when He is talking about this very thing in the Sermon on the Mount: "Lay not up for yourselves treasure upon earth,… but lay up for yourselves treasure in heaven,… for where your treasure is, there will your heart be also" (Matt. 6:19-20). Moses found himself faced with the whole issue of whether or not he was going to refuse the treasures and pleasures of Egypt.

A young man in Scotland was a brilliant university graduate, and as he qualified in medicine, his professors forecast a most distinguished career for him. The whole world in his particular sphere lay at his feet. That young man was converted one day to Jesus Christ, and not long after that he heard the call to the mission field; he was immediately "not disobedient unto the heavenly vision" (Acts 26:19). He turned his back upon fame and fortune and everything else.

One day he was talking among some other students who had a kind of easy-going Christian life that made no difference to them, and they said to him, "But, John, you can't possibly go on with this. Why, look at all that would be before you! Look at all you're turning your back on! You'll never get on in the world out there." He turned and said to them, very quietly, "Which world?"

And that is it, isn't it? Which world are you living for? Jesus points out the folly of investing your whole life and eternal soul in something that has the very marks of rot in it already. "Lay not up for yourself treasures upon earth, where moth and rust doth corrupt, and where thieves break through and steal" (Matt. 6:19), where in the end you are going to discover the utter confusion of having lost everything that you had set your heart on.

Let us bring this down to practical realities. While I said a moment ago, on the one hand, I believe many of us go far too quickly into a round of Christian service neglecting our Christian character, let me say, on the other hand, that I believe the call of God and the Word of God, if it is going to have any practical meaning in our lives, may well mean that some will be changed from one career to another. I wonder if the fact that so many young men are refusing the call of God into the ministry is just precisely this matter: that their heart is in the wrong place. Could it be that this is the call of God for you? What are you going to live for: the things that are temporary, passing, and perishing, or the things that are eternal? Moses refused to be called the son of Pharaoh's daughter.

MOSES'S CHOOSING

Secondly, we have a picture here of the other side of this, the positive side: Moses's *choosing*. Notice it was obedience that Moses chose. We read that Moses chose "rather to suffer affliction with the people of God, than to enjoy the pleasures of sin for a season" (v. 25). What that really means is that Moses was obeying the call of God to him; and this is the essence of his life. If you read through the Book of Exodus, you notice the repetition: "and Moses did as the LORD commanded him." That is the character of the man's life, and this is the very essence, of course, of consecration.

Some people look for consecration in some form of ecstatic experience. They expect themselves suddenly to have a flight of emotion and for some blinding light to strike them. But the essence of consecration is, very simply, obedience. The reason is this: the essence of our sin is rebellion against God. It is revolt—disobedience. So when Jesus Christ comes to undo the works of the devil in our lives, you would expect to find the opposite, wouldn't you? Instead of disobedience, obedience; instead of revolt, submission. Instead of the life that is marked by refusing to listen to the Word of God, we would expect the kind of life that was described: "Moses did as the LORD commanded."

As John Stott used to emphasize, Jesus set us free from the law not in order that we might be free to break it but so that we might be free to obey it. God did two things, therefore, in our hearts when we came to Christ.

First, He redeemed us from the curse of the law. Second, He has written His law in our hearts and begun to produce the kind of prayer we find in Psalm 119:36: "Incline my heart unto thy testimonies." That is the essence of Moses's consecration and obedience. This was what he chose.

But notice that the writer of the Epistle to the Hebrews goes on to talk about the costliness of this choice: "Moses,… choosing rather to suffer affliction." In other words, the choice was a costly choice, and the reason for that takes us to the nature of our rebellion. The nature of our rebellion before we became Christians is that we set ourselves on the throne of our lives, like the people of whom Paul writes who "worshiped and served the creature rather than the Creator" (Rom. 1:25, RSV). And that is the very heart of sin.

The very heart of consecration is that that is reversed: self is dethroned, and Christ is enthroned. It is a tremendously costly and painful thing to allow God to strike that great capital "I" down from the throne of my heart. But it is this that the apostle is speaking about in 2 Corinthians 5:15, when he says that Jesus "died for all, that they which live should not henceforth live unto themselves, but unto him." In other words, I cease living one way and start to live another. That is very costly, because it means that God begins to deal with my most precious possession. What do you think is your most precious possession? Consider that line from Townend's hymn, "The dearest idol I have known, / whate'er that idol be.[57] What do you think the "dearest idol" is? I will tell you. It is not a thing, but it is the great ugly monster of pride and self. That is the "dearest idol" any of us has known. And God wants to cast that down.

This is, I believe, an issue that many of us have to face. It is the most fundamental issue in the whole of the Christian life. That is why Paul

---

57 From Stuart Townend's hymn, "O for a Closer Walk with God."

was able to say, "I die daily" (1 Cor. 15:31) and "death worketh in us" (2 Cor. 4:12)—in other words, the bringing to an end of the enthronement of self in his life. That is why, of course, the most characteristic Christian virtue is humility—not that kind of painful pretense that masquerades under the name of humility and is really pride, but something that derives from a deep work of God in the very citadel of my being, where I have consented to the fact that self is to be dethroned and Christ enthroned in my heart.

MOSES'S ESTEEMING

Not only do we have a picture here of Moses's refusing and of Moses's choosing, but we also have a picture, finally, of Moses's *esteeming*. Here the picture is of Moses having his eyes in the right place again, and this is the characteristic of his faith. He had, in other words, the ultimate situation and not just the immediate situation in view. He esteemed, and the word is a commercial word—"considered" or "accounted"—that the reproach of Christ was greater riches than the treasures in Egypt. Here he is, you see, weighing in the balance one over against the other: the results, the treasures, the rewards of giving himself to the claims of Egypt over against the results and rewards of acceding to the claims of Christ upon his life and body. And he discovers at the end of this accountancy exercise that the rewards and the treasures of Christ are infinitely greater riches than he could ever find anywhere else.

But there was not just an eye for the reward that was eternal, and this is immensely important. In the midst of this fleeting world, when we begin to see how desperately short this life is, we come to the conclusion that only what is done for Jesus will last, and the real issue about your life is this: Is the thing you are investing your life in going to last? On the day when our works and our service are going to be exposed before God, is yours going to be the kind of life that has the quality of eternity about it?

Not only is there an eternal reward on which Moses had his eye, as Paul did too—"I count all things but loss for the excellency of the knowledge of Jesus Christ" (Phil. 3:8)—but there is also a reward here and now. It is twofold. Moses found a reward in his own life, because his life began to be the kind of life that told in the world for God. We read all through Exodus, as I have said, a recurring phrase, "Moses did as the LORD commanded him," and then suddenly we come across this precious jewel again: "The LORD did according to the word of Moses." That is the life that tells for God in the world.

The second thing is this: Moses found that all the allurements and pleasures, as it seemed at first that Egypt held for him—that an unconsecrated life might have given him—were a lie. He discovered that he had been made in such a fashion by God that the only thing that fitted his life was the will of God in all its fullness, and that was the only thing that could give him joy in the ultimate meaning of the word. That is what Jesus means when He says, "My meat is to do the will of him that sent me, and to finish his work" (John 4:34). He meant that the will of God was not something simply to which we submitted ourselves but something in which we found our truest satisfaction. As the Apostle John writes, "His commandments are not grievous" (1 John 5:3).

You know, we sometimes get all mixed up about this, as if God in His grace and love were a God of tyranny who wants to spoil and ruin our lives. The God and Father of our Lord Jesus Christ is the God who wants to remake our lives—to bring them into the true thing for which they were first created. In Him is the fullness of our joy; it is at His right hand that there are pleasures for evermore. And we are robbing ourselves in the deepest sense when we are living outside of the will of God.

My little girl has just been introduced to jigsaw puzzles, and the time I spend going round the floors of our house on my knees looking for the bits and pieces of jigsaws that she scatters all over the place! But eventually it is always daddy who has to finish the jigsaw. One day we were spending a long time looking for just one piece to fit into the very center of the picture, and we could not find it anywhere. We went under the chairs, under the carpets, in the kitchen, in the buckets, even in the waste bin looking for this one piece. Then we found it; and when we put it in, the picture was whole. Now, that is a pretty poor parable of what happens in the life of a man when he is seeking for the will of God. Being in the will of God is the only thing that will fit and complete the picture as God intended it to be.

I lay in dust life's glory dead,
And from the ground there blossoms red
Life that shall endless be. [58]

God's purpose is not that our lives might be dull but that our joy might be full.

---

58   From George Matheson's hymn, "O Love That Wilt Not Let Me Go."

Chapter 23

A New Look at Consecration

For he looked for a city which hath foundations,
whose builder and maker is God.
— Hebrews 11:10 —

We have been taking a fresh look at some of the teaching in the Bible about living the Christian life, trying to discover together some of the things that we need greatly to learn about the kind of life that is pleasing to God. There are two ways of looking at the life that is consecrated and given over to God—at the challenge of the Bible to Christian people to live a life that is pleasing to Him. One of them is to try to sort out some of the great principles that you find in the New Testament and to seek to understand them and apply them to your life. The other way is to see some of these great biblical principles clothed with flesh and blood in the lives of great men of God who were committed and consecrated to the God who had brought them out of darkness into His light.

It is in this second way that I want us to look at the meaning of a consecrated Christian life. I want us to do it by trying to look together at the life of a man whose position in the Bible is probably more significant than that of any other individual, except for our Lord Jesus. I am referring, of course, to the life of Abraham, the man who is described in the Scriptures as our spiritual father, the man from whom we take our roots spiritually, as it were. The story of Abraham is told in the Old Testament from Genesis 12 onwards, but there is an inspired commentary on it in Hebrews 11:8-19, and I want us to see a few verses from there.

First of all, I want to try to say some very simple things gathered from the evidence of the life of Abraham, a man who is described as a "friend of God," a man who is the example of true faith. If you want to live a life that is really faithful to God, look at Abraham. That is the Bible's advice. Well, what are the things that are characteristic of the life of Abraham? Look at Hebrews 11:8-12, 17:

> By faith Abraham, when he was called to go out into a place which he should after receive for an inheritance, obeyed; and he went out, not knowing whither he went. By faith he sojourned in the land of promise, as in a strange country, dwelling in tabernacles with Isaac and Jacob, the heirs with him of the same promise: For he looked for a city which hath foundations, whose builder and maker is God. Through faith also Sara herself received strength to conceive seed, and was delivered of a child when she was past age, because she judged him faithful who had promised. Therefore sprang there even of one, and him as good as dead, so many as the stars of the sky for multitude, and as the sand which is by the sea shore innumerable…. By faith Abraham when he was tried [or tested], offered up Isaac: and he that had received the promises offered up his only begotten son, Of whom it was said, That in Isaac shall thy seed be called: Accounting that God was able to raise him up, even from the dead; from whence also he received him in a figure.

The position that Abraham occupies in the Bible is, I think, something of tremendous importance. If you put it very simply, the biblical record is the account of how God acted in history all down through the years to reclaim men from the ravages of sin and from the damage that sin had done, both to God's creatures and to God's creation.

Here and there throughout the whole of the Bible's records of God's activity in the world to redeem it, you get certain very important moments and certain very significant people. And one of these people is this man Abraham. The choice and call of Abraham in the Bible is, in a sense, a watershed in the history of God's whole purpose to redeem the world from the results of sin. The particular significance of Abraham is that it is out of Abraham's seed that redemption is to come, so that after Abraham there is a gradual expanding, as it were, of the sphere in which God is working—a great nation coming out of this man Abraham and those who were his descendants.

Then, after this expansion—the great company—there is a narrowing down of God's interest, almost like one of these television cameras which goes over the audience, and then suddenly focuses on just one. This is what happens in the Bible: there is a focusing on, first of all, one tribe; and then in that tribe, one family; and then within that one family, one individual, so that when you open your New Testament at Matthew 1:1-2, you find that the concentration is on Christ Jesus, and He is called the son of Abraham.

When the New Testament explains what God is doing when He redeems men by Jesus Christ dying on the cross as "the curse," bearing the curse for our sins, you find it described in these terms. Why did He die? "That the blessing of Abraham might come on the Gentiles" (Gal. 3:14). So the blessing that we have in Jesus Christ is the blessing God promised when He dealt with Abraham in the days of the Old Testament. And the question that I want us to ask of the pages of the

Scriptures we shall be looking at is, How was Abraham blessed by God? As the Reverend Alan Stibbs says in his excellent little book on Abraham, *God's Plan*, "The way for Abraham to be blessed is the way for us to be blessed."

ABRAHAM'S CONSECRATION

Let me point out to you, first of all, why it was that Abraham was called by God, and why it was that God worked in Abraham's life in the way that He did—*the context of his consecration*, if you like. You will see, if you try to get to grips with the story of Abraham, that the purpose God had in all that He did in Abraham was not primarily to make Abraham happy or to solve all Abraham's problems. It was something much bigger than that. I think these things happen, but the basic drive of the purpose of God when He begins to work in your life is not simply to solve all your problems, make you happy, and send you along during the rest of your earthly pilgrimage on a flowery bed of ease. The great point about all this background the Bible gives to Abraham is that God called Abraham to a consecrated committal to Himself, in order that he might be caught up in the great ongoing purposes of a sovereign God who is working out His redemption in the world.

That is why God called Abraham to the place of full and utter committal of himself: because He wanted Abraham to be part of the great ongoing purpose of God. I suppose that none of us is likely ever to reach the prominence and the heights of Abraham—Abraham is a man of unique significance. But the fact is that, no matter how unimportant we may think we are, how young we may be, whatever insignificant kind of sphere we may think we have in life, we all have a place in this great ongoing purpose of God in the world. God seeks for His people to be committed and consecrated to Him in order that they might have His place in His purposes in the world.

There is nothing more tragic than to see Christian men or women in the formative days of their lives missing out on God's great purpose for which He brought them into the world. Just as the bird was made for the air, and the fish was made for the water, you were made for the will of God. And you will never find the true happiness for which so many people are madly rushing here and there to seek—that God meant you to find—unless you are right in the center of His will and purpose for your life, whatever that may be.

Let us look, second, at *the character of Abraham's consecration*. We started with the context of Abraham's consecration; now we come to the character of Abraham's consecration. There are one or two things—I suppose rather negative in one sense, but they have positive truths behind them—that I want us to notice.

The first is this: *the consecration of his heart, life, will, mind, and future to God*. Abraham's was not a wonderful kind of emotional and mystical experience, bringing with it an exhilarating feeling. What does Hebrews 11 tell us was the mark of faith in the life of Abraham? "By faith Abraham, when he was called…, obeyed" (v. 8). For Abraham, consecration to the will and purpose of God was essentially a matter of moral obedience to the will of God. And this is what true faith in the New Testament is; that is why it is married together in the Bible to obedience, and the phrase is used, "the obedience of faith."

There are many people who spend a great deal of their time looking for some kind of exhilaration, but this is not what the New Testament means by "consecration." There are many people who come away from meetings—and I have sometimes spoken to one or two of them—and have said, "I got a glorious feeling there! I felt wonderful when I went out!" But, you know, it is very dangerous to mistake exhilarating experiences for true consecration to the will of God. For Abraham, it was the challenge of moral obedience to what God had to say to him.

This is why it is so important for you to get into the Bible and become a true student of the Word of God, that you might live in obedience to what God is saying. That is how consecration is maintained.

Second, *Abraham was not made a man of God overnight.* His consecration, his godly character, was not the business of a day, but it was the work of a lifetime. This, too, is a matter of great importance, as it seems to me. You see, it is possible for us, and very natural for us, to seek some kind of crisis in our spiritual life which is going to be the answer to all our problems and make us men of God in three short steps. You know the series of books that you sometimes see on the bookstalls: *The Golf Secret, The Exam Secret,* and so on. The implication is that if you just get this read up, your golf handicap will sink overnight; if you just read this, examinations will no longer be any problem. And, of course, some of us have found to our cost that that is not at all true. There are many people who think there is a quick, snappy secret into a consecrated Christian life, but, my dear friends, there is not. It is not the business of a day, but it is the work of a lifetime.

The characteristic New Testament language to describe the work of God in the soul of man bears this out: it is the language of birth and growth. When you come to know God through Jesus Christ, you are born again into His family. The description of young Christians is "babes in Christ," and when we go on it is said in Paul's epistles that we "grow up into him" (Eph. 4:15). Therefore we are told to take food to help us to grow. This is the kind of language. So it is that that wonderful biography that some of you may be acquainted with, the story of Hudson Taylor, was rightly called *The Growth of a Soul.*

Of course, there are crises within this process of growth. Let us never go to the other extreme of error and think that God may not come into our lives with a real crisis to awaken us and do something in us that is going to make it possible for us to grow in a way that we did not before.

Not long ago, I visited our little hospital, not far from my parish, and there I saw a little cot in the middle of the ward. On it was a tiny child—she turned out to be four-and-a-half years of age—and I said to the Sister of the ward, "What's wrong with that child, Sister?" The child seemed shrunken; bones were sticking out; there were bruises here and there; and the little child's stomach was swollen. The Sister replied, "Malnutrition, and we are having a tremendous battle to save the child's life." Surgeons and physicians worked with that child for a long time.

Several weeks later, when I was going to see one of my congregation, I saw the child again; and after the critical days of treatment, she was beginning to grow again. But you see the point. The crisis was not in order to make her a full-grown woman once the hospital treatment was done, but it was to make growth possible. This is a very important thing that I wish I had got sorted out in my own Christian life a long time before I did.

ABRAHAM'S CRISES

Abraham had crises in his life. You only need to read the story very cursorily to find this out. Let me try just to outline for you some of the crises that we sometimes have.

I think one of the crises that matters more than many others in the lives of Christian people is the *crisis of truth,* when suddenly by reading your Bible the truth of some issue dawns upon you. I remember when this happened on so many different occasions in my own life. It may be the deeper truth about the real meaning of the death of Christ and what God has done in Christ—when the truth dawns upon you and somehow or other your soul is liberated to grow and go on with God in a way you were not before.

There are sometimes *crises of trial*—difficulties, adversities, sudden situations with which you are faced—when God speaks to you about something, and it is like a spiritual surgical operation. And through that trial, through that difficult experience, God sometimes brings you on to grow. That was what Abraham was experiencing when he was called upon to face the trial of offering up Isaac, of separating from Lot, and so on.

The third time of crisis is often a *crisis of repentance*. When I have failed, and I see what a wretched flop I am, and how utterly hopeless my life is when I rebel against God and try to go it alone, that can be a crisis which afterwards enables you, when you have turned from your sin and cast yourself on the grace of God, to go on and grow again. There are crises of this kind in spiritual experience.

But let us be very clear that there is no single crisis experience, no matter what you may call it, which is the key to suddenly becoming a mature Christian. I think it was Dr. Barnhouse who said that the graph of Abraham's spiritual life was rather like the graph of the cost of living—it goes up gradually; the overall picture is of a steady rise. Sometimes it stops for a while and remains level; maybe it dips down for a while and then rises again. But the overall picture of Abraham's life goes up in a steady and gradual rise.

ABRAHAM'S FAILURES

Abraham was not a figure of spotless perfection. This is where the honesty of the Bible is so encouraging, don't you find? God openly shows us Abraham's failures. He does not try to cover up the picture in all its reality, but He shows Abraham's failures, and He does so for two reasons. The first is very important: it is *that we might see where Abraham failed, take warning, and cry to God* to be prepared for a similar attack from Satan and for readiness to ward it off.

There is one way in which the failures of the men of God in the Bible are misused, and that is when they encourage us to feel, "Well, we're not so bad after all. We can just lie back on our oars. They were just as bad as I am." That is not why God shows us failures of men of God in the Scriptures. He shows them to us that they may warn us. It could even happen to him, so beware!

The second reason is this: God gives us these pictures of failures of the men of God like Abraham in order *that we might take encouragement* and realize that out of such unlikely material—a man who failed to trust God on a number of occasions—God made such a mighty man as Abraham became. As the Epistle of James expresses it concerning Elijah, Abraham, too, was "a man subject to like passions as we are" (5:17).

Do you think your nature is, perhaps, too difficult for God? Do you think your problems are so exclusive that no Christian has ever experienced them before, and that you can never become the kind of person that you would like to be? The testimony of the men of God in the Bible is that there is no twist in a man's character which God is not able to take, as the potter takes the clay, and make it into a vessel that He can use and bless.

Will you look at some of Abraham's failures, that we might learn from them? First, Genesis 11:31, *the failure of a partial obedience.* "The LORD had said unto Abram, Get thee out of thy country,… unto a land that I will shew thee: And I will make of thee a great nation." The land that God was going to show Abraham was the land of Canaan.

But look what happened to Abraham: he landed not in Canaan but in another place called Haran. "They went forth … from Ur of the Chaldees, to go into the land of Canaan; and they came unto Haran, and dwelt there" (11:31). Why did Abraham stop in Haran? Most people seem to think it was because of a personal relationship. His obedience was incomplete because of a personal relationship—family ties, in this case. May we learn from that the principle that people can keep people from the full will of God for their lives.

Could you be in a personal relationship just now that is doing that? That is the real test, you see, in a very real sense, of the seal of God upon your relationship with somebody of the opposite sex. Are they going to lead me on nearer to God? Are they going to provoke me to godliness? Or are they going to hold me back? People can keep people from God, and Abraham's obedience at the first was a partial obedience.

The second thing you will notice was *Abraham's failure to trust God in days of famine and trial.* It seems as if Abraham had expected, once he set out from Haran stepping forth in obedience to the word of God, that everything would go smoothly—trials and testings, wrestling and adversities were out of place in Abraham's idea of things. Suddenly famine came, and Abraham believed that this grievous famine could not be any part of the purpose of God for him. Wrestling with this was something he was not prepared to continue in; so he went down into Egypt.

But you know, one of the experiences of the saints of God is this: that these very trials and testings—some of the battles that we are waging, whether they are battles with the devil, with the flesh, with the world, whatever they may be; some of the internal conflicts that you are knowing; some of the pressures of the world around you, the society in which you have to live and witness for Christ—can be the very things that God takes and uses to make a real man of God out of you. As we sing in the hymn:

For I will be with thee, thy troubles to bless,
And sanctify to thee thy deepest distress.

When through fiery trials thy pathway shall lie,
My grace all sufficient shall be thy supply;

The flame shall not hurt thee; I only design
Thy dross to consume, and thy gold to refine.[59]

So, says the Apostle Paul, "Therefore will I glory in my infirmities, that the power of Christ may rest upon me" (2 Cor. 12:9).

Abraham's third failure was *failure in the realm of putting himself first*. You remember when he was in the land of Egypt—a place he should never have been in the first place—he found that one sin led to another; one lapse led him into more trouble. And he came to the place where he began to fear for his own skin, that with his beautiful wife Sara he might get into trouble with the king and with the Egyptians. "[They] shall see thee," said Abraham, "that they shall say, This is his wife: and they will kill me, but they will save thee alive. Say, I pray thee, thou art my sister" (Gen. 12:12-13)—a thing that would happen again. So concerned was he for number one (Isn't it interesting that we never need to ask who "number one" is?) that he lied to other people, compromised the position of another, and found himself in the most atrocious spiritual mess. Failure in the realm of putting self first.

He did the same with his plans. When Ishmael was born, this was Abraham's plan of fulfilling God's purpose. He began to rebel against God's idea—God's word, God's plan—and said, "Oh, that Ishmael might live before thee!" (Gen. 17:18). Ishmael was the child of a little plan that Sara and Abraham had together between them. God had another way, but Abraham said, "Here is my plan, God. Will you just put Your seal of approval on this, because I don't really care for Your idea of how I should be consecrated to You and live for You in the world? I prefer my own idea, my own plan." And Abraham failed.

---

59 From Robert Keen's hymn, "How Firm a Foundation."

Just a word about the two sides, positively, of the consecration. There was a cost in the consecrated life that Abraham lived—the cost of being separated from all the luxury and affluence of Ur of the Chaldees which was no broken-down shanty town, but a great civilization. Abraham was called to forgo that and to go out with God.

May I just ask you in a word, have you faced the issue of whether you are living for material gain, comfort, possessions, advancement, ambition, or for the will of God? Abraham found that the purpose of God, as he was again and again separated from things that might have been dear to him, was not to impoverish him but to enrich him. He found that out when he was faced with the question of separating from Lot. You remember in Genesis 13 how he gave Lot the choice of the land and was ready to leave his life in the hands of God; and it seemed as if Lot had taken the fertile plain, and Abraham was left impoverished.

Do you ever feel as if men and women in the world around you are going to have so much more happiness and joy because they are not Christians than you have because you are? It is one of the lies of the devil, you know, and one of his most effective lies: that the purpose of God in calling you to consecrate yourself utterly to Him is to impoverish you of the very things that are going to do you good.

Abraham found, after he had separated from Lot, that God told him, "Lift up now thine eyes, and look from the place where thou art northward, and southward, and eastward, and westward [and it will all be yours]" (v. 14). His design was to enrich rather than to impoverish. There is a fullness in the life utterly given over to the will of God and to His purpose that you will find nowhere else under God's heaven.

I used to have a dentist who was a master at touching his drill on the nerve of my teeth, and when I had come back down from the ceiling, he would say: "Whoo! I think we got the nerve then, didn't we!" God put his finger on the nerve center of Abraham's consecration when He took him out to Moriah with Isaac, his dearest possession. That was the crux of the whole matter.

What is your dearest possession? What is the thing that matters more than anything else in the world to you? I once heard someone say, "You know, what God wants is your Isaac; whatever your dearest possession is in the world—whatever matters to you most—He is calling you to lay it on the altar." But I do not think that is true. I think it is you God wants on the altar; not yours, but *you*. Is that where your life is going to be placed from this day forward?

Chapter 24

The Christian, the World, and the Holy Spirit

*I have said this to you, that in me you may have peace. In the world you have
tribulation; but be of good cheer, I have overcome the world.*
— John 16:33 (RSV)[60] —

John 15 and 16 have been described as chapters of Christian
relationship, and we found earlier that 15:1-17 deal with the
Christian's relationship with Christ, with the Father, and with our
fellow believers. We are to abide in Christ by obeying His Word; we are
to glorify the Father by bearing much fruit through submitting to His
pruning; and we are to love one another by becoming like Jesus in our
sacrificial self-giving.

From 15:18 to 16:15 our Lord goes on to deal with a new set of three
relationships, which we could describe as the relationship between *the
Christian and the world* (15:18-16:6), the relationship between *the world
and the Holy Spirit* (16:7-11), and the relationship between *the Holy Spirit
and the Christian* (16:12-15).

Then from 16:16 to the end of the chapter Jesus outlines some
of the blessings which will be the fruit of His going and the Spirit's

---

60   Unless otherwise stated, Scripture quotations in this chapter are from THE HOLY
BIBLE: REVISED STANDARD VERSION, International Bible Society.

coming. They are *joy out of sorrow*—and verse 20 is the keynote: "Your sorrow will turn into joy"; *understanding out of perplexity*—and verse 23 is the keynote: "In that day you will ask nothing of me"; *triumph in tribulation*—and verse 33 is the keynote: "I have said this to you, that in me you may have peace. In the world you have tribulation; but be of good cheer, I have overcome the world."

Notice our Lord's own explanation in 16:1 of His purpose in all this teaching: that He might succor and buttress the disciples in their weakness and need as they face this horrifying prospect of the departure of the Lord Jesus from them. Jesus says to them, "I have said all this to you [and it is the whole of this Upper Room discourse, I think, to which He is referring] to keep you from falling away." That is our Lord's great burden for the security of His people. And the truth enshrined in that explanation is that it is the ministry of His Word that keeps us from falling: "I have said all this to you to keep you from falling away."

THE CHRISTIAN AND THE WORLD

Let us look at the first of these relationships—*the Christian and the world* (15:18-16:6): "If the world hates you, know that it has hated me before it hated you." It is important to notice that the context in which Jesus begins to expound to the disciples what will be the relationship between themselves and the world is the life of fruit-bearing, of which He has been speaking in the earlier part of the chapter. And the point is that this life of fruit-bearing, and of fellowship with the Father and the Son, is not just to be lived out in the context of the mutual love of believers, but it is to be lived out in the context of the secular society which is fundamentally hostile to the fruit-bearing Christian. That is what Jesus means by "the world." There are various usages of the phrase "the world" in the Scripture, but here, and in so many places in John's writings, it is society as alienated from God and under the sway of Satan as its prince. And it is within the context of this secular society, as we would say, that the life of the fruit-bearing child of God is to be lived.

The position of the Christian in relationship with the world, you will notice, is a threefold relationship. First, *he has been chosen out of the world*: "You are not of the world, but I chose you out of the world" (v. 19). Secondly, *he is therefore not of the world*—that is, he does not belong to it: "If you were of the world, the world would love its own." The counterpart of belonging to Christ and belonging to the vine is that you do not belong to the world. But the third relationship that the Christian has to the world is that *he is a witness to the world*. He is chosen out of it; he is not of it. But that does not mean that he is in isolation. He is sent back into it by the same Lord who has chosen him out of it; and in verse 27 Jesus says, "You also are witnesses, because you have been with me from the beginning."

It is because of what Jesus has done in them, when He chose them out of the world, that the world is hostile to them when He sends them back into it. I wonder if you know that wonderful fairy story of the animal taken out of the herd by a being from another world, and this being ennobles and beautifies the animal until it radiates some kind of strange new glory. Then it returns to the herd, and at first they are curious and intrigued, wondering what has happened to this member of their herd. Then the curiosity and intrigue turn to resentment and anger, until the whole place becomes a cauldron of hatred, and they turn upon it to rend it to pieces. They hate the glory that is shining from it. There is a world of theology in that kind of fairy story, isn't there?

It is because of what He has done in them when He chose them out of the world that the world is hostile to them when they stand in it. This is why Jesus says, "The world hates you." In verses 18 and 19 onwards, this hatred is related to Christ in two ways.

First, the world hates the Christian *as it hated Christ*: "If the world hates you, know that it has hated me before it hated you" (v. 18)—that is, His relationship with the world is the pattern, or prototype, of their experience with the world. How did the world treat Jesus? Well, you see that supremely at the cross. The cross is the great revelation of all things. How did they treat Jesus then? With indifference, you remember: with cynical indifference they gambled at the foot of the cross while He suffered. With contempt: "If thou be the Christ, come down from the cross." With mockery: "Hail, King of the Jews!" With hatred and violence: "They spat upon Him, and took the reed and smote Him." Jesus says that if they did that with Him, do not be surprised that they will do the same with you. " 'A servant is not greater than his master.' If they persecuted me, they will persecute you" (v. 20).

But notice also that the world hates the Christian not only as it hated Christ but also *because it hated Christ*: "All this they will do to you on my account" (v. 21). "If you were of the world, the world would love its own; but because you are not of the world, but I chose you out of the world, therefore the world hates you" (v. 19)—that is, His relationship with the world is not only the pattern and prototype of theirs, but it is also the reason for the world's hatred of them. That is an important truth for us as we think of the relationship of the Christian with the world. It is not, in other words, our oddities and inconsistencies which are to draw upon us the world's opposition; it is our Christlikeness and holiness which is the real motive of the world's opposition. It is a grievous error, beloved, when a man blames opposition that he is receiving upon his relationship with the Lord when really it is the result of the inconsistencies of his own life. You may not blame on the Lord Jesus some of the objectionable things that are in your own life that may draw down the opposition of the world!

Further, Jesus says, you can trace this hatred still deeper. "They hate you because they hate me," but there is in verse 23 a strong hint of the fact that they hate Jesus, really, because they hate His Father: "If

I had not come and spoken to them, they would not have sin; but now they have no excuse for their sin. He who hates me hates my Father also" (vv. 22-23). That is something that Christian people need to learn: that the natural man, nice and upright though he may be, is at heart implacably opposed to God. So when a man says to you, "Oh, I have nothing against God and all that," he does not know himself, beloved. The natural man is implacably opposed to God, to His Son, and to the whole message of the gospel. Once that reality is open to his eyes, the hatred begins to come out of the heart of the natural man.

Further, Jesus says, they hate you, Him, and His Father *because of their blindness and spiritual ignorance*:

All this they will do to you on my account, because they do not know him who sent me. If I had not come and spoken to them, they would not have sin; but now they have no excuse for their sin (vv. 21-22).

Notice that this is willful ignorance of which Jesus is speaking. It is not that they have not heard but that they will not listen. Therefore they are without excuse.

Throughout the Scripture you get illustrations of that kind of thing. Do you remember the experience of Stephen in Acts 7, when he is witnessing to the world of the Lord Jesus Christ and has been preaching Christ in all the Scriptures to them? "When they heard these things they were enraged, and they ground their teeth against him" (Acts 7:54). That was the hatred of the world against God. When Stephen went on to speak, "they cried out with a loud voice and stopped their ears and rushed together upon him" (v. 57). Can you see the picture of these men? They say, "We don't want to listen! We don't want to hear this!" It is a willful ignorance.

It is very significant that Jesus extends this hatred of the world, which the believer will suffer, to the realm of worldly religion: "I have said all this to you to keep you from falling away. They will put you out of the synagogues; indeed, the hour is coming when whoever kills you will think he is offering service to God" (16:1-2). That prophecy was literally fulfilled in the persecuting zeal of Saul of Tarsus. Giving his own account of it in Acts 22:3 and the following chapters, Paul says he was "zealous for God," and in Acts 26:9, "I myself was convinced that I ought to do many things in opposing the name of Jesus of Nazareth." Here is another realm, you see, of the opposition of the world. It is the opposition of worldly religion to the real Jesus in the lives of His disciples. I want to say to you, my Christian friends, that one of the most frightening things in all the world is to see the naked hatred of worldly religion for the real Jesus in the lives of His children. And whether that worldly religion wears liberal clothes or evangelical clothes does not matter.

I was at a conference some time ago, and I met a young man who came to see me in great distress. He was the pastor of a certain congregation, and he began to tell me about this evangelical congregation that he had come to. It was an evangelical congregation that had never been disturbed out of the Word of God. He began to tell me about some of the things that had happened to him, and some of the experiences he had had with officers in that congregation. Do you know what had happened to that young man? They had brought him to the verge of a mental breakdown. What was it? Well, it was because, under this awful, diabolical delusion that they were serving God, they were hounding the young man out of the place. And there is a worldliness even in evangelical religion which can produce a demonic hatred of the real Jesus.

But all that is the negative side of the relation of the Christian to the world. What is the Christian to do in response to the world's hatred? Well, Jesus's answer comes in the context of His words about the ministry of the Holy Spirit, in 15:26-27. The Christian is to go into the world, sent by the Lord Jesus and empowered by the Holy Spirit, to be a witness: "You also are witnesses, because you have been with me from the beginning." So the Christian's response to the world's hostility to God and to the gospel is neither isolation, nor retaliation, but evangelization. And that is the bridge into the next section of the chapter, because you will notice in verse 26 that behind the witness of the disciple is the witness of the Holy Spirit.

This is why Jesus is sending the Holy Spirit. It is He who will be the witness: "When the Counselor comes, whom I shall send to you from the Father, even the Spirit of truth,… he will bear witness to me; and you also are witnesses" (vv. 26-27). This is what Peter and the apostles are testifying to in Acts 5:32, when they say, "We are witnesses to these things, and so is the Holy Spirit." The same Lord Jesus who took them out of the world and incorporated them into the vine, so that they were not of the world, sends them back into the world as His fruitful and fruit-bearing disciples, to bear witness to the world as the instruments of the Holy Spirit.

You see, God's attitude to the world is not that He stands back from it. When He sees the hostility and the rebellion of those who "did not see fit to acknowledge God" (Rom. 1:28), who "worshiped and served the creature rather than the Creator" (Rom. 1:25), what does God do? He does not wash His hands of them and go to some corner and leave them to themselves. He loves the world, and He sent His only begotten Son. Part of that loving and sending is that the Lord Jesus says He is sending you out into the world, equipped by His Holy Spirit to be His witness. And the Book of Acts is really the account of the fulfillment of that promise. It is the story of how the Holy Spirit takes up these poor, weak, frightened men, fills them with power from high, and bears witness to the Lord Jesus through them.

THE WORLD AND THE HOLY SPIRIT

It is that which brings us to the second relationship: *the world and the Holy Spirit*. The Holy Spirit bears witness to Christ; but He does not only conduct Christ's case before the world, to use Dr. Leon Morris's phrase, although this is the first element in the Holy Spirit's witness. You will remember that the word "Paraclete," which is the word John uses for the Holy Spirit, has these legal overtones. The normal idea used of the Spirit's work for the believer in the word "Paraclete" is that He is the One called alongside to buttress the believer, to indwell him, and then to witness to the world concerning Christ. But here in John 16:6-11 he appears to become not so much the Advocate to conduct Christ's case before the world but rather the Prosecutor who secures the world's conviction. Notice verses 7 and 8:

> Nevertheless I tell you the truth: it is to your advantage that I go away, for if I do not go away, the Counselor will not come to you; but if I go, I will send him to you. And when he comes, he will convince the world, [or as the Authorized Version puts it, "He will convict the world"] concerning sin and righteousness and judgment.

This is the Holy Spirit's ministry as the Prosecutor, as it were: to secure conviction in the world. In witnessing to the world, the Holy Spirit is giving evidence; in convicting the world, the Holy Spirit is securing a conviction; and in both cases it is through the believer that He works.

Specifically He convicts the world of three things concerning which it is either heedless or ignorant. First, *the solemnity of sin*: He will convict the world "concerning sin, because they do not believe in me" (v. 9). Secondly, He will convict the world of *the necessity of righteousness*:

"concerning righteousness, because I go to the Father, and you will see me no more" (v. 10). And thirdly, He will convict the world of *the reality of judgment*. So there are the three areas in which the Holy Spirit comes to the world, acting as it were, as a Prosecutor.

You see, the great thing that the believer can never do by himself in the world is to produce this sense of conviction—to bring to the world the sense of the reality of God, the solemnity of sin, the necessity of righteousness, and the certainty of judgment. That is a thing that you can never persuade the world of. You can argue men blue in the face, you can be the most brilliant intellectual in the world, and you will never bring that kind of conviction to the world, because it is the exclusive ministry of the Holy Spirit of God. This is why Jesus says, "It will be to your advantage that I go away. I will send the Holy Spirit"—not only because it will be to their personal advantage but also because He will come to indwell them. It will be the beginning of the ministry which will take this hostile world and bring it to see its sin.

Now let us look at these three things that Jesus says the Holy Spirit will do. I take this to mean the Holy Spirit *convicts the world of the solemnity of sin* in verse 9. The evidence that He uses to secure this conviction is the evidence of unbelief: "concerning sin, because they do not believe in me." The Greek usage probably does not mean that sin consists in unbelief but rather, as Dr. Leon Morris puts it, that unbelief is a classic illustration of sin. Let me quote his words to you:

The basic sin is the sin that puts self at the center of things and consequently refuses to believe. This is the world's characteristic sin, and it received classic expression when God sent his Son into the world and the world refused to believe in him.[61]

---

61 Morris, *The Gospel According to John*, 619.

It is the solemnity of this sin which only the Holy Spirit can drive home to the conscience and stab it awake.

This is what you see happening again in the Book of Acts. It is a glorious thing to see how the Lord Jesus has all these promises laid before the disciples, and in Acts they are fulfilled. I had the great privilege of standing in Philippi in the ruins of Paul's prison. I could almost hear the cries of the jailer as the earthquake came, the prison came clattering down round about him, and he began to discover that the message of these men he had beaten was something other than old wives' tales. He began to see that there was a living God; he began to discover that sin was a black reality, and he cried out, "Men, what must I do to be saved?" (Acts 16:30). That is the Holy Spirit coming to convict the world of the solemnity of sin.

You see this happening not only in the Book of Acts, but you see it happening also in the great revivals. Isn't this what happens when the Spirit of God comes down upon a community: that men and women who lived lightly to sin, who joked about it, probably, who practiced it, apparently with impunity, came to discover the gravity and the reality of sin? Oh, you need to read the story of revival to see something of this! Edwin Orr, in his great book, *The Second Evangelical Awakening*, describes how the Spirit of God came down upon the little fishing town of Cellardyke, on the east coast of Scotland, in 1860. Let me read you one part of it. He says,

On 12 March 1860 a young man under deep conviction went to sea. After three days of struggle he finally appropriated salvation in Christ. The Christian skipper saw in the event the beginning of the outpouring of the Holy Spirit in the community. With the return of the ship and the testimony of the young man, hundreds in Cellardyke became burdened by sin, sending for the ministers, before whom they gave way to tears.... Three hundred adult inquirers were dealt with in this period.... An Army officer of high rank summed up his impressions of what he had seen in Cellardyke thus.... "Those of you who are at ease have little conception of how terrifying a sight it is when the Holy Spirit is pleased to open a man's eyes to see the real state of his heart."[62]

The Holy Spirit convicts the world of the solemnity of sin.

Secondly, the Holy Spirit *convicts the world of righteousness* (v. 10), and I take this to be the necessity of righteousness. The righteousness of which Jesus speaks I would understand to be that righteousness which God demands, which man lacks, and which Christ alone provides. Jesus points us to this in the phrase He uses of righteousness: "because I go to the Father, and you will see me no more." His going to the Father is His atoning work whereby that righteousness which man does not have is provided in the Lord Jesus Christ.

This is the Holy Spirit's convicting ministry. When men become aware of this, you see what happens. It is similar to what happened on the day of Pentecost, when the Word of God was preached, and the glory of God was seen in what He had done in the Lord Jesus Christ, and they were "cut to the heart" (Acts 2:37). A man finds himself saying, "God is a God of righteousness, and I look into my heart and find I do not have righteousness. All my righteousnesses are as filthy rags." He cries out, as they did to Peter on that day, "Brethren, what shall we do?" And the Holy Spirit will say, "Put on the Lord Jesus Christ" (Rom. 13:14). "Christ Jesus, whom God made our wisdom, our righteousness and sanctification and redemption" (1 Cor. 1:30). The Holy Spirit will convict the world "concerning righteousness, because I go to the Father."

---

62   J. Edwin Orr, *The Second Evangelical Awakening in Britain* (London and Edinburgh: Marshall, Morgan & Scott, Ltd, 1949), 72-73.

Thirdly, the Holy Spirit *convicts the world of judgment*: "concerning judgment, because the ruler of this world is judged" (v. 11). He does so by revealing to the world the state of its prince.

One of the great significances, you see, of Christ's saving work is that it is a triumph over Satan. In Colossians 2:15, Paul speaks of Christ's work on the cross in this way: "He disarmed the principalities and powers and made a public example of them, triumphing over them in him"—that is, in His cross. The defeat of Satan is not just an arbitrary act, but it is a judgment, and here Jesus speaks of it as the harbinger and forerunner of the final judgment. Sir Edwin Hoskyns comments that "the dethronement of the devil" must be exposed to the world and become one of the themes of the apostolic teaching.

There is the ministry of the Holy Spirit in the world. He convicts the world of the seriousness of sin, of the necessity of righteousness, and of the reality of judgment. Martin Luther, preaching on this, comes to the end of verse 11 and says, "Now, do I hear someone ask…?" Martin Luther is always hearing somebody asking questions, and conveniently they are always just the questions he wants to answer! At this point he says, "Do I hear someone ask by what means will God perform this convincing work? I answer, by sending the Spirit into the heart of His children." You will notice this in 16:7-8: "If I go, I will send him to you. And when he comes [that is, when He comes to you] he will [convict] the world concerning sin and righteousness and judgment." So that is the Holy Spirit's work: to convict the world through Spirit-filled and Spirit-anointed men and women.

THE HOLY SPIRIT AND THE CHRISTIAN

Now in verses 12 to 15, from the Spirit's work in the world, our Lord turns to *the Spirit's work in the disciple*: "I have yet many things to say to you, but you cannot bear them now. [However] when the Spirit of truth comes, He will *guide you into all the truth"* (italics added). Let me remind you of what our Lord has already taught us about the Holy Spirit's ministry in the believer in these chapters. They are troubled in heart because they are to be bereft of Jesus's physical presence, but Jesus tells them that it will actually be to their advantage when He is glorified. They would have kept Him back, you see; they would have said to Him, "Lord, you mustn't go away!" But Jesus says, "I have a far better plan than that. The Holy Spirit, the other Paraclete, will not just be with you, but He will be everything I am to you, only He will be in you. And He will continue this teaching ministry."

Here in verses 12 to 15 it is the Holy Spirit's teaching ministry on which Jesus lays emphasis. They are not in a position at this moment to receive so much of what He wants to say to them, but the Holy Spirit will exercise a ministry of instruction and illumination: "He will guide you into all the truth.… He will declare to you the things that are to come." That may well mean that the Holy Spirit is going to teach and instruct the disciples on the significance of the death and resurrection and ascension and return of the Lord Jesus.

It seems to me important to distinguish between the fulfillment of that promise of Jesus to the apostles and its fulfillment to believers in future generations. I would put the distinction this way: The Holy Spirit led the apostles into all the truth by enabling them to write Scripture. The Holy Spirit leads *us* into all the truth by enabling us to understand Scripture. That is an important distinction. We need to compare these words with 14:26 where Jesus speaks of the Spirit's twofold ministry—of reminding them of all that Jesus said and of teaching them all things necessary to salvation. In one sense one could say that the fulfillment of that reminding ministry of the Holy Spirit is in the Gospels; and the fulfillment of the further teaching ministry—leading them into all the truth and showing them things that were to come—is in the rest of the New Testament.

But the vital distinction is that the Holy Spirit leads the apostles into the truth by enabling them to write Scripture. He leads us into the truth by enabling us to understand Scripture. That, you see, is why it is so important that we do not seek to degrade the rest of the New Testament below the Gospels. You will find many people who will say, "I accept the words of Jesus very happily; but when you come to the epistles, that's just what Peter thinks, or that's just what John thinks, or that's just what Paul thinks." But Jesus says, "That's where you're wrong. That's what the Holy Spirit says, in fulfillment of my promise, 'He will lead you into all the truth.' "

That is a cardinal matter in our attitude toward the authority and inspiration of the New Testament. When He leads us into the truth and there is a fulfillment of this promise to us, it is not into novel truth. It is not into truth that is different from Scripture; it is certainly never into truth that is contrary to Scripture. Scripture is always the final judge and the ultimate court of appeal for everything the Holy Spirit says to any man. So when somebody says, "The Holy Spirit has said this to me," we always bring that word to the arbitrator of Holy Scripture. The Holy Spirit, therefore, has this double ministry: He is the giver of truth, and He is the guide into the truth. And in all His works, says Jesus, He is self-effacing—"He will not speak on His own authority,… He will glorify me" (vv. 13-14)— and He is Christ-exalting.

There are the three relationships, then, in skeletal outline, of which our Lord speaks from 15:18 to 16:15. And now in 16:16-33 Jesus outlines some of the blessings which will be the fruit of His going and the Spirit's coming.

JOY OUT OF SORROW

The first of these is *joy out of sorrow*, and the key verse is "Truly, truly, I say to you, you will weep and lament, but the world will rejoice; you will be sorrowful, but your sorrow will turn into joy" (v. 20).

It is obvious that it appeared to the disciples as if Jesus was speaking in riddles about "a little while" when they would not see Him, and then another "little while" when they would see Him.

> Some of his disciples said one to another, "What is this that he says to us, 'A little while and you will not see me, and again a little while, and you will see me'; and, 'because I go to the Father'?" They said, "What does he mean by 'a little while'? We do not know what He means" (vv. 17-18).

Dr. Leon Morris comments that it is not surprising that these words of Jesus proved a difficulty to the men in the Upper Room, and they have puzzled Christians ever since. Well, the problem really is, of course, what Jesus means by these two "little whiles" in verse 16. It seems certain that the first "little while" must be the time between the present discourse and His departure: "A little while, and you will not see me." But does He mean by the second "little while" the period between His death and His resurrection, when they saw Him in His resurrection body and rejoiced? Or between His death and Pentecost, when they saw the evidence of His power in the world? Or between His death and His return in glory, when "every eye will see him" (Rev. 1:7)?

It seems most likely that the primary reference may be to the resurrection appearances of our Lord. But ultimately it may be characteristic of John's way of speaking of several things in one compass—to all three—since it is a principle which Jesus is primarily teaching here. And the principle is this: it is the paradox in all Christian experience that life comes out of death, and joy comes out of sorrow. The principle is that God is not bringing them through these days of sorrow without having blessing and glory in view any more than

Christ is passing through His anguish and death without being assured of a resurrection and return in glory.

This is the whole point of the illustration of the travailing woman (v. 21). Jesus has told them that the world is going to rejoice, and they will be sorrowful; and then, when He is come to them in "a little while" they will see Him, and they will rejoice since their sorrow will be turned into joy. Then in verse 21 you get this remarkable picture:

> When a woman is in travail she has sorrow, because her hour has come; but when she is delivered of the child, she no longer remembers the anguish, for joy that a child is born into the world.

That is not only a parable of the experience of the disciples (a sorrow which is going to give way to joy), but it is also a parable of Christian service.

The point is that there is some pain in the world that is apparently meaningless and unproductive. But there is pain of a different order. There is pain in the world which is productive, and productive of life. That is what Paul is speaking about when he tells the Galatians, in the context of his own service—in all the travail and agony that he was passing through—that he can only compare it to one thing: "I … travail until Christ be formed in you!" (Gal. 4:19). In other words, "This pain and agonizing that I'm going through is not meaningless, beloved." He says, "I would go through it again and again, because of the outcome. It is productive pain. Death worketh in us, but life in you."

Let me apply this to some servant of God who is in the midst of travail. I wonder if you have known what it is to be travailing before God in some corner of the world. You may have come back from the mission field on furlough. God knows we do not care nearly enough with a shepherdly heart for men and women who are back in this country, having been in the very front line of the battle in some corners of the world. And you may be wondering how in God's name you are going to go back. You may even bear in your body this kind of agony. My brother or my sister, may I say to you, diffidently (because I am not fit to give counsel to so many of you), can you think of your travail like this: that it may be the birth pangs of a new life that you are experiencing—that this pain, this turmoil, this anguish, if you are in the Lord's hands, is going to be productive? Can you take the Word of God and apply it as a balm to your soul? "He that goes forth weeping, bearing the seed for sowing, shall come home with shouts of joy, bringing his sheaves with him" (Ps. 126:6). "Weeping may tarry for the night, but joy comes in the morning" (Ps. 30:5). Joy out of sorrow.

UNDERSTANDING OUT OF PERPLEXITY

Secondly, *understanding out of perplexity*. Look at the following verses:

You have sorrow now, but I will see you again and your hearts will rejoice, and no one will take your joy from you. In that day you will ask nothing of me…. I have said this to you in figures; the hour is coming when I shall no longer speak to you in figures [or in dark sayings] but tell you plainly of the Father…. His disciples said, "Ah, now you are speaking plainly, not in any figure! Now we know that you know all things" (vv. 22-23, 25, 29).

Do you see the theme that runs through this of an understanding that is beginning to dawn out of perplexity?

In verse 23 there is some doubt again as to what "that day" refers. It seems most likely that "that day" may in a general sense refer to the new age of the Spirit, when the disciples will be led into the truth by the Holy Spirit. But once more it is the principle which is the vital thing. That principle is this: that our procession toward glory as

God's children is accompanied by a gradual dawning of light—by an increasing understanding—until the day will come when we shall see no longer "through a glass, darkly, but then face to face" (1 Cor. 13:12, AV). In the meantime, as Amy Carmichael so beautifully says: "We have our backs to the darkness, and we are walking into the light."

You can trace how this is illustrated in John's Gospel itself. It is almost a minor theme of the Gospel. Let me give you two examples of it briefly. In John 12:14 Jesus is coming into Jerusalem, sitting upon the ass, and the disciples are perplexed. In John 12:16 we read, "His disciples did not understand this at first; but when Jesus was glorified, then they remembered that this had been written of him." Do you see what is happening? They are in the dark; they do not understand; they are perplexed. But they are moving toward the day when Jesus was glorified; and then they remembered, and they understood.

In John 13:7, when Jesus is washing the disciples' feet, Peter says, "I can't understand this. This seems absolutely contrary to everything that I conceived." And Jesus says to him, "What I do thou knowest not now; but thou shalt know hereafter" (AV). At a period in my life when I went through some very dark days through an experience that came into my family, people wrote many different kinds of messages; but there was one that came from a dear brother of mine in Morocco, and it was just a card with these words written on it: "What I do thou knowest not now; but thou shalt know hereafter." That is the way the Lord is dealing with all his children, beloved. We are moving into the light. So He says, "In that day you will ask nothing of me."

But there is another asking for which there is a different word: the asking of prayer. This is part of the whole ministry of leading us from perplexity into understanding. Jesus goes on to tell us how this is to be revolutionized too: "Truly, truly, I say to you, if you ask anything of the Father, he will give it to you in my name" (v. 23).

On the ground of all that Jesus is going to do in His atoning work, the disciples will be able to come to the Father with an assurance that they can ask in Jesus's name, and the Father will give them in Jesus's name. Notice that the proper translation of verse 23 links the giving, rather than the asking, with "in my name"—the name of Jesus. You will see the point. Both the disciples' right to ask and the Father's readiness to give are on the basis of what Jesus is going to do. "Hitherto you have asked nothing in my name; ask, and you will receive, that your joy may be full" (v. 24).

Do you see the linking of this blessed gift of prayer with both the joy that comes out of sorrow and the understanding that comes out of perplexity? "In that day you will ask nothing of me," but there is another kind of asking. He says, "Truly, truly," and they are words that Jesus uses to emphasize something. It is because of this going to the Father, and all that His Father is going to mean to them, that they are going to ask in the name of Jesus. Asking in that name, they will receive, and their joy will be full.

Now, in verses 25 to 28 our Lord is speaking of the new access to the Father which His atoning work will bring: "I came from the Father and have come into the world; again, I am leaving the world and going to the Father" (v. 28). That is one of the great descriptions of the downward and upward reach of the Lord's atoning work. He comes down from the Father into the world and leaves the world and goes to the Father. On the basis of that mighty work of atonement and reconciliation, we have access to the Father for ourselves.

Verses 26 to 27 are not a contradiction of the fact that our Lord has a continuing intercessory ministry for the believer. He says,

In that day you will ask in my name; and I do not say to you that I shall pray the Father for you; for the Father himself loves you, because you have loved me and have believed that I came from the Father.

What does this mean, then? Is Jesus saying, "I am no longer going to have this intercessory ministry" of which we read in chapter 17? Does this mean that our Lord does not intercede for the saints? No, that is not at all what He is speaking about. It is rather an assurance of the glorious direct access to God which Christ's sacrifice will bring. He is drawing them on, you see, even in the same way that a father will say to his child, "Now, you don't need me to pray for you anymore; you can go to the Lord for yourself." Isn't that what we say to our children?

Jesus is saying, "Because of what I am doing—because of my coming from the Father into the world and leaving the world to go to the Father—you may come to the Father; and you will find that you do not need me to persuade the Father to be gracious to you, because His heart is open toward you."

As John Calvin expressed it: "We are taught that we have the heart of God as soon as we place before Him the name of His Son."[63]

TRIUMPH IN TRIBULATION

Joy out of sorrow, understanding out of perplexity, and, finally, *triumph in tribulation* (vv. 31-33). These are Jesus's last words to the disciples. They said to Him, "Ah, now you are speaking plainly, not in any figure! Now we know that you know all things, and need none to question you; by this we believe that you came from God" (vv. 29-30). But in verses 31 and 32 Jesus said, "Do you now believe? The hour is coming, indeed it has come, when you will be scattered, every man to his home, and will leave me alone." In other words, there is a tribulation which is yet before them; and He faces them with the reality of His coming agony and theirs. For Him, this coming agony means that the shepherd will be smitten and the sheep scattered (Zech. 13:7). He says, "You will leave me alone."

---

63   Calvin, *Commentaries*, 130.

Isn't it a very striking thing that Jesus finds throughout the whole of this discourse that the disciples have so little interest in what is going to happen to Him? It is what is going to happen *to them* that they are taken up with. My friends, there is a lesson in that. There is a kind of religion, even evangelical religion, which is very selfish. There is a use of the Word of God, even, that is very selfish: "I come to it to get a little word to help me through the day!" I am not despising that, but I want to say this to you: If somebody were only interested in you for what they could get out of you, would you not begin to suspect them of cupboard love? Why is it that God has given us His Word? It is that we might come to know Him, acquaint ourselves with His will, discover His plan and purpose for ourselves and for the world, and give ourselves to the doing of it.

He says, "I shall be alone, yet not alone, for the Father is with me." But of course the time was to come when even the fellowship of the Father was hidden, and Jesus was to cry, "My God, my God, why hast thou forsaken me?" He knew the ultimate loneliness of being cut off from men by His holiness and from God by our sins.

For the disciples, what does it mean that they are facing tribulation? Jesus had one last word to them, and this brings us to the conclusion of His discourse:

I am leaving the world and going to the Father…. The hour is coming, indeed it has come…. I have said this to you that in me you may have peace. In the world you will have tribulation; but be of good cheer, I have overcome the world. (vv. 28, 32-33).

There is something we need to grasp: we are both in the world and in Christ. In Christ, for the believer, there is glorious and blessed peace: "Peace I leave with you; my peace I give to you" (14:27). There is peace in Christ for the believer. In the world there is tribulation. But the two sides are not equally balanced. Christ has overcome the world, and He says, therefore, "Be of good cheer!"

Notice how He tries to take these men from their sense of defeatism—their sense of abandonment, their sense of weakness and loss—into a sense of abounding confidence. Oh, beloved, we need this spirit of confidence to hear the Lord Jesus come and say, "Be of good cheer. Go out into the world knowing that I have overcome the world. You are going to find tribulation; you are going to find trouble. But I have overcome!"

There was a time when Lord Reith, that giant of a man in so many ways, came to speak to our General Assembly in the Church of Scotland. He was speaking about the spirit that he detected abroad in Christian circles of a sense of the apologetic—of defense, being always on the retreat; of apologizing to people, almost, for the faith; the sense of embarrassment at being in a minority. And he said, "What we need to see happening in Scotland is something of the Dothan sort."

Do you remember what happened at Dothan? That is where Elisha lived, and he was a thorn in the flesh to Ben Hadad, king of Syria. He found that all his plans for attacking Israel were made known. As he had thought and planned, even in his bedchamber before he put the plan into action, the Israelites had known about it.

He turned to his courtiers and said, "Let's come clean. Who is the quisling among us? Who among us is for the enemy? Somebody's taking the plans out and giving them to him, almost before I've thought them up."

They said to him, "My lord, it's not any of us. It is the prophet in Israel who seems to know everything that goes on in the mind of my lord, in his very bedchamber."

The King of Syria said, "Find out where he lives."

And they said, "He lives in Dothan."

"Right," he said. "Gather the army."

They got a vast army together—horses, chariots, troops—and Ben Hadad said, "Send them down to Dothan." This vast army begins to charge out of the capital of Syria. It is an extraordinary picture, almost comic. If somebody were to stop them and say, "Where is this vast army going? What great fortress are you going to attack?" they would say, "We are going down to capture the little prophet down in Dothan!"

There they go, this vast army; and they come and circle the city of Dothan with all the cavalry, artillery, and infantry; they are round about it, this vast host. The servant of Elisha—a young man, inexperienced probably—sees this great array and turns to Elisha and says, "My father, my father, what shall we do?"

And Elisha says, "It's all right. Don't panic!"

The young man could have thought to himself, "The old man's gone off his head! He's not facing reality. He's not facing the facts."

But, ah, beloved, it was the old prophet who was facing the facts. He turns to God and he says, "Lord, open his eyes!" The Lord opened the young man's eyes, and he saw the mountain full of the horses and chariots of the Lord: "Those who are with us are more than those who are with them" (2 Kings 6:16). "Greater is he that is in you, than he that is in the world" (1 John 4:4, AV). Blessed be the God and Father of our Lord Jesus Christ for such a hope and for such a gospel.

Chapter 25

Our Lord's Consecration and Intercession

I made known to them thy name, and I will make it known,
that the love with which thou hast loved me may be in them,
and I in them.
— John 17:26 (RSV)[64] —

Bishop J. C. Ryle has called John 17 "one of the most wonderful chapters in the Bible," adding, with great wisdom, that we have "no line [with which] to fathom" its depths.[65] Shortly before his death, Philip Melanchthon, Martin Luther's colleague, lectured on John 17 and said, "There is no voice which has ever been heard, either in heaven or in earth,... than the prayer offered up by the Son of God Himself."[66] One can scarcely read this chapter without a great sense of the wonder and awe that comes through words like these. As we study it, we shall inevitably discover that we are, indeed, out of our depth here. We have no line with which to fathom it but shall seek to have, as it were, a scratch on the surface. The Lord Jesus has finished His discourse to

---

64　Unless otherwise stated, Scripture quotations in this chapter are from THE HOLY BIBLE: REVISED STANDARD VERSION, International Bible Society.

65　Ryle, *Expository Thoughts on the Gospels*, volume 7, 126.

66　Quoted in James Hastings, *The Great Texts of the Bible: St. John XIII-XXI* (New York: Charles Scribner's Sons, 1912), 261.

the disciples and now turns from instruction to intercession, thereby, as John Calvin points out, giving a great example to ministers of the Word, that "it is by watering the good seed with prayer that power and thrust comes to the Word of the living God." And this is what our Lord does. He turns from instruction to intercession.

It has been customary to call this prayer the High Priestly Prayer of Jesus, and it is certainly helpful and illuminating for us to see our Lord here in the role of the great High Priest. That is a theme which is, of course, so fully and gloriously worked out in the Epistle to the Hebrews. He is distinguished from all other priests in that He is both priest and sacrifice; He is both the offeror and the victim. He is about to bear the sins of His people in His own body as the sacrificial victim; and now, before He comes to the place where this is to be done, He bears the needs of His people before the Father, as the great High Priest and Mediator. The nature of this prayer, therefore, takes on the two activities of the great High Priest: *consecration and intercession*. He is consecrating Himself to be our sin-bearer, and He is lovingly interceding for us as our Mediator.

Bishop Ryle draws attention to one great value of this prayer which it seems to me vital not to neglect. He says, "It is wonderful as a pattern of the intercession which the Son, as a High Priest, is ever carrying on for us in heaven."[67] I have no doubt that this is one of the great blessings we ought to derive from this prayer and from studying it together. We do not think nearly enough of our Lord's present intercessory ministry. We concentrate a great deal on His finished work—His past ministry— and on that work which is still to be consummated by His glorious return in person and in power. But there is a work which our Lord Jesus Christ is doing now for His people: He is making intercession for us. Our salvation, in the present tense, is closely knit with this. How

---

67 Ryle, *Expository Thoughts on the Gospels*, volume 7, 126.

is it that He is able "for all time to save those who draw near to God through him"? It is because "he always lives to make intercession for them" (Heb 7:25). That is what this prayer is a pattern of, in many ways.

What is this intercessory ministry which is patterned here? Well, the high priest's ministry, and the ministry of our Lord, is symbolized in Exodus 28 in the rather strange clothing that Aaron was prescribed to wear, whereby he had a shoulder piece with the names of the people of Israel engraved on two stones; and again, a breastplate in which were embedded stones on which the names of the people of Israel were engraved. He was thus to bear the names of the people of God before God, on his shoulders and on his heart (v. 29).

You see the symbolism. This is God's picture book; this is God's visual aid, as it were. The people of God were to be upheld before God by name, by their names indelibly written in stone. The names of the people of God are upheld before God, and they lie near to the heart of God. That is what this means, and we ought to lay hold of this blessed truth: that the names of every one of the Lord's people are engraved on the heart of God, and our concerns lie close to His heart.

The words in John 17:1, "Father, the hour has come," provide us with the background to the prayer. They are, of course, a reference to the fact that Jesus is on the threshold of His suffering and passion. That phrase "the hour"—or sometimes in John, "my time"—is the hour of the consummation of His ministry. It is a phrase that comes very frequently, but until now that phrase has always had "not yet" attached to it. In the story of the wedding at Cana, Jesus says to His mother, "Woman, what have I to do with thee? mine hour is not yet come" (John 2:4, AV). All through John's Gospel this "not yet" is added to the phrase "mine hour." But here Jesus says, "The hour has come."

It is particularly impressive to notice how it is the Lord Himself who declares the hour has come. He is, in other words, not harried to the cross when it suited men, but He is striding, as it were, with a regal majesty to the cross, moving with the perfect timing of the God who is directing the whole universe on its course. And as He comes into the presence of the Father for His disciples, having in measured tones spoken to them about all that lies before—for them and for Him—it is He who now declares, "The hour has come."

You see, the whole world of men and devils—all the Pilates and Caiaphases, all the prevaricators, the Jews and the Romans—had to wait, as it were, in the wings of the scene of history, until God said, "Now!" This is the real background of this. It is the picture of our Lord's moving to the cross which you find reflected in the language of the apostles. In their prayer in Acts 4, for instance, they ask the Lord for the kind of poise in their own spirits which is in the heart of Jesus as He says to the Father, "The hour has come." You remember how they prayed,

> Truly in this city there were gathered together against thy holy servant Jesus, whom thou didst anoint, both Herod and Pontius Pilate, with the Gentiles and the peoples of Israel, to do whatever thy hand and thy plan had predestined to take place (vv. 27-28).

"Father, the hour has come," says Jesus. He prays as the Son of God and as the King of glory.

One cannot but feel that it is almost unseemly to analyze this prayer in John 17. But there are three areas in which the prayer of our Lord concentrates, conveniently set out, if you have the Revised Standard Version, in three paragraphs. In the first section (vv. 1-5), our Lord is focusing His prayer on the *glory of the Son and of the Father*; in the second section (vv. 6-19), His prayer is focused on the *well-being of the disciples in the world*; and in the third section (vv. 20-26), the prayer is focused on the *unity of the future church universal.*

THE GLORY OF THE SON AND OF THE FATHER

We turn to the first of these sections, the *glory of the Son and of the Father* (vv. 1-5). It is sometimes said that Jesus is here praying for Himself as He begins, "Father, the hour has come; glorify thy Son." But that could be a misleading idea, I would suggest to you, as if there were some kind of self-seeking in our Lord's praying. The burden on His heart, in these first verses, is the glory of the Godhead and the accomplishing of salvation. And this will be not by self-pity but by self-sacrifice. So we need to rid our minds of any idea of a self-seeking if we say our Lord is praying here for Himself.

The petition that Jesus makes in these first verses concerns the glorifying of the Father and the Son. Twice He prays for His own glorification in verse 1: "Father, the hour has come; glorify thy Son." Again in verse 5: "Now, Father, glorify thou me in thy own presence." Twice He relates that prayer to the glorifying of the Father, again in verse 1: "Glorify thy Son that the Son may glorify thee." In verses 4 to 5: "I glorified thee on earth, having accomplished the work which thou gavest me to do; and now, Father, glorify thou me."

There are these two concerns in the heart of our Lord, and there are two questions that we need to ask of these verses. First, what is this glory of which Jesus speaks? Verse 5: "Glorify thou me … with the glory which I had with thee before the world was made." He wants the glory to be manifested. That is the first question: What is this glory of which Jesus speaks? The second question is this: How is this glory manifested, or how is the Father glorified in the Son?

The first of these two questions: What is the glory of which Jesus speaks? The glory of God in Scripture is, of course, the outshining of His character. It is the luster of what the Westminster Shorter Catechism calls "his being, wisdom, power, holiness, justice, goodness, and truth" (WSC 4). It is the outshining of these characteristics of God which is His glory. Hebrews 1:3 tells us that Jesus is the brightness, the effulgence, of this glory. So God is glorified when He is manifested; and when He is manifested in His Son, we read, "The Word became flesh and … we have beheld his glory" (1:14), because the fullness of God dwelt in Jesus Christ.

The second question: Where is that glory of God to be seen, and particularly, how is the Father glorified in the Son? That is what is answered in these verses. There are five things that these verses teach us about this, and I take them in historical order. Where is the glory of God, of which Jesus here speaks, to be seen?

First, notice that the glory of God was *shared by Jesus with the Father in eternity*: "Now, Father, glorify thou me in thy own presence with the glory which I had with thee before the world was made" (v. 5). That is really very striking, because God specifically says in the Scripture that He will not share His glory with another; and yet the Lord Jesus says He shared it from all eternity.

We cannot pretend to understand what this means—what this glory that Jesus shared with the Father before the foundation of the world was. Let me simply pause long enough to point this out: Could there be a clearer claim to deity in the Scripture than this? Can there be any remaining doubt in our minds of what the Lord Jesus Christ Himself claimed in His position with the Father? In His nature He shared the glory of the Father before the world was made. I say again, we cannot understand what this is like; we are like kindergarten children in the university here. But Jesus shared this glory with the Father before the world was made.

Secondly, this glory was *veiled in the flesh of Jesus in the world*: "I glorified thee on earth, having accomplished the work which thou gavest me to do" (v. 4). So the Lord Jesus has been manifesting this glory as He has come into the world and as He has done the work that the Father gave Him to do. That is, of course, what John is speaking about when he tells us in 1:14, "We beheld his glory, the glory of the only begotten of the Father."

Notice that our Lord does not divest Himself of His glory when He comes into His flesh and is born in Bethlehem, but He veils His glory. Wesley is therefore right when he sings about "veiled in flesh the Godhead see."[68] In His flesh our Lord manifested the glory of God in a veiled way. He does it in a veiled way because, of course, men in the world could not have stood it if the glory of God had not been veiled. It would have been impossible for them to have looked upon Him; and sometimes it seems as if that is almost beginning to happen, and the veil is wearing very thin. You remember at the Transfiguration, for example, when our Lord is metamorphosed before them. It seems as if the veil which is hiding His glory is becoming thin, and they bow before Him. He is shining with glory.

You get it in some other places, too. It is very significant, I believe, in John 18 that the men coming in the garden to take Jesus say, "We are seeking Jesus of Nazareth," and Jesus challenges them. They are facing Him at this point, you see. He says to them, "Whom do you seek?" They say, "We seek Jesus of Nazareth," and He confronts them, and says, "I am he!" Now do you remember what you read after that? "They fell back." Why do you think these men fell back? Not with fear—they were with some soldiers to take Him away. No, I will tell you why they fell back. I think it was because when He declared Himself "I am," something of the glory began to break through. But lustrous and blinding though that glory was to men, it was the glory of His humiliation, and was as nothing compared to the "light inaccessible," which was His in eternity. It was veiled in the flesh of Jesus in the world.

---

68   From Charles Wesley's hymn, "Hark! the Herald Angels Sing."

Thirdly, it was *revealed in His saving work on the cross*. This is supremely where Jesus says the Father is to be glorified in the Son. The "hour" and the "glory" are welded together: "I glorified thee on earth, having accomplished the work which thou gavest me to do." What was that work? Well, it is the work that is described in verse 2; it is the giving of eternal life to men, in bringing them to know God: "Thou hast given him power over all flesh, to give eternal life to all whom thou hast given him."

Where was that work finished and accomplished? It was finished and accomplished at the cross, where Jesus cries in triumph, "It is finished!" The glory of God is revealed in the saving work of Christ, because nowhere is the character of God more fully displayed than in His cross and resurrection, where He displays His holiness, His justice, His love, and His tender mercy toward the children of men. This is why in the Book of Revelation—that book of unveiling—you discover that in the center of the glory of heaven is the figure of a Lamb as it had been slain. That is where the glory of God is manifested. Calvin writes, "In the cross of Christ, as in a splendid theatre, the incomparable goodness of God is set before the whole world."[69]

Fourthly, this glory is *unveiled in His ascension into heaven*. That is the point of the prayer in verse 5: "And now, Father, glorify thou me in thy own presence with the glory which I had with thee before the world was made." This is a prayer for our Lord's entering again into that same glory which He shared with the Father before the world began. Yet in a sense, if you think carefully, it is not entirely the same glory.

When the Lord Jesus ascends into heaven it is now as the God-Man; and it is as the God-Man that the Lord Jesus is glorified in His ascension. So not only His deity but also His manhood is vested with

---

69   Calvin, *Commentaries*, 68.

the glory of God. That means that Christ is our forerunner entered into the glory to bring us to glory. It is Christ's ascension into the glory as the God-Man, you see, which gives us the hope of glory. He is engaged in this work now in His ascended might and triumph, "bringing many sons to glory" (Heb. 2:10). We have that glorious hope of the end day for the children of God, which is not the immortality of the soul—that is not the Christian hope—but the Christian hope is the resurrection of the body. A glorified body is possible because the Lord Jesus has had His manhood, as well as His divinity, clothed and vested with glory.

That leads us to the last of these five places where the Son glorifies the Father. It is shared with the Father in eternity; it is veiled in the flesh of Jesus; it is revealed in His saving work; it is unveiled in His ascension into heaven. Could anything be more wonderful than that? Ah, but beloved, there is something still more. If you look at verse 10, there is another place where this glory is to be seen: "All mine are thine, and thine are mine, and I am glorified in them." That is what the work of grace should do: it should bring the glory of God *into the life of the believer*. There is coming a day when we shall behold His glory, but in this day Jesus says, "I am glorified in them." That is the burden of our Lord for the glory of the Father and the Son.

THE WELL-BEING OF THE DISCIPLES

The second section of the prayer is the *well-being of the disciples in the world*. In verse 9, our Lord points to the constituency for which He is now praying: "I am praying for them; I am not praying for the world but for those whom thou hast given me, for they are thine."

First, notice the description that Jesus gives of these men to whom He has revealed the Father. He spends some considerable time describing them. They are, first of all, *the Father's possession*: "I have manifested thy name to the men whom thou gavest me out of the world; thine they were" (v. 6). Believers are described by our Lord as the Father's possession; they belong to Him.

They are not only the Father's possession, but, in the second place, they are also *the Father's love-gift to the Son*. Notice in verse 2, for example: "Since thou hast given him power over all flesh, to give eternal life to all whom thou hast given him." Verse 6: "I have manifested thy name to the men whom thou gavest me out of the world." Verse 9: "I am praying for them; I am not praying for the world but for those whom thou hast given me." Again in verse 24: "Father, I desire that they also, whom thou hast given me, may be with me where I am."

Have you noticed, I wonder, this very remarkable series of givings which are in John's Gospel? First, the Son is the Father's love-gift to the world: "God so loved the world, that he gave his only begotten Son" (3:16, AV). Secondly, believers are the Father's love-gift to the Son: "Thine they were, and thou gavest them to me." Do you grasp what this means? Can you think of this? It is the picture, you see, of the Lord Jesus being given His bride by the Father. Believers are the Father's love-gift to the Son.

There is a gorgeous little picture in the Church of England wedding service, where the minister says to the assembled company, "Who giveth this woman to be married to this man?" And the father, with varying degrees of reluctance or willingness, says, "I do." He brings the bride up and presents her. The father comes with the bride, you see, to the bridegroom. It is a glorious picture, because she belongs to him; but he comes, and this is how the bridegroom gets his bride. It is a blessed picture: the bridegroom gets his bride because the father takes this most precious gift of his and presents it to the bridegroom; and he says, "There you are!"

Beloved, that is how Christ gets His bride, which is the church. The Father takes you, you who belong to the Father, whom He has chosen out of the world, and He presents you to the Lord Jesus, and He says, "There is my love-gift." I cannot fathom that. Can you? This humbles us down into the depths! That is something that sends me into an absolute bewilderment of heart and mind. But it is what the Holy Scripture tells us; it is what the Lord Jesus says. He has gained His bride because the Father has come, taken the believers, and presented us to the Son.

But notice further the Son's love-gift to the believer. Oh, the giving there is in the whole of the Godhead and in the family of God! That is why the essence of the love of God shed abroad in our hearts is giving, not getting. Giving, you see, is the very fiber that seems to make the Godhead what it is. What is the Son's love-gift to the believer? In verse 2 it is eternal life and the knowledge of God: "since thou hast given him power over all flesh, to give eternal life to all whom thou hast given him." Notice it is the Father's name, in verse 6: "I have manifested thy name to the men whom thou gavest me out of the world." He has shown them all the glory of the Father's character. Then in verse 8 it is the Father's words that He gives to them: "I have given them the words which thou gavest me."

You cannot get away from this, you see. The Father has given the bride to the Son; He has given the words to the Son. The Son takes His bride and gives eternal life to them, and He gives the Father's name to them. Then the Father gives Him the words, and He gives the words to the believers. Oh, the giving, the blessed, blessed donations that there are from the heart of God to us!

But what about the believer's love-gift to the Father and to the Son? Verse 6: "Thine they were, and thou gavest them to me, and they have kept thy word." And verse 8: "I have given them the words which thou gavest me, and they have received them and know in truth that I came from thee; and they have believed that thou didst send me." What is it that we can give? God knows there is so little that we have to give, is there not? But what we give to Him is our obedience ("They have kept my words") and our faith ("They have believed that thou didst send me").

Now, having described them, Jesus goes on to pray for them. His prayer is, of course, supremely for their sanctification or holiness. The central theme is found in verses 17 to 19:

> Sanctify them in the truth; thy word is truth. As thou didst send me into the world, so I have sent them into the world. And for their sake I consecrate myself, that they also may be consecrated in truth.

Let me simply point out to you what seem to me to be the three main elements in the sanctification for which Jesus prays in these verses. Sanctification, of course, just means "to make holy." The three elements I see in these verses, in our Lord's prayer for the well-being of the disciples in the world, are, first, *perseverance*: "Father, keep them"; then, *separation*: "They are not of the world. If they were of the world the world would love its own, but they are not of the world"; and, thirdly, *consecration*: "That they also may be consecrated in the truth."

First, let us look at *perseverance*. In verses 11 and 12, Jesus speaks of the need of the disciples to be kept:

> And now I am no more in the world, but they are in the world.… Holy Father, keep them in thy name, which thou hast given me, that they may be one.… While I was with them, I kept them in thy name, which thou hast given me; I have guarded them, and none of them is lost but the son of perdition, that the scripture might be fulfilled.

Judas Iscariot was not one of them; he did not belong to the vine. But Jesus says, "I kept them in thy name, which thou has given me; I have guarded them." Then in verse 15: "I do not pray that thou shouldst take them out of the world, but that thou shouldst keep them from the evil one."

Beloved, it is a very wonderful thing to me that our Lord not only prayed for the disciples in this connection ("Father, keep them"), but He also actually let them hear Him pray for their security. Do you see why He does that? He is praying aloud. That is, of course, why we have the prayer of John 17. He prays for them because the Lord is not just concerned about your security, but He is concerned about your serenity. He lets them hear Him pray, "Father, keep them." He does the same thing for Simon Peter, you remember: "Simon, Simon, behold, Satan demanded to have you, that he might sift you like wheat, but I have prayed for you" (Luke 22:31). That is why it is important not just to pray for people, but to tell them that you are praying for them. I think the Lord means us to do that—if it is true. I tremble when I think of the number of people who have promised and covenanted to missionaries, "We'll pray for you," which they do for a week. But if it is true, we need to tell one another, as the Lord told Peter, and as He told His disciples here—or allowed them to hear, "I will pray for you."

Do you see from this the quite vital issue which derives from our Lord's prayer and His burden for the disciples? What is it that the perseverance of the believer depends on? How can you be sure that you will endure to the end—that you will be kept and guarded from the world, the flesh, and the devil? Well, the answer is, *it is in the keeping power of God*. That is what it depends on. I think the Lord may have been ministering particularly to Simon Peter's need in this connection, for Peter had quite the wrong idea about perseverance. In 13:37, he says, "Lord ... I will lay down my life for you." Peter in effect says, "You are a bit disturbed about what is going to happen to the disciples, and you are talking about us being scattered. Don't have any fear, Lord;

you can count on me. I'm the persevering variety." Oh, how little the man knew his own heart!

But you see, perseverance in the Christian life is not "Lord, you can count on me," but "Lord, there is nothing else in the world that I can count on, but that you are able to keep that which I have committed unto you." It is Paul's testimony in Philippians 3:3: "We … glory in Christ Jesus, and put no confidence in the flesh."

That is why Jesus prays in verse 11, "Holy Father…" He is appealing to the Lord's fatherly grace, to that fatherly grace which will not deny His child any good thing; to the holiness in the Father's character—that is, to everything that God is by nature. He says, "Holy Father, keep them in thy name, which thou hast given me." It is not, I believe, the disciples that Jesus is referring to when He says, "which thou hast given me," but the name of the Father.

Do you see what this means? The Father has given His name to the Son—that is, His nature. The Lord Jesus has manifested all the nature of God, and this is why they wanted Him to stay. They wanted to know the security of the Lord Jesus. They had known His shepherdly care in their lives; they had known His hand stretched out when in their folly they would have run ahead of Him in the energy of the flesh; they had known His hand behind them when, through lack of faith, they would have lagged back from Him. They knew something of the glorious keeping power of the Lord Jesus. "But," He says, "that was the name of the Father that He gave to me." And now He says, "Holy Father, keep them in thy name, which thou hast given me.… While I was with them,… I have guarded them.… But now I am coming to thee." The name of God is the character of God, and our security lies in that.

I can recall attending a prayer conference at a lovely house in the Kent countryside. There was a high tower in the house, and carved on it were the words, "The Name of the Lord Is a Strong Tower. The Righteous

Runneth into It and Is Safe." That is the perseverance of the believer, and our perseverance depends upon what God is and upon what God does. "I have kept them; I have guarded them, Father," He says. Some of our great hymns express this quite wonderfully. Toplady has it right in his great hymn, "A Debtor to Mercy Alone." The last verse declares, "And I to the end shall endure." Why is he so sure? Some people tell me, "That sounds a bit cocky to me, you know: 'I to the end shall endure.' Shades of Simon Peter!" Well, Toplady gives us the answer in these words:

The work which His goodness began,
The arm of His strength will complete;
His promise is Yea and Amen,
And never was forfeited yet.

Things future, nor things that are now,
Not all things below or above,
Can make Him His promise forgo,
Or sever my soul from His love.

My name from the palms of His hands
Eternity will not erase:
Impressed on His heart it remains,
In marks of indelible grace.
And I to the end shall endure,
As sure as the earnest is given:
More happy, but not more secure,
When glorified with Him in heaven.

Specifically, Jesus prays for their perseverance in the face of all the pressure and power of the evil one: "I do not pray that thou shouldst take them out of the world, but that thou shouldst keep them from the evil one" (v. 15)—not in the absence, you will notice, of all the pressures of the adversary but in the face of them. You remember the psalmist's great testimony: "Thou preparest a table ... in the presence of mine enemies" (23:5). Well, there is their perseverance.

The second element in our Lord's prayer for the disciples' well-being is their *separation*. The whole thought of sanctification and holiness in the Scripture—and Jesus's great theme here is, I believe, "Sanctify them in the truth" (v. 17)—is rooted in the idea of separation. Linguistically, that is what the word really means. So in verse 6 the disciples are those "thou gavest me out of the world." This is the negative idea of that separation, for it is important to see that there are two sides to the separation of which the Scripture speaks. We are in this sense separated—translated—out of one kingdom into another. We are cut off, as it were, for God, and that is the positive element in this separation. We are separated unto the gospel. We are separated from the world—from sin and the evil one—unto the Lord Jesus Christ.

But here it is specifically their separation from the world that Jesus is speaking about. The word "world" occurs nineteen times in this chapter, and it is obvious that the disciples' relationship to it is a crucial factor in our Lord's intercession for them. This doctrine of separation ("They are not of the world, even as I am not of the world. Sanctify them") is one which we eclipse, or neglect, at our great peril. There is to be a distinctiveness about the believer's life which is a reflection of the distinctiveness of the life of Jesus: "They are not of the world, even as I am not of the world" (v. 16). That is the real distinctiveness of the believer.

Beloved, you will notice that our distinctiveness is not a matter of being odd or peculiar. There are many people who delight in being, in the worst possible sense of the term, the Lord's "peculiar" people; they think that this is what it means to be separated from the world.

One of the first Christian meetings that I was ever taken to was in a hall in the north side of Glasgow. (I suppose I was in my late teens at the time.) People were seeking to interest me and help me, and they took me to this hall. I shall never forget; it is by the grace of God alone that it did not put me off forever! Over the top of the door was a sign that read, "The Oddfellows Hall." (I discovered later on that the Oddfellows were some kind of society that came from the Victorian era!) It is a great error for us to imagine that being separate from the world makes you an oddity!

Paul's word is the same as that of the Lord Jesus: "Do not be conformed to this world" (Rom. 12:2), and what he means is this: when the Lord God has called you to Himself out of the world, He has called you into something infinitely greater. He does not want you to live like a pauper anymore, now that He has called you to be a royal priesthood. He does not want you to live at that kind of level anymore. He does not want you to live by the standards of the world. He does not want you to live by the criteria of the world. Are you living your life, planning your future, and ordering your priorities by the priorities and standards of the world and the things that are acceptable there—by the lifestyle of the world—or by the lifestyle of the New Testament? That is the separation of the believer, and it is infinitely more costly than some of the rather more trivial things we concentrate on when we speak about separation. You are to be a distinctive people.

That neither implies isolation from the world ("I do not pray that thou shouldst take them out of the world") nor does it imply insulation from reality. Jesus says, "Keep them from the evil one." Evil will be all around them. God knows in these days there are subtle, hidden, persuasive pressures to bring people into conformity. "But neither through isolation nor through insulation," says Jesus, "do I want them to be kept. It's through transformation in their character."

Positively, this separation has two things. It is, firstly, a *spirit of detachment from the world* which gives evidence that they are here as "strangers and pilgrims." It is, secondly, a *spirit of missionary compassion for the world*: "As thou didst send me into the world, so I have sent them into the world" (v. 18). That is the burden that our Lord prays may be in the hearts of His children.

Thirdly, not only perseverance and separation but also *consecration*. There is another meaning given in verse 19 of this word translated "sanctify" in verse 17. It is actually the same word, and that is why you will find that the Authorized Version translates it the same way: "Sanctify them through thy truth: thy word is truth." Then, "For their sakes I sanctify myself, that they also might be sanctified through the truth" (v. 19). But this other translation is a proper and right one.

There are two things to say about it. First, it is clear that the means that God employs for this inward work of sanctification, which is called consecration, is *His Word*: "Sanctify them in the truth; thy word is truth." Now I could not do better than to read to you the words of Bishop Ryle on this: "The Word," he says, "is the great instrument by which the Holy Ghost carries forward the work of inward sanctification. By bringing that Word to bear more forcibly on mind and will, and conscience, and affection, we make the character grow more holy."[70] Here lies the immense importance of regularly reading the written Word and hearing the preached Word. Believers who neglect the Word will not grow in holiness, because the means God employs for this inward work of consecration is His Word.

Also notice that the aim Jesus has in view in His consecration of Himself to suffering and death is *our consecration*. He says, "As thou

---

70   Ryle, *Expository Thoughts on the Gospels*, volume 7, 150.

didst send me into the world, so I have sent them into the world" (v. 18); and in verse 19: "And for their sake I consecrate myself…" He is referring to His consecrating of Himself to His death and suffering as the vicarious atonement for the sins of His people. He is consecrating Himself to be the Sin-Bearer.

Why is He giving Himself to this agony and sin-bearing? Well, says Jesus, it is "that they also may be consecrated in truth." I am sure that that has some reference to their being sent out into the world, but even more primary and fundamental than the sending of the believer out into the world was to create in us a likeness to His consecration to the Father. That is why we have been reading more than once 2 Corinthians 5:15: "He died for all, that those who live might live no longer for themselves, but for him." This is why Jesus says to the disciples that they have to take up the cross. The cross is not only the instrument of our regeneration and justification, but the cross is also the instrument of our sanctification; and the aim with which our Lord goes to the cross is "that they also may be consecrated."

Listen to these words of Samuel Chadwick:

As the Son of God placed all the resources of His glory at the disposal of man's need, so every disciple abandons all to God for the blessing of man…. The Christian undertakes to be as Christ in the world, to do His work, to minister in His Spirit; and for this he lays all at the feet of his Lord.[71]

This is what it is to take up the cross and follow Jesus. Thus does our Lord pray for the well-being of His disciples in the world.

---

71 Samuel Chadwick, *Humanity and God* (London: Hodder and Stoughton, 1904), 124-125.

THE UNITY OF THE FUTURE CHURCH UNIVERSAL

Finally, He prays for the *unity of future believers in the church universal*. The Lord Jesus Christ lifts up His eyes and looks over the centuries to future believers, and His gaze stretches right over the centuries to focus on us. He has the whole church of God in view, His gaze is upon us, and He is speaking of people like ourselves. He encompasses that multitude that no man can number (Rev. 7:9) now in His praying.

Notice there are two distinct sets of people mentioned. They are described as "these" and "those" in verse 20 in the Revised Standard Version: "I do not pray for these only, but also for those who are to believe in me through their word." "These" are the apostles, for whom He has been praying in verses 6 to 19; and "those" are future believers. The "these" and "those" become the "all who are one" in verse 21: "That they may all be one; even as thou, Father, art in me, and I in thee." And the bridge between "these" and "those" is the Word of truth, which they have believed.

That Word, you will notice, has a long history traced in John's Gospel. It is given by the Father to the Son; it is given by the Son to the apostles; and then—notice this bridge—it is given by the apostles to future believers. So the link we have with the apostles—the real apostolic succession, in other words—is the truth which the apostles were given by Jesus, which Jesus had received from the Father, and which the apostles give to future generations in the Word of the New Testament Scripture. That is the great link, you see. It is this Word through which we believe that is the unifying factor. That is what unites us with the apostles, and that is what unites us with each other. That is what makes us all one in Christ Jesus. Both "those" and "these" have received and believed the Word of truth, and that is what makes them one.

This means, you see, that the unity for which our Lord is here praying is not just a unity of spirit. That is a very important distinction. There are several words that are misunderstood and misinterpreted in connection with Christian unity—words like "union," "unity," "unanimity," and "uniformity." Here is unanimity in gospel truth which gives us true unity in Christ. We must never be afraid of this, beloved, because it is one of the central elements in the New Testament teaching about unity. Unanimity in gospel truth is the essence of gospel unity. This unity is patterned upon the unity within the Godhead. Verse 11: "That they may be one, even as we are one." Verse 21: "Even as thou, Father, art in me, and I in thee, that they also may be in us." Verse 22: "The glory which thou hast given me I have given to them, that they may be one even as we are one." This implies for us a unity of heart, mind, and will, in the words of Moulton and Milligan: "all wills bowing in the same direction, all affections burning with the same flame, all aims directed to the same end."[72] That is a blessed thing, isn't it? It does not matter what kind of denomination you belong to, because the thing that unites us is a unanimity in gospel truth—a unity of heart and mind and will.

But note that the ultimate concern of our Lord is a burden for a lost world:

O righteous Father, the world has not known thee, but I have known thee; and these know that thou hast sent me. I made known to them thy name, and I will make it known, that the love with which thou hast loved me may be in them, and I in them (vv. 25-26).

Jesus longs that the apostles may go out, and that the world may know.

---

72 William Milligan and William Fiddian Moulton, *The International Revision Commentary on the New Testament. Based Upon the Revised Version of 1881. The Gospel According to John. Vol IV* (Outlook Verlag, 2024), 354.

That is the work of grace on earth, then: holiness and unity in the church, and evangelism in the world. But there is one last thing: not only the work of grace on earth but also the weight of glory in heaven. Verse 24: "Father, I desire that they also, whom thou hast given me, may be with me where I am, to behold my glory which thou hast given me in thy love for me before the foundation of the world." I said earlier that we could not see this glory. This is something that we do not have the equipment, in this earthly vale of tears, to grasp. But one day we are going to behold His glory.

Let me call upon the help of John Owen to describe this. The last sermon that that great saint of God, with such a giant intellect, preached was on "The Glory of Christ," and he compares the difference between beholding His glory by faith and beholding it by sight. He finds a parable of it in Mark 8, in the experience of the blind man at Bethsaida, whose eyes were opened in two stages. Says Owen, "When he first touched him, his eyes were opened, and he saw,… [He was no longer blind, but yet still there were many things that were obscure.] but upon his second touch he 'saw all things clearly.' "[73] The scales were entirely gone. The first touch is grace; the second touch is glory.

---

73   John Owen, *The Works of John Owen, D.D.: An exposition of the Epistle to the Hebrews, with preliminary exercitations* (London and Edinburgh: Johnstone and Hunter, 1855), 72.